ASIAN LEGENDS FOR KIDS

History Brought Alive

© Copyright 2025 - All rights reserved.

Published 2025 by History Brought Alive

The content contained within this book may not be reproduced, duplicated, or transmitted without direct written permission from the author or the publisher.

Under no circumstances will any blame or legal responsibility be held against the publisher, or author, for any damages, reparation, or monetary loss due to the information contained within this book, either directly or indirectly.

LEGAL NOTICE:

This book is copyright protected. It is only for personal use. You cannot amend, distribute, sell, use, quote, or paraphrase any part, or the content within this book, without the consent of the author or publisher.

DISCLAIMER NOTICE:

Please note the information contained within this document is for educational and entertainment purposes only. All effort has been executed to present accurate, up-to-date, reliable, complete information. No warranties of any kind are declared or implied. Readers acknowledge that the author is not engaged in the rendering of legal, financial, medical, or professional advice. The content within this book has been derived from various sources. Please consult a licensed professional before attempting any techniques outlined in this book.

By reading this document, the reader agrees that under no circumstances is the author responsible for any losses, direct or indirect, that are incurred as a result of the use of the information contained within this document, including, but not limited to, errors, omissions, or inaccuracies.

FREE BONUS FROM HBA: EBOOK BUNDLE

Greetings!

First, thank you for reading our books.

Now, we invite you to join our VIP list. As a welcome gift we offer the History & Mythology eBook Bundle below for free. Plus, you can be the first to receive new books and exclusives! Remember it's 100% free to join.

Simply click the link below to join.

https://www.subscribepage.com/hba
Keep up to date with us on:
YouTube: History Brought Alive
Facebook: History Brought Alive
www.historybroughtalive.com

CHINESE LEGENDS FOR KIDS

EMPERORS, DRAGONS, GODS, HEROES,
MYTHS & MORE FROM ANCIENT CHINA

TABLE OF CONTENTS

INTRODUCTION: WELCOME TO THE WORLD OF CHINESE LEGENDS!... 1

CHAPTER 1: THE LEGEND OF THE DRAGON KING – GUARDIAN OF THE SEAS.. 6

CHAPTER 2: THE STORY OF CHANG'E – THE MOON GODDESS... 12

CHAPTER 3: THE TALE OF THE MONKEY KING – JOURNEY TO THE WEST 19

CHAPTER 4: THE WEAVER AND THE COWHERD – A LOVE ACROSS THE STARS 25

CHAPTER 5: THE LEGEND OF THE WHITE SNAKE – A TALE OF LOVE AND TRANSFORMATION.................. 31

CHAPTER 6: THE STORY OF NIAN – THE MONSTER OF THE NEW YEAR 37

CHAPTER 7: PANGU AND THE CREATION OF THE WORLD 43

CHAPTER 8: THE JADE EMPEROR – RULER OF HEAVEN 48

CHAPTER 9: THE LEGEND OF MULAN – A BRAVE DAUGHTER'S JOURNEY 54

CHAPTER 10: THE LAUGHING BUDDHA – A SYMBOL OF HAPPINESS 60

CHAPTER 11: THE STORY OF YU THE GREAT – TAMER OF THE FLOODS 65

CHAPTER 12: THE STORY OF HOU YI – THE ARCHER WHO SHOT DOWN NINE SUNS 70

CHAPTER 13: THE TALE OF ZAO SHEN – THE KITCHEN GOD. 75

CHAPTER 14: THE LEGEND OF THE BUTTERFLY LOVERS – A TALE OF TRAGIC LOVE.. 81

CHAPTER 15: THE STORY OF THE BAMBOO CUTTER – THE TALE OF KAGUYA..87

CHAPTER 16: THE STORY OF THE CARP THAT BECAME A DRAGON 93

CHAPTER 17: THE LEGEND OF SUN AND MOON CAKES – A HIDDEN MESSAGE 99

CHAPTER 18: THE LEGEND OF THE RED THREAD OF FATE – INVISIBLE CONNECTIONS 103

CHAPTER 19: FESTIVALS AND CELEBRATIONS – HONORING THE LEGENDS..109

CONCLUSION: CREATE YOUR OWN CHINESE LEGEND!.........115

BONUS SECTION: FUN ACTIVITIES INSPIRED BY CHINESE LEGENDS 120

FUN FACTS ABOUT CHINESE CULTURE AND MYTHOLOGY.. 126

REFERENCES...132

INTRODUCTION: WELCOME TO THE WORLD OF CHINESE LEGENDS!

Imagine a world where dragons soar through the skies, mischievous monkeys leap from treetop to treetop, and brave heroes save entire kingdoms! Legends are magical stories that have been passed down from generation to generation. These stories are not only fun to hear but also teach us valuable lessons about life, friendship, courage, and kindness. A legend might tell the tale of a clever trickster, a powerful emperor, or a magical goddess living on the moon. But no matter what the story is about, it always holds a hidden lesson for us to discover.

Chinese legends are some of the oldest stories in the world. Many of them began thousands of years ago, long before the modern cities of today existed. Back then, people told stories to explain how the world worked—like how the sun rises, why the seasons change, or what happens when we are kind to others. These tales also helped people learn what it means to be brave, wise, or kind. By reading these stories, you'll explore a world full of magic, courage, and imagination.

A Peek into China's Ancient History and Traditions

China has a rich and ancient history. Long ago, China was ruled by mighty emperors who built great palaces and walls to protect their people. It was a place where scholars studied the stars, farmers grew rice by the river, and merchants traveled along the Silk Road, bringing treasures from distant lands. Throughout all these years, stories were told to make sense of the world around them.

CHINESE LEGENDS FOR KIDS

In ancient times, people believed that dragons brought rain to help crops grow, and the moon held a beautiful goddess named Chang'e. Heroes like Mulan fought for their families and kingdoms, while gods like the Jade Emperor ruled from the heavens. Even animals, like the carp that transformed into a dragon, found their place in these stories, teaching important lessons about perseverance and bravery.

These legends connect with Chinese traditions in so many ways. Festivals, like the Mid-Autumn Festival, celebrate the tale of Chang'e, and the Chinese New Year brings the story of Nian, the monster who feared fireworks and red decorations. Through these stories, children and adults alike understand the meaning behind many customs, foods, and celebrations that are still enjoyed today. By reading these legends, you'll see how China's past is woven into its present.

How These Tales Shape Chinese Culture Today

Even today, the wisdom found in Chinese legends is all around us. You might spot statues of the Laughing Buddha in homes and temples, bringing joy and good fortune. During the Lunar New Year, families celebrate with bright red lanterns and lion dances to keep away bad luck, just like the villagers did in the story of Nian.

CHINESE LEGENDS FOR KIDS

These stories are not just about entertainment—they show us how to live. The tale of the Monkey King teaches us to never give up, even when the journey is tough. The story of Mulan reminds us that anyone, no matter who they are, can be a hero. Legends like these help people, young and old, understand values such as kindness, bravery, and respect for others. They also encourage us to dream big and believe that anything is possible.

What's wonderful about these legends is that they continue to inspire new stories. You'll see traces of these old tales in books, movies, and TV shows today. Maybe you've heard of Kung Fu Panda or seen the live-action Mulan movie—these are modern retellings inspired by ancient Chinese stories. Legends live on because they spark imagination and teach lessons that never grow old.

This book is your gateway to a world full of adventure! As you turn each page, you'll meet dragons that bring rain, gods who rule the heavens, and tricksters who love to stir up trouble. You'll read about heroes like Mulan and the Monkey King, who show us how to be courageous and clever. You'll explore the story of the Jade Emperor and discover how the animals of the Chinese zodiac earned their place in the calendar.

CHINESE LEGENDS FOR KIDS

As you read each chapter, think about the lessons hidden in these stories. What can you learn from the Monkey King's mischievous ways? How does the tale of the carp becoming a dragon inspire you to keep trying, even when things seem hard? These legends are not only fun to read but also full of ideas that you can use in your own life.

You'll also discover some of the traditions and festivals that keep these legends alive today. Maybe you'll want to celebrate the Mid-Autumn Festival with mooncakes or try creating your own dragon mask for Chinese New Year. Each story opens a door to understanding more about Chinese culture and the values that have been passed down for generations.

So, get ready to dive into a world of wonder! With each story, you'll travel to magical places, meet unforgettable characters, and discover valuable lessons along the way. Whether you want to laugh with the Monkey King, dream with Chang'e on the moon, or battle alongside Mulan, this book has something for everyone.

Let your imagination take flight like a dragon in the clouds! The adventure starts now—are you ready to begin?

CHAPTER 1: THE LEGEND OF THE DRAGON KING - GUARDIAN OF THE SEAS

Deep beneath the waves of the ocean, in a palace made of shimmering pearls and coral, lives the Dragon King—one of the most powerful and respected figures in Chinese mythology. The Dragon King is not just one dragon but a title passed among several rulers of the seas, with each Dragon King governing a different ocean. Together, these mighty dragons are protectors of the water, rain, and all creatures that swim below. They have long, serpent-like bodies, shining scales, and long whiskers that flow gracefully with the currents.

In Chinese legends, dragons are not fire-breathing monsters like those found in other myths. Instead, they are wise and powerful beings associated with water and life. The Dragon King is known to be a fair ruler who ensures the seas remain calm and provides much-needed rain to nourish the crops on land. If treated with respect, the Dragon King offers blessings. But if angered, his rage could stir up storms and massive waves! This makes the Dragon King both admired and feared.

Tales of the Dragon King's Adventures Beneath the Waves

The Dragon King's palace is hidden at the bottom of the sea, surrounded by fish, sea turtles, and glowing jellyfish. Here, he rules over his watery kingdom and listens to the needs of sea creatures and fishermen. Many stories tell of his adventures and the times he came to help both the people on land and the creatures of the sea.

One of the most famous stories tells how the Dragon King helped a young boy named Liu. During a terrible drought, the rivers dried up, and the crops withered under the blazing sun. The villagers prayed for rain, but none came. So Liu decided to venture to the Dragon King's palace beneath the ocean to ask for help. Brave and determined, Liu swam deep into the sea, dodging schools of fish and swirling currents, until he found the Dragon King's palace.

When Liu asked the Dragon King to bring rain, the mighty dragon listened carefully. Touched by the boy's bravery and concern for his village, the Dragon King agreed to send rain clouds to the land. Soon after, the skies darkened, and rain poured down, saving the crops and filling the rivers once again. Liu returned to his village a hero, and the people celebrated the Dragon King's kindness.

In another story, the Dragon King faced off against a sea monster that was terrorizing ships. The creature had sharp teeth, glowing red eyes, and a terrifying roar that could shake the ocean floor. But the Dragon King, with his majestic power, summoned waves and lightning to battle the monster. After a long struggle, the Dragon King emerged victorious, restoring peace to the sea. This tale teaches us that the Dragon King is not only wise but also courageous, willing to protect those in need.

The Importance of Dragons in Chinese Culture

In Chinese culture, dragons are seen as symbols of power, protection, and good fortune. Unlike the scary dragons of other cultures, Chinese dragons bring blessings and are often called upon during festivals and ceremonies. The Dragon King himself is believed to have control over water, rain, and weather, which are essential for a good harvest. This connection between dragons and nature is why many farmers prayed to the Dragon King to send rain during dry seasons.

Dragons are also celebrated during the Dragon Boat Festival, where people race beautifully decorated boats shaped like dragons across rivers and lakes. This tradition is not only exciting but also honors the spirit of the dragon and brings the community together. In ancient times, emperors considered themselves to be like dragons—powerful rulers who protected their people and kept the land prosperous.

Even today, the image of the dragon appears everywhere in Chinese art, architecture, and clothing. You'll see dragons on temple roofs, festival decorations, and even embroidered on the robes of ancient emperors. The Dragon King's presence is still felt in modern China, where dragons are a beloved symbol of strength, luck, and protection.

Lessons from the Dragon King: Protection, Power, and Respect

The stories of the Dragon King are not just exciting tales—they also carry important lessons. One of the most important lessons is about protection. The Dragon King uses his power to protect both the sea creatures and the people on land, showing us that true strength lies in caring for others. Just like the Dragon King calmed the storms and brought rain to the villagers, we can help those around us by being kind and supportive.

Another lesson we learn from the Dragon King is about responsibility and power. The Dragon King has the power to create storms and calm the seas, but he must use his abilities wisely. This teaches us that having power comes with responsibility. It's not enough to be strong—we must use our strength to do good and make the world a better place.

Finally, the Dragon King's stories remind us about the importance of respect for nature. The sea is vast and powerful, and we must treat it with care, just as the villagers respected the Dragon King by offering prayers and thanks. When we respect nature—

whether it's the ocean, rivers, forests, or animals—we help keep the world balanced and healthy.

The Dragon King's tales encourage us to be kind, brave, and respectful. Just like Liu, who bravely asked the Dragon King for rain, we can all make a difference when we show courage and care for others. And like the Dragon King, we can use our talents and strengths to protect the world around us.

So, the next time you see a dragon decoration or watch the rain fall from the sky, think of the Dragon King swimming beneath the waves, watching over the seas and rivers, and bringing balance to the world. His story is a reminder that even the most powerful beings can choose kindness, courage, and wisdom—and so can we!

CHAPTER 2: THE STORY OF CHANG'E - THE MOON GODDESS

High up in the night sky, far above the clouds and stars, lives Chang'e, the Moon Goddess. Her story is one of love, sacrifice, and magic, and it has been told for centuries. On nights when the moon is full and bright, people in China remember her legend. They gather with their families, eat delicious mooncakes, and look up at the moon, wondering if they might catch a glimpse of Chang'e or the Jade Rabbit hopping by her side. Let's dive into this beautiful story and discover how Chang'e became the Moon Goddess and what lessons her tale teaches us!

How Chang'e Flew to the Moon

A long, long time ago, Chang'e was the wife of Hou Yi, a famous archer. Hou Yi was known throughout the land for his incredible skill with a bow and arrow, and he was celebrated as a hero. One day, the Jade Emperor—who ruled both the heavens and the earth—noticed that ten suns had risen in the sky instead of just one. The heat from these suns was scorching the land, drying up rivers, and withering crops. The people were desperate for help.

The Jade Emperor asked Hou Yi to use his skills to save the world. Hou Yi took his mighty bow and shot down nine of the suns, leaving just one in the sky to provide light and warmth. The people were saved, and Hou Yi became a beloved hero. As a reward, the Jade Emperor gave Hou Yi a special gift—a potion of immortality. This magical potion would allow the person who drank it to live forever and ascend to the heavens.

However, Hou Yi did not want to leave Chang'e behind. Instead of drinking the potion, he decided to keep it safe and hidden. But one day, a greedy man tried to steal the potion while Hou Yi was away. To protect it, Chang'e made a bold decision—she drank the potion herself. Suddenly, Chang'e began to float, rising higher and higher into the sky. She flew all the way to the moon, where she would stay forever.

Even though Chang'e became immortal, she missed Hou Yi deeply. Alone on the moon, she gazed down at the earth every night, longing to be with the people she loved. But from that moment on, the moon became her home, and she became known as the Moon Goddess.

The Legend of the Jade Rabbit and Its Friendship with Chang'e

Living alone on the moon could have been a very lonely experience for Chang'e, but she was not completely alone. According to legend, a kind and magical Jade Rabbit lives on the moon with her. The story of the Jade Rabbit begins with three animals—a rabbit, a fox, and a monkey—who were asked by the gods to find food to help a hungry traveler. The fox and monkey brought food they had found, but the rabbit, having nothing to give, offered himself. Touched by the rabbit's selflessness, the gods transformed him into the Jade

Rabbit and gave him a home on the moon, where he became Chang'e's companion.

Together, Chang'e and the Jade Rabbit became close friends. It is said that the Jade Rabbit spends his days mixing potions, grinding herbs, and preparing magical elixirs in a large mortar. Sometimes, people on earth even imagine they can see his shadow when the moon is full—if you look carefully, you might spot the outline of a rabbit!

Chang'e and the Jade Rabbit share stories, watch over the world below, and remind us that even in times of loneliness, friendship and kindness can bring comfort. Their tale teaches us the importance of companionship and how even the smallest acts of kindness, like the rabbit's, can have lasting meaning.

Celebrating the Mid-Autumn Festival in Her Honor

Every year, on the 15th day of the eighth lunar month, people in China and other parts of Asia celebrate the Mid-Autumn Festival to honor Chang'e. This special festival is a time for family reunions, delicious food, and looking at the moon. Families gather under the night sky, eat mooncakes (round pastries filled with sweet or savory fillings), and share stories about the Moon Goddess.

During the Mid-Autumn Festival, children carry colorful lanterns shaped like animals or stars, adding magic to the night. Some families light incense and offer fruits to Chang'e as a way to show their respect. It is a time for people to reflect on the importance of family and togetherness, just as Chang'e wishes to be reunited with her loved ones on earth.

The mooncakes eaten during this festival are more than just tasty treats—they are also symbols of unity and completeness. Just like the round shape of the moon, these cakes remind us that even though Chang'e is far away on the moon, the bond between loved ones remains strong.

Lessons from Chang'e: Love, Sacrifice, and Longing

The story of Chang'e is not just a beautiful tale—it also teaches us valuable lessons about love and sacrifice. Chang'e's choice to drink the potion was an act of bravery and protection. She gave up her life on earth to keep the magic potion safe and ensure that it would not fall into the wrong hands. Through her story, we learn that love sometimes means making difficult sacrifices to protect those we care about.

Chang'e's time on the moon also teaches us about longing and how important it is to cherish the moments we share with the people we love. Even though she became immortal, Chang'e's heart still longed for the company of Hou Yi and the people on earth. Her story reminds us to value our time with family and friends because those moments are precious.

The friendship between Chang'e and the Jade Rabbit offers another important lesson—kindness and companionship can help us through even the loneliest times. The Jade Rabbit's selflessness shows us that acts of kindness, no matter how small, can bring joy and meaning to others.

Finally, Chang'e's story teaches us about hope and renewal. Just as the moon changes from new to full each month, we are reminded that life is always moving in cycles. Even when we experience sadness or separation, there is always the hope of new beginnings, just like the moon reappearing after a dark night.

The story of Chang'e and the Jade Rabbit has captured the imaginations of people for generations. When you look up at the moon, think of Chang'e sitting in her palace with the Jade Rabbit by her side. Their story teaches us that even when we feel far from the ones we love, the light of friendship, love, and kindness will always shine through.

So, the next time you see the full moon glowing in the sky, make a wish for Chang'e and the Jade Rabbit. And who knows? Maybe, just maybe, she'll send a little moonlight your way to remind you that you are never truly alone.

CHAPTER 3: THE TALE OF THE MONKEY KING - JOURNEY TO THE WEST

Have you ever imagined what it would be like to meet a mischievous monkey with magical powers? In Chinese legends, the Monkey King—also known as Sun Wukong—is one of the most exciting and beloved characters of all time. He is clever, funny, and full of energy, but he also learns important lessons about bravery, wisdom, and growth during his adventures. So, let's swing through the trees and dive into the incredible world of the Monkey King!

Who Is the Mischievous Monkey King?

The Monkey King's story begins on a magical mountain where a special stone gave birth to a monkey. This was no ordinary monkey—he was destined for greatness. He could talk, walk upright, and jump higher than any other creature in the forest. The monkeys of the mountain quickly made him their king because he was so smart and fearless.

But being king of the monkeys wasn't enough for Sun Wukong. He wanted to become even more powerful. He traveled far and wide, learning magical skills from wise masters and becoming stronger with each new adventure. The Monkey King could transform into different animals, summon clouds to ride through the sky, and even make himself invisible!

With all these abilities, Sun Wukong became quite confident—maybe a little too confident! His playful tricks soon became trouble, as he began to challenge the gods and cause mischief in the heavens. But every legend needs a twist, and the Monkey King's story is all about how he learns to use his powers for good.

His Magical Staff and Incredible Adventures

One of the most famous parts of the Monkey King's story is his magical staff, called the Ruyi Jingu Bang. This wasn't just any ordinary staff—it could shrink to the size of a needle or grow as tall as a mountain! The staff became Sun Wukong's favorite weapon, and with it, he fought off powerful enemies, including demons and monsters.

But the adventures didn't stop there. Sun Wukong became famous for his strength and cleverness. One of his most exciting adventures is told in the legend of Journey to the West. In this story, the Monkey King joins a monk named Xuanzang on a long journey to find sacred Buddhist scriptures. Along the way, Sun Wukong faces many challenges, from fighting fierce demons to solving tricky puzzles.

On this journey, the Monkey King teams up with two companions: Pigsy, a greedy pig spirit, and Sandy, a river demon. The three of them help Xuanzang on his mission, protecting him from danger and learning important lessons about friendship, patience, and teamwork. While Sun Wukong's mischievous side causes trouble now and then, his clever tricks often save the day.

How the Monkey King Learned to Be Wise and Brave

Even though the Monkey King started out as a mischievous troublemaker, his adventures taught him some valuable lessons. During his journey with Xuanzang, Sun Wukong learned that being strong isn't just about having magical powers—it's also about using those powers wisely.

One of the hardest lessons for the Monkey King was learning to control his temper. In the beginning, he would rush into fights without thinking, using his strength to defeat anyone in his way. But as he traveled with Xuanzang, he realized that bravery also meant knowing when to be patient and finding peaceful solutions.

By the end of his journey, Sun Wukong had grown from a mischievous monkey into a wise hero. He earned the respect of the gods and found peace within himself. Through his adventures, the Monkey King discovered that true strength comes not just from power, but from wisdom, kindness, and understanding.

Lessons from the Monkey King: Strength, Cleverness, and Growth

The tale of the Monkey King is more than just an exciting adventure—it's also filled with important lessons that we can all learn from.

First, the Monkey King teaches us about the power of cleverness. Even though Sun Wukong was smaller than many of his enemies, he often outsmarted them with his quick thinking. His story reminds us that brains can be just as important as brawn, especially when we face challenges.

Second, the Monkey King's journey shows us the importance of growth and learning from our mistakes. Sun Wukong wasn't perfect—he made a lot of mistakes along the way. But each time he faced a challenge, he became wiser and stronger. His story encourages us to keep learning, even when things get tough.

Finally, the Monkey King's tale is a reminder that strength isn't just about fighting—it's also about kindness and self-control. Sun Wukong started his adventures thinking that power meant winning battles, but he learned that true strength comes from using his abilities to help others.

Sun Wukong's adventures have been told and retold for centuries, and his story remains one of the most popular in Chinese culture. Kids and adults alike admire the Monkey King's daring spirit, quick wit, and big heart. His journey from a mischievous troublemaker to a wise hero shows us that anyone can grow, change, and become better with time.

So, the next time you feel like mischief is calling, think of the Monkey King. Use your cleverness, but don't forget to be kind and wise too! And who knows? Maybe you'll go on your own adventure one day—just like Sun Wukong on his journey to the West.

CHAPTER 4: THE WEAVER AND THE COWHERD - A LOVE ACROSS THE STARS

Long ago, in the vast sky, there lived a beautiful young girl named Zhinu, the Weaver Girl. She was no ordinary girl—Zhinu was a goddess who could weave the most beautiful clouds in the heavens, creating colors and patterns that sparkled like rainbows. Her job was to weave the sky with these magical clouds, filling it with light and wonder. But despite all the beauty she created, Zhinu felt lonely. She spent her days weaving and dreaming of something more—she longed for love and adventure beyond the heavens.

Down on Earth, there lived a kind-hearted young man named Niulang, the Cowherd. Niulang was a humble farmer who took care of a small herd of cows. Though his life was simple, he was happy, surrounded by nature and his animals. But, like Zhinu, he too dreamed of love—of someone to share his life with.

And so, the stars aligned, and fate brought the two together.

How the Weaver Girl and the Cowherd Fell in Love

One day, Zhinu's curiosity got the best of her. She decided to leave the heavens and visit the Earth disguised as a mortal girl. As she wandered through a beautiful forest, she met Niulang by chance. From the moment they saw each other, it was as if the stars themselves had connected their hearts. Zhinu and Niulang fell deeply in love, and they decided to stay together, creating a happy life on Earth.

Niulang's cows loved Zhinu just as much as he did. With her by his side, life seemed perfect. The Weaver Girl and the Cowherd spent their days laughing, farming, and sharing stories under the bright sky. They were inseparable, and together they built a life full of joy and love.

But love between a goddess and a mortal was not something the gods would easily allow. When the mighty Queen Mother of the West, Zhinu's mother, found out that her daughter had fallen in love with a human, she became very angry. She believed that gods and mortals could not live together, so she ordered Zhinu to return to the heavens, separating her from Niulang forever.

Heartbroken, Niulang refused to give up. With the help of a magical cow from his herd, Niulang flew to the heavens, determined to be reunited with his beloved Zhinu. But just as they were about to embrace, the Queen Mother of the West drew a river of stars across the sky, creating the Milky Way to keep them apart.

The Bridge of Magpies and the Qixi Festival

Even though Zhinu and Niulang were separated by the Milky Way, their love was so strong that it touched the hearts of the animals and birds. Every year, on the seventh day of the seventh lunar month, magpies from all over the world would gather to help the two lovers meet again. They would form a bridge across the Milky Way, allowing

Zhinu and Niulang to cross the river of stars and be together for just one night.

This magical night became known as Qixi, the Chinese Valentine's Day. To this day, people celebrate the Qixi Festival by looking up at the night sky, hoping to catch a glimpse of the stars where the Weaver Girl and the Cowherd meet. Children make wishes, and couples exchange gifts, just like Zhinu and Niulang shared their love across the stars.

The stars Altair and Vega—which represent Niulang and Zhinu—shine brightly in the night sky, separated by the Milky Way but forever connected in spirit. On the night of Qixi, it's said that if the sky is clear and the stars are bright, the magpies have built their bridge once again, reuniting the lovers for their special night.

Lessons from the Weaver and the Cowherd: Patience, Love, and Hope

The story of the Weaver Girl and the Cowherd teaches us that true love is patient and never gives up, even when faced with challenges. Zhinu and Niulang's love was so powerful that even a river of stars could not keep them apart forever. Their story reminds us that love is worth waiting for, and that sometimes, patience is the greatest strength of all.

The tale also shows us the importance of hope. Even though Zhinu and Niulang could only meet once a year, they never lost hope. They believed in their love, and the animals around them believed in it too. Just like the magpies who built a bridge across the Milky Way, we can always find a way to bring people together if we have hope in our hearts.

Finally, this story reminds us to treasure the moments we share with the people we love. Even though the Weaver Girl and the Cowherd could only be together for one night each year, they cherished every second. Whether we have a lot of time or just a little, it's important to make the most of it and show kindness and love to those around us.

The legend of the Weaver Girl and the Cowherd has been passed down for generations, inspiring people with its message of love, patience, and hope. Their story shines brightly in the night sky, reminding us that no matter how far apart we may be, love can always bring us together.

So, the next time you see the Milky Way stretching across the sky, think of Zhinu and Niulang. Look for the stars of Altair and Vega, and make a wish.

Who knows? Maybe the magpies are building their bridge at that very moment, reuniting the two lovers under the watchful gaze of the night sky.

And remember, just like the Weaver Girl and the Cowherd, we too can create bridges with patience, love, and hope—bridges that connect us to the people we care about, no matter where they are.

CHAPTER 5: THE LEGEND OF THE WHITE SNAKE - A TALE OF LOVE AND TRANSFORMATION

Long ago, in ancient China, there lived a powerful spirit in the form of a white snake. But this was no ordinary snake—she was a magical being who had lived for thousands of years, studying the ways of the universe and growing wise and powerful. One day, she transformed into a beautiful woman named Bai Suzhen, leaving behind her snake form to experience life among humans. What she did not expect was to fall deeply in love with a mortal man, and so begins the legend of the White Snake—a story of love, transformation, and courage.

Who Was the White Snake Spirit?

The White Snake Spirit, known as Bai Suzhen, was a magical being that had lived for centuries. Over the years, she learned many skills, including the arts of healing and medicine, using her powers to help others. Unlike other spirits who may have used their magic selfishly, Bai Suzhen wanted to do good. Her heart was filled with kindness, and she longed to see what it would be like to live among people.

One spring day, as Bai Suzhen wandered the world in her human form, she arrived at West Lake near the city of Hangzhou. It was a place of incredible beauty, with peaceful waters and blossoming flowers. There, she met a kind and gentle man named Xu Xian, a scholar who worked as an herbalist. From the moment they met, Bai Suzhen and Xu Xian felt a connection that neither of them could explain. Their love story began that day by the shimmering waters of West Lake.

Her Forbidden Love with a Human

Although Bai Suzhen looked like a human woman, she carried a secret—she was still, in essence, a spirit in the form of a snake, and in ancient times, spirits were not supposed to live among humans or fall in love with them. But Bai Suzhen's heart told her otherwise. She knew her love for Xu Xian was real, and she wanted to spend her life with him.

After meeting, Xu Xian quickly fell in love with Bai Suzhen's beauty and kindness. He admired her ability to heal others and was amazed by how gentle she was with every living thing. It wasn't long before the two decided to get married and live a peaceful life together.

For a time, their love seemed perfect. Bai Suzhen and Xu Xian worked side by side, helping people with their herbs and medicines. Their little home was filled with happiness, and it seemed like nothing could come between them. But there was one person who did not approve of their love—a powerful monk named Fa Hai.

How the White Snake Overcame Challenges for Love

Fa Hai, the monk, believed that spirits like Bai Suzhen did not belong in the human world. He was convinced that Bai Suzhen's presence would bring harm to Xu Xian and everyone around them. Determined to break the couple apart, Fa Hai tricked Xu Xian into giving his wife a special wine during the Dragon Boat Festival.

The wine, known for its mystical properties, forced Bai Suzhen to transform back into her white snake form in front of Xu Xian. Xu Xian was terrified. He couldn't believe that his beloved wife was, in fact, a magical snake spirit. Overwhelmed with fear, Xu Xian collapsed and fell into a deep sleep.

Heartbroken but determined to save her husband, Bai Suzhen embarked on a dangerous journey to find a cure. She traveled far and wide until she reached the sacred Kunlun Mountains, where she found a magical herb capable of reviving Xu Xian. Using all her courage and love, she brought the herb back and saved his life.

However, their troubles were far from over. Fa Hai captured Xu Xian and took him to a temple, locking him away so that Bai Suzhen could never see him again. Despite the obstacles, Bai Suzhen refused to give up. With the help of her loyal friend, the Green Snake Spirit, she stormed the temple, using her magic and bravery to free her husband from Fa Hai's clutches. Even though she faced great danger, Bai Suzhen fought not out of anger, but out of love and determination.

Lessons from the White Snake: Compassion, Change, and Bravery

The story of the White Snake teaches us many important lessons. Bai Suzhen's love for Xu Xian showed that true love can overcome even the greatest challenges. She never gave up on her husband, even when things seemed impossible. Her story reminds us that love is not always easy, but it is worth fighting for.

Bai Suzhen also teaches us about compassion. Even though she had great power, she used it to help others. Instead of being selfish with her abilities, she chose to heal and protect the people around her. This part of the legend reminds us that kindness is one of the greatest strengths anyone can have.

The legend also shows the importance of change and growth. Bai Suzhen transformed from a spirit into a human, learning new things along the way. Just like Bai Suzhen, we too can change and grow, learning from our experiences and becoming better people. The story encourages us to embrace new challenges and believe in the power of transformation.

Finally, Bai Suzhen's story is one of bravery. She faced great dangers to protect the person she loved, showing that bravery isn't just about strength—it's about standing up for what matters most. The White Snake's journey teaches us that courage comes in many forms, whether it's fighting for someone we love or simply being kind in a difficult world.

A Love That Stands the Test of Time

The legend of the White Snake is one of China's most beloved stories, passed down through generations as a tale of love, sacrifice, and transformation. Even today, it continues to inspire books, operas, and movies, reminding people of the power of love and the importance of compassion.

So, the next time you see a beautiful lake or a white snake gliding through the grass, think of Bai Suzhen and her story. Remember the lessons of patience, kindness, and bravery, and know that love—just like Bai Suzhen's—can overcome even the greatest challenges. And who knows? Maybe, like Bai Suzhen, you too will find that with compassion and courage, anything is possible.

CHAPTER 6: THE STORY OF NIAN - THE MONSTER OF THE NEW YEAR

A long, long time ago, in a small village in ancient China, the people lived in fear of a terrifying monster called Nian. This was no ordinary creature—Nian was enormous, with sharp claws, glowing eyes, and a mouth large enough to swallow anything in its path. Each year, during the coldest winter night, Nian would awaken from his sleep in the mountains and come down to the village, destroying crops, homes, and scaring the people away. For many years, the villagers had no idea how to stop him. But one day, they discovered a way to defeat the fearsome monster using courage, cleverness, and celebration.

How the Villagers Defeated Nian with Fireworks and Drums

Every year, when Nian came down from the mountains, the people would flee in fear, leaving their homes behind. They hid in the forest, hoping that Nian wouldn't find them. But one year, a wise old man came to the village. He told the people that they didn't have to live in fear of Nian anymore.

"I've heard stories about Nian," the old man said. "This monster is afraid of loud noises, the color red, and bright lights." The villagers were surprised. How could a powerful creature like Nian be afraid of such simple things? But they trusted the old man and decided to try his plan.

The villagers began decorating their homes with red paper and ribbons. They hung bright red lanterns outside their doors and wore red clothing to scare Nian away. They also gathered all the drums and cymbals they could find. On the night of Nian's expected arrival, the villagers stayed in the village instead of running away.

When Nian appeared, roaring and stomping through the streets, the villagers beat their drums and banged their cymbals as loud as they could. Firecrackers exploded in bursts of light, and lanterns glowed brightly in the night. The sudden noise, lights, and flashes of red terrified Nian, and the monster ran back to the mountains, never to return. From that day on, the villagers celebrated their victory over Nian with a great celebration, which became known as Chinese New Year!

Celebrating Chinese New Year with Traditions and Customs

The story of Nian is why Chinese New Year, also called the Spring Festival, is celebrated with fireworks, red decorations, and loud music. Families come together to welcome the new year and drive away any bad luck—just like the villagers once scared off the monster Nian.

On New Year's Eve, families gather for a big feast with delicious foods. Dumplings, fish, noodles, and sweets are all part of the celebration, with each dish carrying its own special meaning. For example, long noodles symbolize long life, while fish represents prosperity.

People also give out red envelopes called "hongbao" with money inside. These envelopes are given to children as a way of wishing them good fortune for the year ahead. Another important tradition is cleaning the house before the new year begins. This symbolizes sweeping away the old and making room for good luck and new beginnings.

The most exciting part of the celebration is the fireworks and lion dances! The sound of firecrackers, drums, and cymbals fills the air as performers dress up as lions to dance through the streets, bringing joy and chasing away bad spirits—just like the villagers did to defeat Nian.

Chinese New Year is not just about loud noises and fun decorations; it's also about family, friendship, and new beginnings. It's a time to reflect on the past year and look forward to the future with hope and joy.

Lessons from Nian: Courage, Celebration, and Community

The story of Nian teaches us that even the scariest challenges can be overcome with courage and cleverness. At first, the villagers ran away from Nian, afraid of what he might do. But when they worked together, they found a way to face their fears. This part of the story reminds us that we don't have to face difficult times alone—with the help of others, we can overcome anything.

The story also teaches us about the importance of celebration. The villagers' joy and excitement didn't just defeat Nian—they also brought the community together. Celebrating with family and friends is a way to remind ourselves of the good things in life and share those moments with the people we love.

Another important lesson from the story of Nian is that traditions help keep us connected. The villagers' clever use of red decorations, loud music, and bright lights became the foundation of Chinese New Year traditions. Even today, people follow these customs to welcome good fortune and happiness into their lives.

The story of Nian encourages us to be brave in the face of challenges, celebrate life's victories, and cherish our communities and traditions. Just like the villagers who defeated Nian, we too can find joy, hope, and strength by working together and embracing new beginnings.

Today, the story of Nian lives on through the joy and excitement of Chinese New Year celebrations. Whether it's through the booming sounds of fireworks, the colorful parades, or the warmth of family gatherings, the spirit of the villagers' victory over Nian continues to inspire people of all ages.

So, the next time you hear fireworks popping or see a bright red lantern glowing in the night, think of the brave villagers who defeated Nian. Remember that courage and community can help us overcome any challenge, and celebrations bring us together to share life's joys. And who knows—maybe one day, you'll create your own tradition to share with others, just like the story of Nian became a tradition for people all over the world!

CHAPTER 7: PANGU AND THE CREATION OF THE WORLD

Long ago, before the world we know existed, there was only darkness—a swirling, silent chaos with no sky, no land, and no sea. But deep within this chaos, something extraordinary began to form: an egg, filled with all the energy of the universe. Inside the egg slept a giant named Pangu, waiting for the right moment to awaken and begin his great task—the creation of the world.

How Pangu Shaped the Heavens and the Earth

After thousands of years inside the egg, Pangu finally opened his eyes. He looked around and saw the swirling darkness around him. But Pangu knew that this chaos had to be separated to create something new. With a mighty swing of his axe, he cracked the egg in two, dividing it into two parts: the light part floated up to become the sky, while the heavier part sank to form the earth.

Pangu knew that the sky and the earth needed to be kept apart, so he stood between them, holding the heavens high above his head. Every day, Pangu grew a little bit taller, pushing the sky higher and higher to make sure it would never fall back down onto the earth. For 18,000 years, Pangu stood like this, separating the heavens from the earth and giving shape to the world we know today.

The Myth of Pangu's Body Becoming Mountains, Rivers, and Trees

Eventually, after many centuries of hard work, Pangu grew tired. His great task was complete—the sky was high, the earth was solid, and the world was ready. So, Pangu gently laid down to rest, knowing that his job was done.

But Pangu's story doesn't end here. In fact, his giant body became the world around us! The legends tell us that when Pangu passed away, his breath became the wind and clouds, and his voice became the thunder that rolls across the skies. His mighty arms and legs transformed into the mountains that rise from the earth, and his blood flowed into rivers that bring life to the land.

Even Pangu's hair and beard found a place in the world—they grew into lush forests and fields. His bones became the precious stones and minerals hidden deep beneath the earth, and his sweat became the morning dew that glistens on leaves and flowers.

And so, every part of Pangu's being became a part of the world, connecting nature to his spirit and leaving behind a beautiful creation filled with life.

Lessons from Pangu: Creation, Endurance, and the Beauty of Nature

The story of Pangu teaches us many important lessons about life, work, and the natural world around us. First, it shows us the power of creation—how everything in the universe has a place and purpose. Pangu's work reminds us that with effort, dedication, and care, we too can shape the world around us and bring good things to life.

This legend also teaches us about endurance. Pangu stood between the heavens and the earth for thousands of years, knowing that his task was too important to give up. Even though it was hard work, Pangu stayed strong until his mission was complete. His story shows us the importance of patience and persistence, especially when we are working on something big or important. Just like Pangu, we can achieve great things when we keep going, even when things are difficult.

Finally, Pangu's story helps us see the beauty of nature. His body becoming mountains, rivers, and trees reminds us that everything in nature is connected. The wind, the rain, the forests, and the animals all work together in harmony. This legend encourages us to respect the natural world and take care of the environment, just as Pangu gave his life to create it.

Pangu's story may be ancient, but it continues to inspire people of all ages. It teaches us that hard work and determination can create something beautiful and that everything around us—mountains, rivers, trees—has its own magic and importance. Whether we are planting a tree, helping a friend, or working on a project, Pangu's legend reminds us to put our hearts into everything we do.

So, the next time you look up at the sky or feel the wind on your face, think of Pangu, the giant who shaped the world with his strength and love. His spirit lives on in the beauty of nature, encouraging us to be kind to the earth and create something wonderful with our own hands. And who knows? Maybe one day, you'll create your own legend, just like Pangu did, leaving a mark on the world for generations to come.

CHAPTER 8: THE JADE EMPEROR - RULER OF HEAVEN

Long, long ago, before there were rulers in the heavens, the earth and the skies were filled with chaos. There were gods, but none of them was powerful enough to bring order. The Jade Emperor wasn't always the most important god. In fact, he was once a kind and wise spirit living a humble life on earth, helping people and creatures wherever he went.

The Jade Emperor's journey to becoming the ruler of all the heavens started with his deep sense of fairness and his love for harmony. After many lifetimes of spreading kindness and wisdom on earth, he earned the respect of the gods. When the time came to choose a ruler for the heavens, the gods all agreed that this gentle but just being should become the Jade Emperor—the Supreme God who would bring peace to the universe.

The Jade Emperor ruled with patience and wisdom, ensuring that every god and spirit knew their duties. But he wasn't just a distant ruler; the Jade Emperor also kept a watchful eye over the people on earth, making sure there was balance between heaven and earth. To keep things in order, he sometimes needed to solve tricky problems, like choosing the animals of the Chinese zodiac—a task that required both fairness and creativity.

The Story of the Great Race and the Chinese Zodiac

The Jade Emperor wanted to create a way for people to measure time and seasons, so he decided to name a year after twelve different animals. But how would he choose which animals to include? He came up with a fun and exciting solution: a great race! The first twelve animals to cross a mighty river would each get a place in the zodiac, with the order of their arrival determining their position.

The animals lined up at the riverbank, eager to start the race. Among them were the rat, ox, tiger, rabbit, dragon, snake, horse, goat, monkey, rooster, dog, and pig. The Jade Emperor watched as the animals prepared to leap into the water and begin the exciting challenge.

As the race began, the ox quickly took the lead, swimming steadily across the river. But unknown to the ox, the clever rat had secretly climbed onto his back! Just before the ox reached the other side, the rat jumped off and scurried to the finish line, becoming the first animal in the zodiac. The ox came in second, followed by the powerful tiger and the quick rabbit, who had hopped from stone to stone to avoid the rushing water.

One of the crowd favorites was the dragon, who came fifth—not because he was slow, but because he had stopped along the way to help villagers by bringing rain to their fields. The rest of the animals arrived in their own time, each with a story about how they overcame challenges during the race. The cheerful pig was the last to arrive, but the Jade Emperor welcomed him with a smile, saying, "Even the slowest has a place."

And so, the twelve animals of the Chinese zodiac were chosen, with each animal symbolizing a different year. The race wasn't just about speed—it was a test of cunning, bravery, teamwork, and perseverance.

Lessons from the Jade Emperor: Leadership, Fairness, and Harmony

The Jade Emperor teaches us many valuable lessons about how to lead with wisdom and kindness. As the Supreme God, he didn't use his power to control others. Instead, he worked to create harmony between the gods, nature, and people on earth. He shows us that being a leader isn't about being the loudest or strongest—it's about making fair decisions that help everyone.

The story of the Great Race teaches us the importance of fairness. The Jade Emperor gave each animal an equal chance, no matter how big or small they were. Even the slow and lazy pig found his way into the zodiac, proving that everyone has value, no matter how long it takes them to reach their goal.

Another lesson from the Jade Emperor is about the importance of teamwork and helping others. The dragon could have easily flown to the finish line first, but he chose to help the villagers in need. This teaches us that sometimes, the right thing to do isn't about winning—it's about making a difference.

The Great Race also reminds us that everyone has their own strengths. The rat's cleverness, the ox's strength, and the rabbit's quick thinking all helped them cross the river in different ways. In life, just like in the race, we all have unique qualities that can help us overcome challenges.

The Jade Emperor's leadership continues to inspire people today, especially during the Lunar New Year celebrations. The Chinese zodiac is not just about marking time—it's also a way to celebrate each person's strengths and the qualities that make us who we are. Each animal in the zodiac teaches us something about ourselves and others, helping us understand the importance of patience, kindness, and hard work.

The Jade Emperor's story also reminds us that life is a journey. Whether we reach our goals quickly, like the rat, or take our time, like the pig, what matters most is that we keep moving forward and help others along the way.

So, the next time you hear a New Year's celebration filled with fireworks and joy, think of the Jade Emperor and his wise leadership. Just like the animals in the zodiac, you have your own special qualities that make you unique. Whether you're brave like the tiger, patient like the ox, or clever like the rat, there's always a place for you in the story of life.

And who knows—maybe one day, you'll find yourself leading with wisdom, just like the Jade Emperor did, bringing harmony and happiness to everyone around you.

CHAPTER 9: THE LEGEND OF MULAN - A BRAVE DAUGHTER'S JOURNEY

Long ago in ancient China, the land faced a great threat. The Emperor sent out a decree calling on all men to join the army and protect their homeland. Every family had to send one man to fight. When the message reached the home of a young girl named Mulan, she knew her family was in trouble. Mulan's father, though brave, was old and weak. He had fought in battles before, and now he was too frail to do so again. But since he had no sons, there was no choice—he would have to go to war.

Mulan couldn't stand the thought of her father suffering on the battlefield. She loved her father dearly and knew he wouldn't survive another war. So, with a brave heart, Mulan made a daring decision—she would go in his place! She put on her father's armor, tied her hair back, and took his sword. Disguising herself as a young man, she quietly left her home under the cover of night, ready to face whatever challenges lay ahead.

Mulan knew the risk she was taking. If anyone discovered that she was a girl, she would be in serious trouble. But Mulan's love for her family gave her the courage to press on. She was determined to do everything she could to protect her father and honor her family.

Her Adventures and Battles in Disguise

When Mulan joined the army, no one suspected her secret. She trained hard alongside the other soldiers, running drills, practicing sword fighting, and preparing for battle. At first, it was tough—Mulan wasn't used to the harsh conditions of army life. But she didn't give up. She worked harder than anyone else, determined to prove herself, and little by little, she gained the respect of her fellow soldiers.

Soon, Mulan found herself marching into battle. Her heart pounded with fear, but she reminded herself why she was there—for her father, her family, and her country. In every fight, Mulan showed bravery and skill, leading her comrades to victory. Her quick thinking saved lives, and she fought fiercely against the enemies threatening her homeland.

One of Mulan's most famous moments came when her army was ambushed by enemies in a narrow mountain pass. Trapped and outnumbered, things looked hopeless. But Mulan came up with a clever plan. Using fireworks and signal flares, she caused an avalanche that swept the enemy soldiers away, giving her army a chance to escape. Thanks to her courage and smart thinking, they won the day!

As time went on, Mulan's reputation as a brave and capable warrior spread throughout the army. She became a trusted leader, helping guide her comrades through many difficult battles. But all this time, no one knew her true identity. Mulan kept her secret close to her heart, knowing that it could cost her everything if it were revealed.

Lessons from Mulan: Courage, Family, and Honor

After years of service, the war finally came to an end. Mulan and her comrades returned home as heroes. The Emperor, hearing of Mulan's bravery, called her to the palace to offer her a great reward. But instead of riches or titles, Mulan asked for only one thing—to return home to her family.

It was then, surrounded by her comrades, that Mulan revealed her true identity. To everyone's amazement, the fierce warrior who had fought alongside them was not a man, but a young woman. The soldiers and the Emperor were stunned, but instead of punishment, they honored Mulan for her bravery and selflessness. She had risked everything, not for fame or fortune, but for love and loyalty to her family.

Mulan's story teaches us many valuable lessons.

Courage is not about being fearless—it's about doing the right thing even when you're scared. Mulan knew the dangers she faced, but she was brave enough to stand up for what she believed in and protect the people she loved.

Family plays a central role in Mulan's story. She chose to fight in place of her father, showing us that family comes first and that love for those we care about can give us strength.

Lastly, honor is an important lesson from Mulan's story. Even though she had to break the rules by disguising herself as a man, Mulan's actions were driven by a deep sense of responsibility. She honored her family, her comrades, and her country by fighting with bravery and loyalty.

A Hero for All Time

Mulan's story has inspired people for centuries. She is a symbol of strength, courage, and love—qualities that remind us all that anyone, no matter their size or appearance, can become a hero. Mulan teaches us that being true to yourself and following your heart can lead to incredible things. Whether you're facing a tough challenge at school or helping a friend in need, you can channel Mulan's bravery and do what's right, even when it's hard.

And just like Mulan, you don't need armor or a sword to be a hero. All it takes is kindness, courage, and a willingness to help others. So, the next time you feel nervous or unsure, think of Mulan and her journey from a quiet village to the battlefield. You have the same bravery inside you—all you need to do is believe in yourself.

Mulan's tale will always remind us that greatness comes from the heart, not from appearances. And as long as we carry her story with us, we'll always remember that we, too, can be heroes in our own unique way.

CHAPTER 10: THE LAUGHING BUDDHA - A SYMBOL OF HAPPINESS

The Laughing Buddha, known as Budai in Chinese, is one of the most beloved figures in Chinese culture. He is not the same Buddha who founded Buddhism, but a joyful monk who became a symbol of happiness, kindness, and good fortune. You've probably seen statues of him before—he has a round belly, a wide grin, and carries a big cloth bag.

So why is the Laughing Buddha always smiling? Well, it's said that Budai found joy in simple things like making people laugh, sharing stories, and helping those in need. His smile reminds us that happiness comes from within and that kindness can bring light to others' lives. Wherever he went, Budai spread joy, laughter, and generosity, making him a beloved figure in both temples and homes.

People believe that rubbing the Laughing Buddha's belly brings good luck! This cheerful monk is also known as the "patron of children and the poor," as he cared deeply for those who had little, always sharing what he had with a happy heart.

Tales of the Laughing Buddha's Travels and Generosity

The Laughing Buddha didn't stay in one place for long—he loved to travel. With nothing more than his big cloth bag and a walking stick, Budai wandered from town to town, meeting new people and spreading joy wherever he went.

One popular story tells of Budai arriving in a small village where people were worried about a bad harvest. The villagers were sad, but Budai sat under a tree, smiling and laughing as if all their problems had already disappeared. Curious, the children of the village gathered around him. Budai told funny stories and gave them small gifts from his bag. Soon, the whole village was filled with laughter, and even the adults began to smile.

Budai didn't have much, but he shared whatever he could—sometimes coins, sometimes toys or food. Whenever he gave something away, his joy seemed to grow even bigger, teaching everyone that true happiness comes from sharing what you have with others.

Another tale says that one day, Budai found a group of people arguing over a small amount of money. He opened his bag and gave away the last of his coins to stop the argument. "Happiness is better than gold," he said with a chuckle, and the people felt ashamed of their greed. They promised to value kindness over wealth, thanks to Budai's wise and cheerful example.

Lessons from the Laughing Buddha: Kindness, Joy, and Sharing

The Laughing Buddha's tales are more than just funny stories—they carry important life lessons for all of us.

First, Budai teaches us the importance of kindness. He didn't wait to be asked for help—he gave freely, whether it was food, a coin, or a smile. His kindness shows us that small acts of generosity can make a big difference in someone's life.

The Laughing Buddha also reminds us that joy is something we can share. No matter where Budai went, he found a reason to smile, even during tough times. His laughter was contagious, helping others see the good in every situation. From Budai, we learn that even when things aren't perfect, a positive attitude can brighten our day and the lives of those around us.

Lastly, Budai's stories teach us about the importance of sharing. He didn't hold on to what he had—he gave it away freely and found happiness in doing so. Budai shows us that sharing isn't just about giving objects—it's also about sharing time, laughter, and kindness with others. Whether it's a kind word or a helping hand, sharing makes the world a better place.

The Laughing Buddha reminds us that happiness isn't found in things—it's found in how we treat others. You don't need a big bag of gifts or gold to spread joy like Budai did. A smile, a kind word, or a simple act of generosity can brighten someone's day.

Think about a time when you made someone smile. How did it make you feel? Just like the Laughing Buddha, you can make the world a little brighter by spreading kindness wherever you go. Whether it's helping a friend, sharing a snack, or telling a funny story, your actions can make a difference.

And remember, the Laughing Buddha teaches us to find joy in simple things—a sunny day, a friendly hello, or the sound of laughter. Even when things are hard, try to find something to be thankful for. Just like Budai's smile brought hope to those around him, your joy can inspire others to find their own happiness.

The Laughing Buddha's story is a reminder that life is better when we share kindness and joy with others. Whether we're facing a challenge or enjoying a happy moment, we can all learn from Budai's example:

Be kind to others and help whenever you can.

Share your happiness and make someone smile.

Find joy in the little things, and spread that joy wherever you go.

The next time you see a statue of the Laughing Buddha, remember his stories and the lessons he teaches. Try rubbing his belly for good luck, and then go out and spread some joy, just like Budai did long ago. And who knows? Your kindness might just make someone's day a little brighter!

CHAPTER 11: THE STORY OF YU THE GREAT - TAMER OF THE FLOODS

A long, long time ago in ancient China, a terrible flood covered the land. The waters rose higher and higher, washing away homes, farms, and villages. Crops couldn't grow, people had to flee from their homes, and no one knew how to stop the endless rain. The flood seemed unstoppable, causing misery for everyone—until a hero named Yu stepped forward.

Yu the Great was not just an ordinary man—he was known for his bravery, wisdom, and unshakable determination. The Emperor asked Yu to find a way to stop the flood and save the land. It was a difficult task, but Yu accepted the challenge, knowing that the fate of China depended on it. Instead of trying to block the water, which had failed many times before, Yu came up with a clever plan.

Yu believed the best way to fight the flood was to work with the water, not against it. He noticed how rivers naturally flowed towards the sea and decided to guide the floodwaters safely instead of stopping them. For thirteen long years, Yu traveled across China, digging canals, building dams, and shaping rivers so the water could flow freely without causing harm. He worked tirelessly, sometimes using just a simple shovel and his own hands to carve out new paths for the water.

His Wisdom in Building Canals and Dams

Yu's most important lesson was that understanding nature's rhythms was the key to success. Instead of trying to block the flood all at once, he guided the water into different paths, letting it flow safely back to rivers and the sea. Every canal Yu built allowed the water to spread out evenly, and dams helped hold back the strongest currents.

Yu didn't just work alone—he inspired people across the land to help. Villagers and farmers worked side by side with Yu, digging canals and building dams that would protect their homes and crops. They trusted Yu because he never gave up, even when the work seemed impossible. Yu's leadership showed everyone that when people work together, even the greatest challenges can be overcome.

It wasn't easy, though. Yu traveled through rugged mountains, dense forests, and dangerous rivers.

Sometimes he slept on the ground under the stars, too focused on his task to return home. In fact, Yu was so dedicated to his work that he didn't return to his family for many years, knowing that the safety of the entire country depended on his efforts. He sacrificed his comfort and time with his loved ones to make sure the land would be safe for future generations.

Lessons from Yu the Great: Hard Work, Leadership, and Responsibility

Yu's story teaches us many important lessons that are still valuable today. One of the biggest lessons is about the importance of hard work. Yu didn't solve the problem overnight—he worked for thirteen years, day and night, until the flood was under control. His story shows that patience and perseverance are essential when tackling big challenges.

Another lesson from Yu the Great is about leadership. A true leader, like Yu, doesn't just give orders—he works alongside others, inspires them, and never gives up, even when things get tough. Yu's actions show us that a good leader cares about others and works for the greater good.

Yu's story is also about responsibility. He could have chosen to return home and live a quiet life with his family, but instead, he took on the enormous task of saving the land from the flood. Yu teaches us that taking responsibility for problems—even when they seem overwhelming—makes a difference. Each of us can make the world a better place by doing our part, just as Yu did.

A Hero Who Built a Legacy

Because of Yu's hard work, the canals and dams he built saved countless lives and allowed the land to flourish once again. The crops began to grow, rivers flowed peacefully, and people could rebuild their homes and villages. Yu the Great's achievements were so remarkable that the people of China named him their leader, and he became the founder of the Xia Dynasty, the first dynasty in Chinese history.

Even today, Yu the Great is remembered as a hero. His story reminds us that no matter how big the challenge, with hard work, leadership, and a sense of responsibility, we can overcome any obstacle. Yu didn't just fight the flood—he taught people how to live in harmony with nature, setting an example for future generations.

The next time you face a challenge, big or small, think of Yu the Great. He teaches us that problems can be solved with patience, teamwork, and smart thinking. Whether you're working on a school project, helping a friend, or finding a solution to a problem at home, you can make a difference—just like Yu did.

And remember, you don't need to tame a flood to be a hero. You can be a hero by taking responsibility, leading with kindness, and working hard to make things better, even in small ways. Yu the Great shows us that the greatest heroes are those who care for others and never give up, no matter how hard the journey may be.

So, as you explore the world of Chinese legends, keep Yu's lessons in mind. Be brave, be kind, and be responsible—and who knows? Maybe one day, you'll create your own story of greatness!

CHAPTER 12: THE STORY OF HOU YI - THE ARCHER WHO SHOT DOWN NINE SUNS

A long, long time ago, ancient China had not one, but ten suns in the sky. These ten suns were brothers who lived high in the heavens. They took turns rising each day, bringing light and warmth to the world. Each sun would shine on a different day, making sure the land and rivers had just the right amount of sunlight.

But one day, the ten brothers grew restless. They decided it would be fun to rise into the sky all at once! The moment they did, the world became unbearably hot. Rivers dried up, crops withered, and animals had no place to hide from the scorching heat. Even the people couldn't find relief, and it seemed like everything would soon be destroyed by the blazing suns.

No one knew what to do. The people prayed to the gods, begging for help. It seemed that no one could stop the suns—until a hero named Hou Yi stepped forward.

How Hou Yi's Skill Saved the Earth

Hou Yi was a famous archer, known throughout the land for his unmatched skill with the bow and arrow. He was not only strong but also brave and determined to save the earth. When the gods saw how desperate the people were, they gave Hou Yi a magical bow and a quiver of enchanted arrows. With these tools, Hou Yi would have the power to stop the ten suns.

Hou Yi climbed to the top of the highest mountain, where he could see all ten suns shining fiercely in the sky. He knew that if he didn't act quickly, the world would be lost. He pulled out his first arrow, aimed carefully, and let it fly.

With a sharp whistle, the arrow soared through the sky and struck one of the suns. The sun flickered and then fell from the sky, disappearing over the horizon. The temperature cooled slightly, but it was still too hot. Hou Yi knew he had to shoot down more suns to save the earth.

One by one, Hou Yi shot down the suns, each time making the world a little cooler. The rivers began to flow again, the crops perked up, and animals returned to their homes. But soon, only one sun remained in the sky. Hou Yi realized that if he shot down the last sun, the world would be covered in darkness forever.

So, with great wisdom, Hou Yi spared the final sun. He let it shine gently over the land, knowing that the people needed both light and warmth to survive.

Lessons from Hou Yi: Heroism, Balance, and Sacrifice

Hou Yi's story is about more than just bravery. It teaches us many important lessons about balance, sacrifice, and what it means to be a hero.

First, Hou Yi showed incredible courage by facing a challenge that seemed impossible. Even though he was just one man, he didn't hesitate to take action when the world needed him. This teaches us that heroes aren't always the strongest or the biggest—they are the ones who act bravely when it matters most.

Hou Yi also teaches us about balance. He could have shot down all ten suns, but he realized that the earth needed light to survive. This reminds us that too much of anything—even something good—can be harmful. Life needs balance, just like the world needs both day and night.

Finally, Hou Yi's sacrifice shows us the importance of putting others before ourselves. After saving the earth, Hou Yi could have been celebrated as a hero. But instead of resting, he continued to use his skills to help others. In some versions of the story, Hou Yi even gives up his immortality for the sake of love, choosing to live as a mortal with his wife, Chang'e. His actions remind us that true heroism comes from selflessness and compassion.

Hou Yi's story has been told for generations in China, inspiring children and adults alike. He is remembered as a hero who saved the earth and restored balance to the world. His bravery and wisdom teach us that even in the face of overwhelming challenges, we can find solutions if we are willing to act with courage and thoughtfulness.

Today, the story of Hou Yi is still celebrated during festivals and holidays, reminding people to appreciate the sun that shines above them and the balance that makes life possible. Whenever you see the sun rising in the morning, you can think of Hou Yi and the moment he chose to save the earth—not by destroying all the suns, but by finding the right balance between light and darkness.

And who knows? Maybe one day, when you face a challenge of your own, you'll remember the story of Hou Yi and find the courage to act with bravery, wisdom, and kindness—just like the great archer who shot down nine suns.

CHAPTER 13: THE TALE OF ZAO SHEN - THE KITCHEN GOD

A long time ago, in ancient China, people believed that every household had a special guardian—Zao Shen, the Kitchen God. Unlike mighty warriors or fierce dragons, Zao Shen's job was a little different but just as important. He watched over the everyday lives of families, making sure that their homes were peaceful, their meals were nourishing, and their hearts were full of gratitude.

Zao Shen didn't live in the heavens like the other gods. He lived right in the kitchen of every home, where families cooked their meals and gathered to eat. In Chinese culture, the kitchen is more than just a place to make food—it's the heart of the household, where people connect, share stories, and show care for one another. This made Zao Shen's role very special because he was believed to protect and guide families in their daily lives.

But Zao Shen didn't just sit quietly in the kitchen. He observed everything that happened—the good and the bad. If a family worked together, treated each other with kindness, and prepared meals with love, Zao Shen was pleased. But if there were arguments, dishonesty, or laziness, Zao Shen noticed that, too. He kept a record of everything, ready to report back to the Jade Emperor, the ruler of heaven.

The Ritual of Sending Zao Shen's Spirit to Heaven on New Year's Eve

Every year, on New Year's Eve, something exciting happened. Families believed that Zao Shen traveled to the heavens to give a report on everything he had seen in the household throughout the year. The Jade Emperor would listen carefully to Zao Shen's report, and based on what he heard, he would decide whether the family deserved blessings or needed to work on becoming better in the new year.

So, as New Year's Eve approached, families prepared for Zao Shen's journey. They wanted to make sure that he delivered a positive report! To keep Zao Shen happy, families would clean their homes from top to bottom, showing that they were ready for a fresh start.

One of the most important parts of the New Year's Eve ritual was the offering made to Zao Shen. Families would prepare sweet, sticky treats, like malt sugar cakes, and place them on the altar next to the stove. Why? The sweets were said to "sweeten" Zao Shen's mouth—so when he spoke to the Jade Emperor, he would only have kind things to say! Some families even believed that the sticky cakes would keep Zao Shen's mouth too full to mention anything negative.

When everything was ready, families would light incense and say a prayer of gratitude to Zao Shen for watching over their home. Then, they would burn a special paper image of the Kitchen God, symbolically sending his spirit to the heavens.

But don't worry—Zao Shen didn't stay in the heavens for long. On the first day of the new year, his spirit returned to the household, ready to watch over the family for another year. Families welcomed him back with a fresh paper image, hung proudly near the kitchen stove, so Zao Shen would feel at home once again.

Lessons from Zao Shen: Honesty, Home, and Gratitude

Zao Shen's story may be about a small, humble kitchen, but the lessons it teaches are big and meaningful. One of the most important things we learn from Zao Shen is honesty. Just like Zao Shen observed everything in the kitchen, the story reminds us that our actions matter, whether someone is watching or not. It teaches us that it's important to do the right thing—not just to impress others, but because it's the right thing to do.

Another lesson from Zao Shen's story is about the importance of home and family. The kitchen is where people gather to share meals, stories, and moments of joy. Zao Shen's presence reminds us to care for one another and to make our homes places of love, respect, and kindness. When families work together and support each other, it creates a peaceful, happy home.

Finally, gratitude is at the heart of Zao Shen's story. Every year, families took time to say thank you to the Kitchen God and reflect on the blessings they had received. This teaches us the importance of being grateful for what we have—whether it's the food on our table, the people we love, or the small moments of happiness that make life special.

Even today, many families in China and other parts of the world celebrate the Kitchen God during the Lunar New Year. It's a time to reflect on the past year, make new goals, and show gratitude for the blessings of family and home. And while not everyone believes in Zao Shen anymore, his story lives on, reminding people of the importance of honesty, kindness, and gratitude.

The next time you sit down for a family meal or help in the kitchen, think of Zao Shen, the Kitchen God who quietly watches over every home. How would your actions make Zao Shen feel? Would he be proud to report your kindness and hard work to the Jade Emperor?

Through the story of Zao Shen, we learn that every small action—like sharing a meal, being kind to a family member, or saying thank you—matters. And just like the Kitchen God keeps watch over the heart of the home, we, too, can look out for those around us, making our homes and communities places of warmth and care.

So, as you enjoy your next meal, take a moment to think about what you're grateful for. Whether it's your family, your friends, or even just the food on your plate, a little bit of gratitude goes a long way. And who knows—maybe Zao Shen is still watching, ready to bring good fortune to those who live with kindness and joy!

CHAPTER 14: THE LEGEND OF THE BUTTERFLY LOVERS - A TALE OF TRAGIC LOVE

Long ago, in ancient China, there lived a young woman named Zhu Yingtai. Zhu was kind and curious, with a heart full of dreams. But in her time, girls weren't allowed to go to school. Zhu Yingtai, however, was determined to learn, so she came up with a clever plan. She dressed as a boy and set off to study in a distant academy, disguising her true identity so she could follow her dream.

At the academy, Zhu met Liang Shanbo, a bright young man with a gentle soul. The two students quickly became best friends. They studied together, laughed together, and shared many adventures. But as time passed, Zhu Yingtai's feelings for Liang Shanbo grew deeper. She wasn't just his friend—she had fallen in love with him.

Sadly, Liang Shanbo didn't know that Zhu Yingtai was really a girl. He thought they were simply two close friends, bound by loyalty and trust. As the seasons changed, Zhu's heart grew heavier. She knew that one day, her disguise would be discovered. But how would Liang Shanbo feel when he learned the truth?

The Power of Love That Transcends Life and Death

After three years of studying together, it was time for Zhu Yingtai to return home. She still couldn't bring herself to tell Liang Shanbo who she really was. Before she left, she gave him a clue—she hinted that she would love for them to meet again one day, not as friends, but as something more. Liang Shanbo, however, didn't understand her meaning right away.

It wasn't until much later, when Liang Shanbo visited Zhu's home, that the truth was finally revealed. When he saw Zhu dressed in her beautiful robes, not as a boy but as herself, he realized that she had been the love of his life all along. His heart filled with joy, but that joy was short-lived—there was terrible news waiting for him.

Zhu's family had already arranged for her to marry another man. Though Zhu and Liang's love for each other was pure and true, her family's decision could not be undone. Liang Shanbo's heart was shattered. The thought of losing Zhu was too much for him to bear. Unable to live without her, Liang Shanbo fell gravely ill and soon passed away, his spirit longing for the love he could never have.

When Zhu Yingtai heard the news of Liang's death, she was devastated. On the day of her wedding, she went to visit Liang Shanbo's tomb, dressed in her bridal gown. Standing by his grave, Zhu prayed with all her heart, wishing that they could be together in some way, even if not in this life. Her love for Liang Shanbo was so powerful that the ground began to tremble, and the tomb opened up.

Without hesitation, Zhu Yingtai leapt into the tomb, joining her beloved in death. In that moment, something miraculous happened—two beautiful butterflies emerged from the tomb, fluttering together into the sky. The two lovers, reunited at last, had transformed into butterflies, free to fly wherever they wished. In the form of butterflies, their love was no longer bound by life, death, or earthly rules.

Lessons from the Butterfly Lovers: Freedom, Love, and Acceptance

The story of Zhu Yingtai and Liang Shanbo is often called the "Chinese Romeo and Juliet," but it offers its own unique lessons about love, freedom, and acceptance. Their tale teaches us that true love cannot be stopped—not by rules, not by distance, and not even by death. It shows us that love is powerful enough to transcend all boundaries and that when two hearts are truly connected, they will always find a way to be together.

The transformation of the two lovers into butterflies carries deep meaning. Butterflies are a symbol of freedom and change. Just as a caterpillar transforms into a butterfly, Zhu and Liang's love transformed them, setting them free from the limitations of the world. Their spirits were no longer bound by family expectations or earthly struggles—they were free to fly together forever.

This story also teaches us about acceptance and letting go. Though Zhu and Liang faced many obstacles in their lives, their love endured. And even when it seemed like everything was lost, their transformation into butterflies reminds us that every ending can be a new beginning. Love has the power to transform even the saddest moments into something beautiful.

Through the legend of the Butterfly Lovers, we learn that it's okay to follow our hearts, even when the path is difficult. True love requires patience and courage, just like Zhu Yingtai showed when she leapt into Liang's tomb, trusting that they would find a way to be together.

The Legacy of the Butterfly Lovers

The story of the Butterfly Lovers has been told for centuries, inspiring plays, songs, and dances across China. Even today, their tale continues to capture the hearts of people all over the world. During the spring, when butterflies flutter through gardens and fields, people often remember Zhu Yingtai and Liang Shanbo, imagining their love story flying with the wind.

This story is also celebrated in Chinese opera and music, reminding people of the importance of love, freedom, and loyalty. Many couples visit shrines and temples dedicated to the Butterfly Lovers, offering prayers for lasting love and happiness.

So, the next time you see two butterflies dancing in the air, think of Zhu Yingtai and Liang Shanbo. Remember that love, just like butterflies, is delicate but strong, capable of soaring through any challenge. And if you ever face difficulties in your own life, remember the lesson of the Butterfly Lovers—even in the hardest times, love and hope will always find a way to shine through.

CHAPTER 15: THE STORY OF THE BAMBOO CUTTER - THE TALE OF KAGUYA

Long ago, deep in the heart of a quiet forest, there lived an old bamboo cutter and his wife. Every day, the bamboo cutter went into the forest, carefully slicing down tall bamboo stalks to sell. One day, something extraordinary happened. As he was working, the old man noticed a faint glow coming from one of the bamboo stalks. Curious, he cut it open, and to his amazement, inside the glowing bamboo, he found a tiny, beautiful girl no bigger than his hand.

The old couple had no children, so they took the tiny girl home, believing she was a gift from the heavens. As soon as they brought her into their home, the little girl magically grew into a normal-sized baby. Overjoyed, the bamboo cutter and his wife named her Kaguya, which means "shining light," because of how she had come to them, glowing inside the bamboo.

Kaguya was no ordinary girl. She was as beautiful as the moon and as graceful as a spring breeze. As she grew, her beauty became even more radiant, and soon, news of the mysterious girl spread across the land. Suitors and noblemen traveled from far and wide to ask for her hand in marriage, but Kaguya was kind but distant. She loved her adoptive parents dearly but didn't seem to belong entirely to the world of humans. There was always a spark of mystery about her, as if her heart were connected to something far beyond the earth.

Kaguya's Magical Journey to the Moon

Many suitors tried to win Kaguya's heart, but she refused them all, setting them impossible tasks. One nobleman was asked to find the Jewel of the Dragon King's Palace beneath the sea, while another was told to bring her a branch of silver from a distant mountain. One by one, the suitors failed, proving they were not worthy of her. Kaguya remained alone, but not sad—there was a secret longing in her heart.

One night, during the full moon, Kaguya stood outside her home, gazing up at the glowing sky. Her parents noticed tears in her eyes and asked her what was troubling her. It was then that Kaguya revealed the truth.

"I am not from this world," she said softly. "I come from the moon, and soon, the time will come for me to return." The bamboo cutter and his wife were heartbroken. They loved Kaguya as their daughter and could not bear the thought of losing her. Kaguya, too, was filled with sorrow, for she had come to love her life on Earth.

As the full moon approached, a golden chariot descended from the sky, sent by the moon people to bring Kaguya back to her true home. Kaguya's parents tried to hold on to her, but they knew they couldn't stop destiny. With tears in her eyes, Kaguya bid farewell to the kind couple who had taken her in and loved her as their own. She gave them a letter and a special gift—a bottle of the Elixir of Immortality, which she hoped would bring them comfort after she was gone.

Kaguya stepped into the glowing chariot, and with one final glance at the Earth she had come to love, she rose into the night sky, disappearing into the soft glow of the moon. The bamboo cutter and his wife watched her until she was out of sight, their hearts heavy with both sadness and gratitude.

Lessons from Kaguya: Magic, Mystery, and Destiny

The tale of Kaguya teaches us many valuable lessons about the wonders of life, the magic of kindness, and the importance of accepting what we cannot change. Though Kaguya's life on Earth was brief, she brought joy and love to those around her. Her story reminds us that even the smallest moments with those we love can leave a lasting impact.

One of the most powerful lessons in Kaguya's story is accepting destiny with grace. Even though Kaguya didn't want to leave her life on Earth, she understood that some things are beyond our control. Her return to the moon reminds us that life is full of changes, and sometimes, we must let go of what we hold dear.

Kaguya's story is also about the beauty of mystery and magic. Not everything in life can be explained, and that's what makes it so magical. Just like the moon shines brightly in the night sky, Kaguya's story reminds us to find wonder in the world around us, even in the moments that seem sad or difficult.

The Elixir of Immortality that Kaguya left behind for her parents symbolizes the eternal power of love and memory. Even though Kaguya returned to the moon, her love for her earthly parents remained with them forever, showing that love transcends time and distance.

The Legacy of Kaguya

The tale of Kaguya, also known as "The Tale of the Bamboo Cutter," is one of the oldest legends in Chinese and Japanese storytelling. It has inspired countless stories, plays, and even movies, reminding people to embrace life's mysteries and cherish the people they love.

To this day, when people look at the moon, some say they can see the outline of Kaguya, watching over the Earth she once called home. Her story is especially remembered during Mid-Autumn Festival celebrations, when people gather to admire the full moon and share mooncakes with family and friends.

So, the next time you look up at the moon, think of Kaguya and her magical journey. Remember that life is full of wonder, even when things don't go the way we expect. And just like Kaguya's love for her parents, the bonds we share with others can last forever, no matter where life takes us. After all, the moon always shines down, even on the darkest nights—just like love and memories stay with us, lighting up our hearts.

CHAPTER 16: THE STORY OF THE CARP THAT BECAME A DRAGON

Long ago, in a sparkling river nestled between towering mountains, there lived a small carp. The carp was no ordinary fish—it was filled with dreams of greatness. Day by day, it watched the waters flow past, yearning to reach the source of the river at the top of the great waterfall. The carp heard an ancient legend: any fish that could swim all the way upstream and leap over the waterfall would be transformed into a mighty dragon.

Though many laughed at the idea, the little carp refused to give up its dream. It knew the journey would be tough, but it was determined to try. One bright morning, the carp set off, swimming against the current. The river was filled with challenges—swift currents pushed the carp backward, and sharp rocks threatened to block its way.

Some of the bigger fish mocked the carp. "You'll never make it up the waterfall," they sneered. But the small carp kept swimming, saying to itself, "I may be small, but I am strong in spirit!" Every time the current pushed it back, the carp swam harder. It dodged rocks, jumped over rapids, and swam past creatures much larger than itself.

At last, the carp reached the base of the great waterfall. It looked up, and the water thundered down like a giant curtain of silver. The carp knew that this would be the hardest part of the journey. Many fish had tried to leap over the waterfall before, but none had ever succeeded.

With a burst of energy, the little carp leaped into the rushing water. It jumped once—only to fall back down. It jumped again, only to be swept away by the force of the waterfall. But the carp refused to give up. With each attempt, it grew stronger and more determined.

Finally, after what seemed like countless tries, the carp made one last mighty leap. It soared through the spray, higher and higher, until it reached the top of the waterfall. And in that moment, something incredible happened.

The heavens rumbled, and a dazzling light surrounded the little carp. Its scales shimmered like gold, and its small body began to grow and change. The carp transformed into a majestic dragon, with gleaming horns, powerful wings, and a long, flowing tail. The new dragon roared with joy, swirling through the clouds and soaring across the sky. It had achieved its dream—and in doing so, it became a symbol of transformation and triumph.

The Symbolism of Perseverance and Transformation in Chinese Folklore

The story of the carp that became a dragon has been told for centuries in Chinese folklore. It is a tale about transformation, perseverance, and never giving up, no matter how hard the challenge. The small carp represents anyone with a big dream, while the rushing river and the waterfall symbolize the obstacles that stand in the way.

In Chinese culture, dragons are powerful creatures that symbolize strength, luck, and success. The transformation of the carp into a dragon reminds us that even the smallest of us can achieve great things if we work hard and stay determined. The journey of the carp is also a lesson about personal growth. Sometimes, we must go through tough times and face difficult challenges before we can become the best versions of ourselves.

This legend is often used to encourage students, athletes, and anyone working toward a goal. It shows that true success comes from hard work and persistence, even when things seem impossible. Just like the carp that swam upstream, we all have the potential to achieve something amazing if we believe in ourselves and keep trying.

Lessons from the Carp: Determination, Hard Work, and Success

The story of the carp teaches us many important lessons that we can use in our own lives:

1. Determination is Key: The little carp never gave up, even when the waterfall seemed impossible to climb. It teaches us that if we want to achieve something, we have to keep going, no matter how hard it gets.

2. Hard Work Pays Off: Just like the carp's repeated attempts made it stronger, the effort we put into our goals helps us grow and learn. Each step, even a small one, brings us closer to success.

3. Success Comes from Within: The carp may have started as a small, ordinary fish, but it had a powerful spirit. The legend reminds us that true strength comes from within, and that greatness is not about size or appearance but about heart and determination.

4. Embrace Transformation: Just as the carp transformed into a dragon, we can also change and grow through our experiences. Every challenge we

face helps us become stronger, wiser, and more prepared for what's ahead.

The Legacy of the Carp and the Dragon

The story of the carp's transformation into a dragon is celebrated in many ways in Chinese culture. It serves as a symbol of success and is often associated with achievements in education, career, and personal growth. People often say, "May you leap over the dragon's gate," as a way of wishing someone good luck and success in their journey.

During the annual Dragon Boat Festival, brightly decorated boats shaped like dragons race along rivers, celebrating the power and energy of the dragon. The festival also reminds people of the importance of working together, just as the carp worked with the river and its currents to achieve its dream.

This legend continues to inspire people of all ages, encouraging them to face challenges with courage and determination. Whenever life feels tough, just remember the little carp—keep swimming, keep trying, and one day, you too might find yourself soaring like a dragon.

So, the next time you feel like giving up, think of the small carp standing at the base of the waterfall. With patience, effort, and belief in yourself, you can conquer even the greatest challenges—and who knows, you might just discover your own dragon waiting within you!

CHAPTER 17: THE LEGEND OF SUN AND MOON CAKES - A HIDDEN MESSAGE

Long ago, in ancient China, people lived under the rule of a cruel emperor who treated his subjects unfairly. Life was hard for many, and the people longed for freedom. But how could they fight against such a powerful emperor? The answer came in the form of a clever plan—and some delicious moon cakes.

During the Mid-Autumn Festival, people would exchange moon cakes, round pastries filled with sweet fillings like lotus seed paste or red bean paste. These cakes were more than just treats; they held a secret. A group of rebels, who wanted to free the people from the emperor's harsh rule, came up with an idea: they would hide messages inside the moon cakes, spreading the word about their plan for a rebellion.

Inside each moon cake was a small piece of paper with instructions. The messages told people to rise up against the emperor on the night of the next full moon. Because the moon cakes were part of the festival traditions, the emperor's guards didn't suspect a thing. The rebels handed out the cakes across the land, and soon, the message reached every corner of the empire.

On the night of the full moon, the people rose together in unity, following the instructions hidden inside the moon cakes. Their plan worked! The emperor was overthrown, and the people celebrated their freedom. Ever since that day, moon cakes have been more than just a sweet treat—they are a symbol of unity, hope, and freedom.

The Traditions of Eating Moon Cakes During Festivals

Today, the legend of the moon cakes lives on through the Mid-Autumn Festival, also called the Moon Festival. Every year, families come together to eat moon cakes and celebrate under the bright, full moon. The round shape of the cakes represents unity and togetherness, reminding everyone of the importance of family and community.

During the festival, children carry colorful lanterns and listen to stories about the moon and the stars. The festival is also connected to the legend of Chang'e, the Moon Goddess, who flew to the moon and now watches over the Earth from the night sky. People gather to admire the moon, share stories, and enjoy delicious moon cakes with their loved ones.

Moon cakes come in many flavors, with fillings like sweet red bean paste, nuts, and even salted egg yolks to represent the moon. Each bite of a moon cake is a reminder of the festival's history and the legends passed down through generations. Families often give moon cakes as gifts, symbolizing love and respect for one another.

Lessons from the Moon Cake Legend: Unity, Freedom, and Tradition

The story of the moon cakes teaches us many important lessons. First, it shows the power of unity. Just like the rebels worked together to achieve their goal, we can accomplish great things when we come together with a common purpose. Whether it's standing up for what is right or helping someone in need, unity makes us stronger.

The legend also reminds us about the value of freedom. The people in the story fought bravely to free themselves from the emperor's rule. Freedom is a gift that should be cherished, and it's important to remember the courage of those who stood up for what they believed in.

Finally, the story of the moon cakes teaches us about tradition. Festivals like the Mid-Autumn Festival are not just celebrations—they are a way to connect with our history and pass down stories from one generation to the next. By celebrating traditions, we honor our ancestors and keep their wisdom alive.

So, the next time you enjoy a moon cake during the Mid-Autumn Festival, think about the hidden messages that once helped start a rebellion. Remember the power of unity, the importance of freedom, and the joy of sharing traditions with those around you. And who knows—maybe there's a little bit of magic in every moon cake!

CHAPTER 18: THE LEGEND OF THE RED THREAD OF FATE - INVISIBLE CONNECTIONS

A long, long time ago, in ancient China, there was a legend about an invisible red thread that connected people. This thread was no ordinary string—it was a magical thread of fate, binding together two people who were destined to meet. No matter how far apart they lived or how different their lives were, the thread would eventually bring them together.

The legend says that the red thread is tied to a person's ankle or finger by the gods at the moment they are born. As the years go by, the thread may twist and tangle, but it will never break. The two people connected by the thread might meet as friends, family members, or even soulmates. Sometimes they might not meet until many years later, but they are always meant to find each other in the end.

The story goes that one day, a boy asked an old matchmaker how love and friendships were formed. The matchmaker, a wise old man with a bag of red thread, explained the magic of the invisible connections. "Even though you can't see it," the matchmaker said, "the red thread guides your heart and brings you to the people who matter most." The boy was amazed, wondering where his own thread would lead him one day.

The Power of Fate and Destiny in Chinese Beliefs

The red thread of fate is not just a story about love—it is a symbol of fate and destiny in Chinese culture. Many believe that the people we meet in life are not by chance, but are meant to be a part of our journey. Whether it's a friend who helps us through tough times, a teacher who guides us, or someone who makes us laugh, the red thread pulls these people into our lives at just the right moment.

In Chinese tradition, the red thread reminds us that some things in life are beyond our control. No matter how much we plan or worry, fate will play a role in our journey. But this doesn't mean we should sit and wait for things to happen. Instead, the red thread teaches us to trust that the right people will come into our lives when the time is right.

Many people in China still believe in the idea of fate, especially when it comes to friendships and love. Parents might tell their children that everyone has a red thread connecting them to someone special, giving them hope and excitement about the future. Couples sometimes give each other gifts tied with red thread, symbolizing their bond and destiny.

Lessons from the Red Thread: Patience, Trust, and Destiny

The legend of the red thread teaches us many important lessons. First, it reminds us to be patient. Just like a tangled thread takes time to unravel, finding the people we are meant to meet can take time. Sometimes, we might feel lonely or frustrated, but the red thread teaches us to trust that good things will come.

Trust is another lesson from the red thread. Even when we can't see it, the thread is always there, silently connecting us to the right people. This teaches us to have faith in the journey, even when things don't happen the way we expect. Life might have twists and turns, but the red thread shows us that everything happens for a reason.

Finally, the red thread helps us understand the idea of destiny. It teaches us that every friendship, every relationship, and every encounter matters. Even if someone is only in our life for a short time, they play a role in our story. Every twist in the thread is part of the adventure.

A Story of Two Friends Brought Together by the Red Thread

Once, there were two children named Mei and Tao who lived in different villages, far from each other. One loved to write stories, and the other dreamed of becoming an artist. Though they didn't know it, the red thread of fate had already connected them.

One day, Tao's family moved to Mei's village, and the two children met at a market. Mei showed Tao her favorite books, and Tao gave Mei a small drawing as a gift. From that moment on, the two became best friends, spending hours creating storybooks filled with drawings and adventures.

Years later, when they were older, they opened a bookstore and art studio together, sharing their creativity with the world. Mei and Tao often laughed about how lucky they were to have found each other, but deep down, they knew it wasn't luck—it was the magic of the red thread, guiding them to the friendship they were always meant to have.

The legend of the red thread teaches us that even when we feel lost or alone, we are never truly disconnected. The thread winds through our lives, weaving together people, places, and experiences that shape who we are. Every friendship, every act of kindness, and every challenge is part of the journey, and the people we meet along the way are part of our story.

So, the next time you make a new friend or meet someone special, imagine the invisible red thread that brought you together. And remember—just like Mei and Tao, the right people will find their way into your life, even if it takes a little time.

The red thread of fate is a reminder that we are all connected by love, friendship, and hope. It teaches us to trust the journey, be patient with life's twists and turns, and embrace the magic of meeting the people we were always meant to know.

CHAPTER 19: FESTIVALS AND CELEBRATIONS - HONORING THE LEGENDS

China's festivals are magical times when communities come together to celebrate legends, traditions, and heroes. These festivals not only honor the past but also help families and friends create joyful memories. Two of the most exciting and colorful festivals are the Lantern Festival and the Dragon Boat Festival. These celebrations are rooted in Chinese history and tell stories that have been passed down for centuries.

The Lantern Festival, celebrated on the 15th day of the Lunar New Year, is like a grand finale to the Chinese New Year celebrations. Families gather to light lanterns of all shapes, sizes, and colors, creating a glowing sea of lights. According to legend, lighting lanterns helps guide spirits back to the heavens and symbolizes hope and brightness for the year ahead. Children often carry animal-shaped lanterns, while adults write wishes and riddles on theirs. The festival also honors Zao Shen, the Kitchen God, and celebrates unity and the renewal of life.

CHINESE LEGENDS FOR KIDS

The Dragon Boat Festival is another vibrant celebration held in honor of the poet Qu Yuan, who gave his life for his country. Legend says that after Qu Yuan drowned in a river, the villagers raced in boats to save him. Today, people honor his bravery with thrilling dragon boat races, colorful parades, and zongzi, a special rice dumpling wrapped in bamboo leaves. The races are not only exciting to watch but also symbolize the strength of community and teamwork. The rhythm of the paddlers rowing to the beat of drums creates an unforgettable atmosphere.

How Communities Keep Their Legends Alive With Dance, Music, and Food

Chinese festivals are not just about decorations and races—they are filled with dances, music, and delicious foods that bring the legends to life. Lion dances are a must-see during festivals, with performers wearing giant lion costumes and dancing to the rhythm of drums and cymbals. According to legend, the lion's dance scares away evil spirits and brings good luck to the community. Children and adults cheer and clap as the colorful lions leap and twirl through the streets.

Music also plays a big part in these celebrations. Traditional instruments like drums, gongs, and flutes fill the air with joyful sounds. Folk songs are sung to honor legendary heroes, and each melody tells a story about the bravery, kindness, or wisdom of the past. Some festivals even include storytelling sessions where elders share ancient legends with children, keeping the stories alive for future generations.

Food, of course, is at the heart of every celebration! During the Lantern Festival, people enjoy tangyuan, sweet glutinous rice balls, symbolizing unity and family togetherness. At the Dragon Boat Festival, zongzi is shared with friends and neighbors, reminding everyone of the importance of tradition and kindness. Festival foods not only taste delicious but are also filled with meaning. Each dish tells a story, connecting the people who prepare and share it to the legends of the past.

What Festivals Teach Us: Gratitude, Joy, and Cultural Pride

Festivals are not only about fun and feasting—they also teach important lessons about gratitude, joy, and pride in one's culture. The legends celebrated during these festivals remind people to be thankful for the heroes and traditions that have shaped their lives. The Lantern Festival teaches gratitude for new beginnings and the light that guides us forward. The Dragon Boat Festival reminds us to be grateful for the sacrifices made by those who came before us, like Qu Yuan.

Joy is another important lesson of these celebrations. Festivals are times to set aside worries and celebrate life with laughter, music, and dance. They bring communities together, showing that happiness is best when shared with others. Whether it's children running with lanterns or families enjoying festival meals, these joyful moments remind everyone of the beauty of togetherness.

Finally, festivals inspire pride in one's heritage and traditions. Through these celebrations, people connect with their roots, learning about the stories, values, and customs passed down from their ancestors. Cultural pride helps people understand who they are and where they come from, fostering a sense of belonging and unity. For children, participating in these festivals is a chance to feel proud of their culture and share it with friends from different backgrounds.

At the heart of every Chinese festival is a deep connection to the past, the present, and the future. The stories and traditions celebrated during these times remind us of the heroes and values that shape our lives. Through dance, music, food, and fun, these festivals keep legends alive, passing their wisdom to each new generation.

Whether it's the glowing lanterns lighting up the night sky or the splash of dragon boats racing down a river, each celebration is a reminder that legends live on in our hearts and communities. The joy, gratitude, and pride shared during these festivals help people connect with one another, fostering unity and happiness.

So, the next time you see a glowing lantern or hear the beat of a drum during a festival, remember the legends that inspire these celebrations. And who knows—maybe one day, you'll create your own traditions and stories to pass down, becoming part of the magical world of legends that keeps our cultures alive!

CONCLUSION: CREATE YOUR OWN CHINESE LEGEND!

Chinese legends have been told for thousands of years, and they still captivate our imaginations today. Why do these stories continue to inspire so many people across generations? The answer lies in the way these legends combine adventure, magic, and important life lessons. Each tale carries values like kindness, bravery, respect, and wisdom—qualities that are just as important now as they were in ancient times.

When you read the story of the Monkey King learning to control his wild nature or Chang'e flying to the moon, you feel connected to characters from a distant time who still face challenges similar to ours. These stories remind us to dream big, be kind, and never give up, no matter how difficult things get. Legends are more than just entertainment—they teach us how to live, how to grow, and how to make the world a better place.

Every generation has added its own voice to these legends, keeping them alive and relevant. Now it's your turn! Just like ancient storytellers, you have the power to create your own legends and share them with the world.

How to Craft Your Own Stories Using Chinese Themes and Characters

Creating your own Chinese legend is easier than you might think! Every great legend starts with imagination. Think about the elements you love from the stories you've read—maybe it's a magical dragon, a clever trickster, or a brave hero like Mulan. You can use these characters or themes as inspiration to build your very own story.

Here are a few fun ideas to get you started:

- Create a New Dragon Hero: Imagine a dragon that controls the wind and embarks on a mission to restore peace between the heavens and the earth.
- Invent a Festival: What if your legend explains how a brand-new festival came to be? Maybe it celebrates a brave child who saved their village from a terrible monster!
- Tell the Story of a Magical Object: Just like the Monkey King's magical staff, your story could feature an enchanted item with extraordinary powers.

You can also mix traditional themes with new ideas. Maybe your character is a modern-day kid who discovers they are connected to an ancient legend and goes on an adventure to fulfill their destiny. You can draw inspiration from Chinese symbols, like dragons (which represent strength), the moon (which symbolizes change), or the red thread of fate (which connects people who are destined to meet). The possibilities are endless!

The Power of Storytelling: Passing Traditions from One Generation to the Next

Storytelling has been one of the most important ways people have shared knowledge, wisdom, and values across generations. In ancient China, stories weren't just for fun—they were a way to teach children about their history, culture, and traditions. By telling these stories to the next generation, families ensured that their values and beliefs would never be forgotten.

When you write or tell your own stories, you're becoming part of a tradition that stretches back thousands of years. Storytelling connects us to our ancestors and helps us understand who we are. And the best part is, you can use stories to pass on important lessons to others! Whether you share a story about courage, friendship, or kindness, your words have the power to inspire people just like the legends of the past.

As you've seen throughout this book, Chinese legends are filled with adventure, magic, and meaning. Now it's your turn to become a storyteller! Don't worry if your story isn't perfect at first—even the greatest legends began as simple ideas. The most important thing is to have fun and let your imagination soar.

So, grab a notebook or sit down with a friend, and start dreaming up your own Chinese legend. Will your story feature a heroic dragon flying through the skies? Or maybe a clever trickster who teaches everyone a lesson about kindness? No matter what you choose, remember that there's no limit to where your imagination can take you.

Just like a dragon soaring through the clouds or a hero braving an impossible challenge, your creativity knows no bounds. Who knows? Maybe one day, your story will be told for generations to come, inspiring others just as these legends have inspired you.

Now, it's time to begin your storytelling adventure. Dream big, write boldly, and let your imagination fly like a dragon! Your legend awaits!

BONUS SECTION: FUN ACTIVITIES INSPIRED BY CHINESE LEGENDS

Welcome to the Bonus Section! Now that you've read about brave heroes, clever tricksters, and magical creatures, it's time to have some fun and let your creativity shine. This section is packed with activities inspired by the stories in this book. Grab your art supplies, pens, and paper—let's jump into the world of Chinese legends and create something amazing!

Create Your Own Dragon Mask: Design a Dragon Mask with Colors and Meaning

In Chinese culture, dragons are powerful symbols of strength, good luck, and protection. Now it's your turn to create your very own dragon mask! When making your mask, think about what kind of dragon it represents. Is it a water dragon swimming through rivers or a fire-breathing dragon soaring through the skies?

What You'll Need:

- A large piece of paper or cardboard
- Markers, crayons, or paint
- Scissors (ask an adult for help!)
- String or elastic to tie the mask
- Feathers, glitter, or anything else to decorate

Steps:

- Draw the shape of your dragon's face. Is it long and serpentine, like the traditional Chinese dragon? Or does it have a fierce snout and sharp horns?
- Color your dragon mask. Use bright colors like red and gold to symbolize good luck, or blue and green for a water dragon.
- Add special details. Glue on feathers for eyebrows or use glitter for scales.
- Cut out your mask and attach the string or elastic to wear it.

Now you're ready to roar like a mighty dragon! Show your family and friends your mask, and maybe even perform a dragon dance.

Write Your Own Trickster Tale: Make Up a Story Starring the Clever Monkey King

The Monkey King is one of the most beloved characters in Chinese mythology. He's mischievous, clever, and always ready for an adventure. Now, it's your turn to come up with your own story featuring this tricky hero!

How to Write Your Trickster Tale:

- Think of a problem. Maybe the Monkey King gets into trouble with another powerful god or needs to rescue a friend.
- Give the Monkey King a clever plan. Remember, he's not the strongest, but he's always the smartest!
- Add some obstacles. Every good story needs a challenge—will the Monkey King's plan work, or will he get caught?
- End with a lesson. Trickster tales often teach something important. Maybe your story is about teamwork, honesty, or thinking before you act.

When you finish, share your story with your family or friends. You might just inspire someone else to become a storyteller too!

Draw Your Favorite Zodiac Animal: Explore the Chinese Zodiac with Art

The Chinese zodiac is made up of twelve animals, each representing a year in a twelve-year cycle. Which animal are you? Here's a chance to explore the zodiac and draw your favorite animal.

Chinese Zodiac Animals:

- Rat
- Ox
- Tiger
- Rabbit
- Dragon
- Snake
- Horse
- Goat
- Monkey
- Rooster
- Dog
- Pig

What to Do:

Pick an animal that speaks to you. Maybe you feel as brave as a tiger or as loyal as a dog.

Use your imagination to give your animal special details. Does your dragon have colorful wings? Is your tiger wearing a crown?

Draw your zodiac animal and give it a name and a personality. You can also write a story about your animal and its adventures in the zodiac.

When you're finished, hang your artwork somewhere special. Your zodiac animal can be a reminder to stay strong, kind, and adventurous—just like the legends!

Map of China: Mark the Places Mentioned in the Legends

Many of the legends in this book take place in beautiful locations across China. Let's make a map to mark the spots where the stories happened!

What You'll Need:

- A printed or hand-drawn map of China
- Markers or stickers
- A list of the legends and the places they are connected to
- Legends and Their Locations:
- The Dragon King: The seas and rivers of southern China

- Chang'e, the Moon Goddess: The sky and the moon
- The Monkey King: The Flower Fruit Mountain and the West
- Yu the Great: The rivers of ancient China
- The Jade Emperor: Heaven and the celestial palace
- The Legend of Mulan: Northern China

Mark each of these places on your map with a star or sticker. You can even decorate your map with small drawings of the characters from the stories!

These activities are just the beginning of your creative journey into Chinese legends. Now that you've designed a dragon mask, written a trickster tale, drawn your favorite zodiac animal, and explored China on a map, what will you do next?

Remember, legends aren't just stories from the past—they are living tales that continue to inspire people today. You can be a part of this tradition by creating your own stories, art, and adventures. So keep dreaming, creating, and sharing your ideas with the world. Who knows? One day, your own legend might inspire others too!

FUN FACTS ABOUT CHINESE CULTURE AND MYTHOLOGY

Welcome to the world of amazing facts about Chinese culture and mythology! Did you know that the legends you've read in this book have been passed down for thousands of years and still inspire art, dance, and movies today? Let's dive into some fun facts about Chinese calligraphy, music, and dance, discover how Chinese myths influence modern stories, and explore famous places where you can experience these legends for yourself.

Amazing Facts About Chinese Calligraphy, Music, and Dance

Chinese culture is full of beauty and tradition. From elegant writing to lively dances, every art form tells a story.

Chinese Calligraphy – The Art of Beautiful Writing

Chinese calligraphy isn't just about writing words; it's a form of art! The brushstrokes represent the writer's emotions and thoughts. There are five main styles of calligraphy, each with its own character. Some are bold and powerful, while others are soft and flowing, just like a river.

Did you know? Calligraphy was so important in ancient China that it was taught alongside reading and math!

Some calligraphy scrolls even tell stories of gods, like the Jade Emperor, or great heroes, such as Mulan. Try practicing calligraphy yourself—you might feel like you're writing your own legend!

Chinese Music – Sounds of the Past

Traditional Chinese music has instruments that create sounds as ancient as the legends. Some popular instruments include the guqin, a seven-string zither, and the erhu, a two-stringed fiddle. Music often tells stories—some songs celebrate brave warriors, while others capture the magic of the moon and stars.

Did you know? Chinese music was believed to connect people with nature and the universe. A performance could reflect the change of seasons or tell the story of the stars.

You might even find songs about Chang'e, the Moon Goddess, or hear sounds inspired by the

Monkey King's adventures in some traditional tunes!

Chinese Dance – Telling Stories Through Movement

Chinese dance is more than just movement—it's storytelling in action. Some dances are energetic and acrobatic, like the Lion Dance performed during the New Year, while others are slow and graceful, like the Fan Dance. These dances are often inspired by legends, animals, and nature.

Fun fact! The Dragon Dance, with performers inside a giant dragon costume, symbolizes power and good luck. It's often performed to scare away bad spirits, just like how the villagers scared away Nian, the New Year monster.

How Chinese Myths Have Influenced Modern Movies and Books

You might not realize it, but some of your favorite books and movies were inspired by ancient Chinese stories!

Movies Inspired by Chinese Myths

The Monkey King has become a well-loved character around the world. His adventures inspired movies like Journey to the West and even influenced the character of Goku in Dragon Ball Z.

The story of Mulan was turned into a famous Disney movie. Her bravery and dedication to family have captured the hearts of people everywhere.

Chinese Symbols in Stories

Dragons, magical creatures, and heroes from Chinese mythology also appear in modern books and games. The idea of a red thread connecting people, as seen in the Legend of the Red Thread of Fate, often shows up in romantic stories. Zodiac animals have also become popular characters in stories for children and adults alike.

Did you know? Even superhero stories often borrow themes from Chinese myths, such as the battle between good and evil or the importance of harmony.

Places to Visit: Famous Temples and Museums to Explore Chinese Legends

If you ever get a chance to visit China, there are some incredible places where you can see history and legends come to life.

The Forbidden City in Beijing

The Forbidden City was once the home of emperors and is filled with statues, art, and stories of the past. You might spot dragons carved into the walls and roofs, guarding the palace just like the Dragon King guards the seas.

The Jade Emperor Pagoda in Shanghai

This beautiful temple is dedicated to the Jade Emperor, the ruler of heaven. Visitors come here to pray for good luck and learn about the Chinese zodiac.

The Temple of the Moon in Beijing

This temple is a perfect place to celebrate the Mid-Autumn Festival and honor Chang'e, the Moon Goddess. It's especially beautiful during the full moon when people gather to enjoy mooncakes and gaze at the night sky.

Museums That Celebrate Chinese Legends

The National Museum of China in Beijing has exhibits about ancient myths, including artifacts related to heroes like Yu the Great and Pangu.

The Shanghai Museum is a treasure trove of Chinese art, including paintings and sculptures that tell legendary stories.

These places are perfect for learning more about the legends that shaped Chinese culture—and maybe even discovering some new ones!

CHINESE LEGENDS FOR KIDS

Chinese legends are more than just stories; they are a way to connect with the past and understand the values that shape Chinese culture today. Whether through calligraphy, dance, or a good story, there are many ways to bring these legends to life.

Now it's your turn! Grab a brush and practice writing a message in calligraphy, listen to traditional music, or act out the tale of the Monkey King with your friends. Who knows what kind of legend you'll create? Remember, stories are meant to be shared—so keep exploring, keep creating, and keep passing these amazing tales on to others!

REFERENCES

Below is a list of resources that provided valuable information for the creation of Chinese Legends for Kids. These references include historical texts, cultural studies, folklore collections, and trusted websites dedicated to Chinese history and mythology. They helped ensure the stories and lessons in this book were both accurate and engaging for young readers.

Books and Academic Publications

- Birch, Cyril. Stories from a Ming Collection: The Art of the Chinese Storyteller. New York: Grove Press, 1958.
- Eberhard, Wolfram. Chinese Folktales. University of California Press, 1965.
- Wu Cheng'en. Journey to the West (translated by Arthur Waley). London: Penguin Classics, 1942.
- Idema, Wilt L. Mulan: Five Versions of a Classic Chinese Legend, with Related Texts. Hackett Publishing, 2010.
- Christie, Anthony. Chinese Mythology. Hamlyn, 1975.

Web Resources and Articles

- China Culture. "Chinese Festivals and Their Meanings." www.chinaculture.org.
- Chinese Folk Religion. "The Jade Emperor and the Origins of the Chinese Zodiac."
- China Highlights. "The Legend of Hou Yi and the Ten Suns." www.chinahighlights.com.
- UNESCO World Heritage. "Exploring the Myths Behind the Forbidden City."
- Museums and Cultural Institutions
- The National Museum of China, Beijing. Exhibits on Chinese mythology and folklore.
- Shanghai Museum, Shanghai. Collections of ancient Chinese art reflecting legendary stories.
- Smithsonian Institution, Washington, D.C. Online exhibits featuring traditional Chinese festivals and artifacts.

Documentaries and Media

- Legends of China, documentary series by CCTV.
- The Myth and the Zodiac, educational program by the History Channel.

Traditional Chinese Texts and Translations

- Classic of Mountains and Seas (Shanhaijing), translated by Anne Birrell.
- Records of the Grand Historian by Sima Qian, focusing on legendary rulers.

These references ensured that the book is both entertaining and educational, providing authentic insights into the rich world of Chinese legends. We hope they inspire readers to continue exploring the magic and wisdom of Chinese mythology for years to come.

INDIAN LEGENDS FOR KIDS:

GODS, GODDESSES, WARRIORS, SAGES, MYTHS, EPICS & MORE FROM ANCIENT INDIA

TABLE OF CONTENTS

INTRODUCTION 1

CHAPTER 1: THE CREATION OF THE UNIVERSE –
VISHNU AND THE COSMIC OCEAN 8

CHAPTER 2: THE ADVENTURES OF HANUMAN –
THE MONKEY GOD 15

CHAPTER 3: GANESHA AND THE RACE AROUND
THE WORLD 26

CHAPTER 4: KRISHNA AND THE BUTTER THIEVES 34

CHAPTER 5: THE LEGEND OF SAVITRI AND
SATYAVAN – A TALE OF LOVE AND DEVOTION 43

CHAPTER 6: THE CLEVER JACKAL –
FOLKTALES FROM THE JUNGLE 54

CHAPTER 7: ARJUNA AND THE MAGIC BOW –
HEROES FROM THE MAHABHARATA 62

CHAPTER 8: HOLIKA AND PRAHLAD –
THE ORIGINS OF HOLI 71

CHAPTER 9: THE CHURNING OF THE OCEAN –
THE QUEST FOR IMMORTALITY 80

CHAPTER 10: THE NAGA AND THE WISE FARMER –
MYTHICAL SERPENTS OF INDIA 87

CHAPTER 11: THE SEVEN SISTERS AND THE STARRY SKY 95

CHAPTER 12: THE STORY OF BUDDHA –
A PRINCE WHO FOUND PEACE 101

CHAPTER 13: THE BIRTH OF DURGA –
THE GODDESS OF POWER 111

CHAPTER 14: THE LEGEND OF THE BAMBOO
PRINCESS – A FOLKTALE FROM ASSAM 117

CHAPTER 15: THE TALE OF KING HARISHCHANDRA –
THE VALUE OF HONESTY 123

CHAPTER 16: PARVATI AND SHIVA –
A LOVE STORY OF THE MOUNTAINS 130

CONCLUSION 137

BONUS: ACTIVITIES 144

BONUS: FACTS 149

REFERENCES 153

INTRODUCTION

Welcome to the world of Indian legends!

Hello, young explorers! Are you ready to dive into a world filled with heroes, monsters, gods, and magic? You're about to discover Indian legends—ancient tales passed down through generations. These are stories filled with wonder, wisdom, and excitement, where animals talk, gods visit Earth, and ordinary kids become extraordinary heroes! In this book, you'll meet kings who ride on flying chariots, magical creatures hiding deep in the forests, and gods with powers beyond your imagination.

You'll visit lands where every river, mountain, and tree has its own story to tell. Some legends are over thousands of years old! So grab your favorite snack, sit back, and let your imagination take flight.

What makes Indian legends special?

Indian legends are more than just fun stories—they carry lessons that have been teaching children (and adults, too!) how to live, love, and grow for centuries. These stories are part of India's rich culture and history, told in temples, homes, and classrooms. So what makes these legends so special? Let's find out!

1. Magic Everywhere!

In Indian legends, magic isn't hidden—it's everywhere! You'll read about gods like Krishna, who make mischief with his flute, or Hanuman, the mighty monkey god who can leap across oceans. Magical objects like flying carpets, enchanted bows, and golden lotuses add excitement to every story.

You'll discover that in these tales, even animals like elephants, snakes, and tigers have magical abilities and speak just like humans. Imagine a talking snake giving advice or a clever jackal teaching a greedy lion a lesson!

2. Bravery and Adventure

These stories are packed with thrilling adventures. Brave princes fight powerful demons, heroes face fearsome monsters, and clever kids outsmart grown-ups. You'll learn about Rama, a prince who went on an epic journey to save his wife from a ten-headed demon king named Ravana. And you'll meet Arjuna, a warrior so skilled that he could shoot an arrow straight through the eye of a spinning fish!

Through these tales, you'll see how courage and determination can help anyone—even you—

overcome the biggest challenges life has to throw at you.

3. Wisdom for Life

Many Indian legends carry messages that are as important today as they were long ago. These stories teach us about kindness, honesty, teamwork, and staying true to yourself. Take Ganesha's story, for example. Even though he's a small, chubby god with the head of an elephant, his cleverness helps him win a race against his much stronger brother. The message? Brains can sometimes beat brawn!

These stories show us that being kind and wise is just as important as being strong and brave. And often, the most powerful magic is the love we share with family and friends.

A Journey Through Stories of Bravery, Magic, and Wisdom

Are you ready to meet some of the most amazing characters from Indian legends?

Here's a sneak peek at the incredible stories waiting for you:

- Fly with Hanuman, the mighty monkey who shrinks himself down to the size of a fly and grows as big as a mountain!

INDIAN LEGENDS FOR KIDS

Discover how his loyalty and strength help save the day in one of the greatest adventures ever told.

- Race around the world with Ganesha, the elephant-headed god who teaches us that being smart can sometimes win over being fast. Can you guess how he beat his brother in a race around the universe?

- Meet Krishna, the butter-loving, flute-playing god who can make cows dance and rivers change direction. You'll read about his tricks and adventures and maybe even learn a thing or two about spreading joy and happiness wherever you go.

- Help Rama defeat Ravana, the ten-headed demon king, in an epic battle to save the princess Sita. Get ready for flying chariots, enchanted weapons, and heroic deeds in this exciting tale from the Ramayana.

- Learn from the Clever Jackal, who uses his wits to outsmart a greedy lion. His adventures will make you laugh—and teach you that sometimes thinking fast is the best superpower of all!

- Travel to the magical land of Tir Na Nog, where faeries dance under the moonlight and time flows differently. This tale will show you that every story holds a little magic, just waiting to be discovered.

What You'll Learn Along the Way

This book is more than just stories—it's filled with lessons that can help you in real life, too.

- **Be Brave:** You'll see that even the smallest heroes can do big things when they believe in themselves.
- **Stay Curious:** Like young Ganesha, ask lots of questions and always look for new things to learn.
- **Help Others:** Just like Hanuman, true heroes use their strength to help their friends.
- **Believe in Yourself:** Krishna's adventures show us that we should always trust our own abilities, even when others doubt us.
- **Have Fun:** And, most importantly, these stories remind us that life is an adventure meant to be enjoyed!

Your Adventure Begins Now!

Each chapter in this book is a doorway to a new adventure, a magical world filled with ancient secrets and timeless wisdom. These stories aren't just for kids in India—they're for kids everywhere!

So, are you ready to meet mighty warriors, mischievous gods, and clever animals? Do you want to ride flying chariots, explore enchanted forests, and discover treasures hidden beneath the ocean? Then turn the page, and let the adventure begin! Your journey through the world of Indian legends awaits.

CHAPTER 1:
THE CREATION OF THE UNIVERSE - VISHNU AND THE COSMIC OCEAN

Long, long ago—before the Earth, the sun, or the stars existed—there was only water. Just an endless ocean that stretched in every direction. It was quiet and peaceful. But something wonderful was about to happen.

Deep in this endless ocean floated Vishnu, one of the greatest gods in Indian mythology. He rested on the coils of a giant serpent named Ananta, whose name means "endless." This serpent had a thousand shimmering heads that swayed gently, rocking Vishnu as he slept. The ocean waves sparkled as the serpent's coils shimmered like precious jewels.

Vishnu's eyes were closed, but he wasn't just sleeping—he was dreaming. And in his dream, he could see the entire universe waiting to come to life. And it all began with a beautiful golden lotus flower.

The Lotus Blooms – The Birth of Brahma

One day, as Vishnu lay on the cosmic ocean, a lotus flower began to grow from his navel! The lotus slowly rose from the ocean's surface, glowing brighter than the sun. Its petals unfolded, and right in the center of the flower sat Brahma, the god of creation, with four heads, each looking in a different direction. Brahma blinked in surprise as he found himself sitting on the lotus, surrounded by water as far as the eye could see.

"What am I supposed to do?" Brahma wondered. But just then, a voice—gentle and wise—came from Vishnu below.

"Brahma, it is time to create the universe," Vishnu said with a smile. "Everything you need is already within you. Use your imagination and bring the world to life."

Brahma took a deep breath. He looked around, closed his four eyes, and began to think deeply. "What should the world look like?" he wondered. "What creatures should live in it?" With each thought, new things began to appear:

- Mountains and rivers sprang into existence.
- Oceans and forests took shape.
- The sun and moon were placed in the sky to light up the world day and night.

And then came the animals: lions, elephants, tigers, deer, fish, birds, and insects. People also appeared, ready to start their journey. As Brahma thought, the universe unfolded like a giant painting. Every star, every cloud, every tree was carefully imagined by him. The once-empty ocean was now filled with color, life, and sound!

Vishnu – The Preserver of the Universe

Vishnu smiled as he watched Brahma create the universe. But his work wasn't done yet. "A world that is created must also be protected," Vishnu thought. And so, Vishnu took on a new role—he became the Preserver of the Universe.

Whenever the world was in trouble, Vishnu would leave the cosmic ocean and come to Earth. He promised to help maintain a balance between good and evil, making sure that life could go on peacefully. Vishnu would take on many different forms to help the world when needed. These forms are called avatars.

One of Vishnu's most famous avatars is Krishna, the playful god with a flute, who helped defeat an evil king and taught people how to live happily. Another is Rama, a brave prince who fought demons to rescue his wife. Each time Vishnu came to Earth, he restored peace and kept everyone safe.

The Cycle of Time – Creation, Preservation, and Renewal

In Indian legends, the universe doesn't stay the same forever. Time moves in cycles, like the hands of a clock. Just as a flower blooms, withers, and blooms again, the universe also goes through phases. There are times of creation, times when life flourishes, and times when things come to an end—only to begin all over again.

Vishnu's role as the Preserver is important during the times when the world is in danger. When things go out of balance—like when greedy kings or powerful demons try to take over—Vishnu comes to the rescue.

Even though the world may face challenges, Vishnu teaches that everything is part of a bigger plan. Just like night follows day, difficult times are always followed by better ones. And in the end, after every cycle, the universe is renewed and reborn, just like the blooming lotus flower.

A World Connected by Stories and Dreams

Just as Vishnu dreamed of the universe, our dreams and stories are powerful too. Every time we share a story or imagine something new, we help create our own little piece of the universe. Vishnu's story reminds us that the world is full of possibilities, and it's up to us to dream big and make good choices.

Whenever you feel small or unsure, remember Vishnu resting on the endless ocean. Even when it seems like nothing is happening, great things are unfolding quietly—just waiting for the right moment to bloom.

What Can We Learn from Vishnu and Brahma?

These legends might be ancient, but their lessons are still useful.

- **Be patient:** Just like Vishnu waited on the ocean, sometimes we need to be patient for the right time to act.
- **Use your imagination:** Brahma created the universe by using his imagination. Your ideas can shape the world too!
- **Protect what you create:** Vishnu teaches us that once something is created, it must be cared for and protected—whether it's a friendship, a project, or even the environment.

Even though this is just the beginning of our journey through Indian legends, you can already see how rich and magical these stories are. Vishnu and

Brahma show us that creation never really ends—there are always new worlds, new adventures, and new things to learn.

What's Next?

Now that you've learned how the universe began, it's time to meet some of the most exciting characters in Indian legends. In the next chapter, you'll fly through the sky with Hanuman, the mighty monkey god. Get ready for bravery, adventure, and a little bit of monkey mischief!

CHAPTER 2: THE ADVENTURES OF HANUMAN - THE MONKEY GOD

Meet Hanuman, the monkey god, one of the most beloved heroes in Indian mythology! Hanuman wasn't just any monkey—he was strong enough to move mountains, fast enough to fly across oceans, and brave enough to face even the most fearsome demons. But what made Hanuman truly special wasn't just his strength; it was his loyalty, courage, and kind heart.

Before he became a great hero, Hanuman was a playful little monkey with a love for adventure. His story begins in the jungles of India, where his childhood was filled with mischief and marvelous feats.

Hanuman's Mischievous Childhood

When Hanuman was born, he wasn't just any ordinary baby monkey—he was the son of the wind god, Vayu, which gave him incredible strength and speed. But young Hanuman didn't always use his powers wisely. He was curious and full of energy, always getting into trouble.

One of the most famous stories from his childhood happened when Hanuman saw the sun rising. To Hanuman, the sun looked like a giant, glowing fruit. "I'm hungry! I want to eat that delicious fruit!" he thought. Without hesitation, Hanuman leaped into the air and flew straight toward the sun, his arms stretched wide.

He soared higher and higher until he reached the sky. Just as he was about to take a big bite of the sun, Indra, the king of the gods, stopped him. Indra threw his thunderbolt, and it struck little Hanuman on the jaw, sending him tumbling down to Earth.

When Hanuman's father, the wind god Vayu, saw his son hurt, he was furious! In his anger, Vayu stopped all the winds from blowing, making it impossible for anything on Earth to move or breathe. The other gods quickly apologized and blessed Hanuman with even more powers, including the ability to change size, become invisible, and never be defeated in battle.

From that day on, Hanuman became stronger and wiser—but he never lost his playful spirit!

The Quest to Rescue Sita – Hanuman Meets Prince Rama

Hanuman's greatest adventure began when he met Prince Rama, a noble warrior searching for his wife, Sita. Sita had been captured by the evil demon king Ravana, who ruled the island of Lanka. Ravana was powerful, and his fortress was heavily guarded by terrifying demons.

The moment Hanuman saw Rama, he felt an instant connection. He knew that Rama was not just a prince—he was an incarnation of Vishnu, the great god who preserves the universe. Hanuman pledged his loyalty to Rama and promised to help him rescue Sita.

Hanuman Leaps Across the Ocean

Hanuman knew that the island of Lanka was far across the sea, too far to swim. But he wasn't worried. With his mighty strength, Hanuman grew as tall as a mountain. Then, with a powerful leap, he soared through the sky like a rocket, flying over forests, rivers, and waves.

The birds and clouds watched in amazement as Hanuman streaked through the sky. After traveling for hours, he finally reached the shores of Lanka. But the hardest part of his mission was still ahead—he had to sneak past Ravana's army of demons to find Sita.

The Search for Sita

Once inside Ravana's palace, Hanuman shrank to the size of a mouse to move unseen through the halls. He searched every corner of the massive fortress until, at last, he found Sita sitting beneath a tree in a beautiful garden. But Sita looked sad and lonely, waiting for Rama to save her.

"Sita, don't be afraid," Hanuman whispered. "I am Hanuman, Rama's loyal friend. I've come to take you home." Sita was overjoyed to hear Rama's name, but she told Hanuman that Ravana's guards were everywhere and that it wasn't safe for her to leave just yet.

Hanuman gave her Rama's ring as a sign of hope. "Stay strong," he said. "Rama will come soon, and together, we will defeat Ravana and bring you home."

Hanuman's Fiery Escape

Before leaving the palace, Hanuman couldn't resist causing a little trouble for Ravana. He wanted to send a message to the demon king that Rama's army was coming. So, Hanuman let himself be captured by Ravana's guards.

The demons tied him up and brought him before Ravana, who laughed at the sight of the monkey. "What can a silly monkey like you do against me?" Ravana sneered. To punish Hanuman, Ravana ordered his guards to set Hanuman's tail on fire.

But Hanuman wasn't worried. With his magical powers, he escaped from the ropes and grew as large as a mountain again. Then, with his tail still blazing, Hanuman leaped from rooftop to rooftop, setting Ravana's palace on fire. Flames roared through the fortress, and the demons ran in fear as the mighty monkey flew back across the ocean to deliver his message to Rama.

The Battle Against Ravana

With Hanuman's help, Rama and his army crossed the ocean to Lanka, where they fought a fierce battle against Ravana and his demon soldiers. Hanuman was at the front lines, leaping and smashing through the demons. He carried huge boulders and knocked down enemy soldiers with ease.

But during the battle, Rama's brother Lakshmana was wounded by a powerful arrow. Rama was heartbroken—Lakshmana's life was slipping away, and only a rare herb found in the Himalayas could save him. Without hesitation, Hanuman volunteered to fetch the herb.

Hanuman raced to the Himalayan mountains, moving faster than the wind itself. But when he arrived, he wasn't sure which plant was the right one! Instead of wasting time, Hanuman lifted the entire mountain and carried it back to Rama's camp.

With the magical herb, Lakshmana was healed, and the battle continued. Thanks to Hanuman's courage and quick thinking, Rama's army defeated Ravana, and Sita was finally reunited with her beloved Rama.

The Lesson of Loyalty and Courage

Hanuman's adventures show that real courage isn't just about being fearless—it's about doing what's right, even when it's hard. Courage means taking the first step, even when you're scared. It's standing by your friends, family, and the people you care about, no matter what challenges come your way. Hanuman could have given up when things got tough, but he didn't. He faced storms, demons, and dangers head-on, because he knew Rama and Sita were counting on him.

Hanuman's courage was not only in his battles but also in the little things he did along the way. When Sita was feeling hopeless in Ravana's garden, Hanuman comforted her with kind words and gave her Rama's ring as a sign of hope. This small act of kindness gave Sita the strength to hold on until Rama came to rescue her. Courage isn't always about fighting—it's also about bringing comfort to those in need.

The Strength of Loyalty

Hanuman's loyalty to Rama is another powerful part of his story. Loyalty means sticking with someone through good times and bad, just like Hanuman stayed by Rama's side no matter what challenges came their way. Even though the mission to rescue Sita was dangerous and difficult, Hanuman never thought of giving up. He didn't ask, "What's in it for me?" Instead, he stayed committed to helping Rama because that's what true friends do.

This kind of loyalty is rare and special. In today's world, it's easy to get caught up in our own problems and forget to help others. But Hanuman reminds us that being loyal to the people we care about makes us stronger. Whether it's standing up for a friend at school, helping someone who's struggling, or being there for a family member in need, loyalty is a superpower that we all have inside us.

Everyone Has a Special Power

What makes Hanuman's story so exciting is that he didn't realize how powerful he was at first. In one story, when Hanuman was young, the other gods placed a spell on him to make him forget his incredible strength. It wasn't until later, when the world needed him most that Hanuman remembered the great power inside him. That's an important lesson for all of us.

You might not know it yet, but you have your own special powers, too. Maybe you're great at making people laugh, or maybe you have a talent for solving problems. You don't have to be able to lift mountains or fly across oceans to be a hero. Every time you use your gifts to help someone—whether it's being a good listener, helping a friend with homework, or standing up for what's right—you are showing the same kind of bravery and strength that Hanuman did.

A Hero for All Time (Continued)

Hanuman's story has lasted through the centuries because his qualities are timeless. He shows us that strength comes from kindness, and that true heroes are those who help others without expecting anything in return. In temples and homes across India and beyond, people worship Hanuman, not just because of his great strength, but because of his big heart and his example of selfless service.

People pray to Hanuman when they need courage or strength to face challenges. His statues often show him standing tall, with his chest puffed out and his heart open, ready to serve. This reminds us that we don't have to be perfect to be heroes. We just have to be willing to try our best, stay loyal to those we care about, and believe in ourselves.

The Spirit of Hanuman in Everyday Life

Even though Hanuman's adventures happened long ago, the lessons from his story can guide us in our everyday lives. The next time you face something scary—whether it's a school project, meeting new people, or trying something new—think of Hanuman. Remember how he crossed the ocean, not because it was easy, but because he believed in his mission. You can face your challenges, too, one step at a time.

And when your friends or family need your help, be like Hanuman. Lend a helping hand, stay loyal, and do what's right, even when it's hard. You never know—your small act of kindness might make a big difference in someone's life, just like Hanuman's kindness gave Sita the hope she needed to stay strong.

You Can Be a Hero, Too

The world still needs heroes today, and you don't have to look far to find ways to be one. Every time you choose kindness over anger, friendship over selfishness, and courage over fear, you are being just like Hanuman. His story shows us that no challenge is too big when we believe in ourselves and support each other.

So, the next time you need a little extra courage, close your eyes and imagine Hanuman—the mighty monkey with a big heart, flying across the sky, lifting mountains, and helping his friends. And remember: there's a bit of Hanuman in all of us.

CHAPTER 3: GANESHA AND THE RACE AROUND THE WORLD

Ganesha is one of the most popular gods in Indian mythology. You might recognize him right away—he has the head of an elephant, a round belly, and a kind smile.

Ganesha is known as the god of wisdom, and wherever he goes, he brings good luck. That's why people pray to him before starting something new—whether it's a project, a journey, or the first day of school.

But what makes Ganesha so wise? To find out, let's dive into one of his most famous adventures: The Race Around the World!

The Challenge – A Race Between Brothers

Once upon a time, Ganesha and his younger brother Kartikeya had a friendly rivalry. Kartikeya, also known as Murugan, was a mighty warrior god. He rode a beautiful peacock and was always ready for an adventure. One day, the two brothers were arguing over who was the fastest and the smartest.

"I'm definitely the fastest!" Kartikeya said proudly, fluffing the feathers of his peacock.

"And I'm the wisest," Ganesha replied with a grin.

Hearing the argument, their father, Shiva, the great god of destruction, and their mother, Parvati, the goddess of love and devotion, decided to settle the matter with a race.

"All right, boys," Shiva announced. "Here's the challenge: the first one to circle the entire world and return will be the winner!" Kartikeya leapt onto his peacock, grinning from ear to ear. "I'll be back before you know it!" he called, as his peacock spread its wings and soared into the sky.

Meanwhile, Ganesha watched his brother fly off into the distance. He scratched his head and looked down at his chubby belly and short legs. "Hmm," he thought. "How am I supposed to beat Kartikeya? He's so fast, and I'm not exactly built for speed."

But Ganesha knew one thing—he didn't need to be fast if he was clever.

The Clever Plan

Instead of running or flying off like his brother, Ganesha sat down calmly and began to think. He knew that the point of the race wasn't just to run around the world. It was about something deeper—something more meaningful. And then, with a twinkle in his eye, Ganesha came up with a brilliant idea.

He stood up, smiled at his parents, and walked slowly around Shiva and Parvati. Not just once, but three times. Then he folded his hands and said, "I have finished my race."

Shiva and Parvati exchanged amused looks. "But you haven't left yet," Parvati said kindly. "How can you say you've won?"

Ganesha smiled. "You and Father are my entire world," he explained. "By circling you, I have traveled the most important path of all."

Shiva and Parvati were delighted by his answer. They realized that Ganesha had used wisdom, not speed, to win the race.

Meanwhile... Kartikeya's Long Journey

Far away, Kartikeya was still flying on his peacock, racing around mountains, rivers, and oceans. He zoomed across deserts and forests, determined to win the race. "This is easy!" he thought. "I'll get back before Ganesha even leaves!"

But as the journey dragged on, Kartikeya grew tired. Flying around the whole world was harder than he had expected. When he finally returned home, he found Ganesha sitting peacefully beside their parents, looking relaxed.

"I did it!" Kartikeya announced, panting as he jumped off his peacock. "I flew around the entire world!"

But before Kartikeya could celebrate, Shiva smiled and said, "I'm afraid your brother has already won."

"What?" Kartikeya gasped, eyes wide. "How is that possible? He never even left!"

Ganesha smiled gently. "I used my mind, Kartikeya. Mother and Father are my entire world, so I circled them instead."

The Lesson of Wisdom over Strength

Kartikeya stared at Ganesha in disbelief, but soon his surprise turned into admiration. "I thought the only way to win was to be fast," Kartikeya admitted. "But you showed me that wisdom can be even more powerful than strength."

This story teaches us an important lesson: sometimes it's not the fastest or strongest person who wins—it's the one who uses their mind. Ganesha didn't need wings or speed to win the race. He used his wisdom and understood that honoring his parents was more meaningful than flying around the world.

This story also reminds us that different kinds of strengths are important. Kartikeya was fast and brave, which are great qualities for a warrior. But Ganesha's cleverness and calm thinking helped him find a smarter way to win. Both brothers had their own strengths, and both were special in their own way.

Why Ganesha is Worshiped Before New Beginnings

Ganesha's wisdom and creativity make him the perfect guide for new beginnings. In India, people believe that Ganesha helps remove obstacles from their path, just like he found a clever way to win the race.

You might notice statues or pictures of Ganesha in homes, temples, and schools. People light lamps and offer sweets like modak, Ganesha's favorite treat, to ask for his blessings. They believe that with Ganesha's help, they can overcome any challenge—whether big or small.

So, the next time you start something new, think of Ganesha. Whether it's your first day at school or a new hobby, stay calm, think wisely, and believe in yourself. Just like Ganesha, you might find a clever way to succeed that no one else has thought of!

A God with a Big Heart (and a Big Appetite!)

Apart from his wisdom, Ganesha is also known for his kindness and love for sweets. He always has time for friends and family, and he teaches us that life should be enjoyed with joy and laughter. Ganesha shows that being wise doesn't mean you have to be serious all the time—you can still have fun, enjoy sweets, and celebrate with loved ones!

In fact, one of the reasons people love Ganesha is because of his friendly and approachable nature. He reminds us that being smart and kind go hand in hand. Whether you're solving a tricky puzzle or sharing a treat with a friend, Ganesha encourages everyone to use their gifts to spread happiness.

A Lesson for All of Us

Ganesha's race around the world shows us that there are many ways to win in life. You don't always have to be the fastest, strongest, or loudest. Sometimes, all it takes is a little bit of thought and creativity. And most importantly, it reminds us that family and love are at the heart of everything.

The next time you feel stuck or face a challenge, remember Ganesha's story. Think carefully, look for new ways to solve the problem, and don't forget to ask for help when you need it. With a little wisdom and a lot of heart, you can overcome anything—just like Ganesha!

CHAPTER 4:
KRISHNA AND THE BUTTER THIEVES

In a small, peaceful village called Vrindavan, there lived a little boy named Krishna. But Krishna was not an ordinary child—he was special. With his sparkling eyes, curly black hair, and a flute tucked under his arm, Krishna could win anyone's heart. Yet, there was something else that everyone in the village knew about him—Krishna was as mischievous as he was charming. And oh, how much he loved butter!

This is the story of how Krishna, the butter thief, became the most beloved little troublemaker in the entire village.

Krishna's Love for Butter

From the moment Krishna could crawl, he was drawn to the pots of fresh, creamy butter the villagers made every day. Butter, or "makhan" as it is called, was a favorite treat for everyone, but no one loved it more than Krishna.

Krishna's mother, Yashoda, churned butter every morning. She kept it in tall pots, high on shelves, thinking that would keep her mischievous little boy away. But Krishna was clever. As soon as his mother wasn't looking, he'd gather his friends and they would plan their butter-stealing adventures.

They sneaked into kitchens, climbed on each other's shoulders, and reached the pots hanging from the ceiling. And when they finally dipped their hands into the cool, creamy butter—oh, what a delight!

The Great Butter Heist

Krishna wasn't just good at stealing butter—he made it a fun game. His friends called themselves the Butter Thieves, and wherever there was butter, they were sure to follow. The villagers tried everything to stop them. They tied the pots with ropes, locked their kitchens, and even set traps. But Krishna always found a way.

One day, Yashoda caught Krishna and his friends red-handed, their faces smeared with butter. "Krishna! What am I going to do with you?" Yashoda sighed, trying to sound stern. But it was hard to stay angry with him, especially when Krishna gave her his most innocent smile and said,

"Mother, the butter was too delicious. It called to me!"

Yashoda shook her head and laughed. How could anyone resist his charm?

Krishna's Pranks and the Villagers' Laughter

Krishna's mischief didn't stop with butter. He loved playing pranks on the villagers, too. He would untie their cows, hide their flutes, and splash them with water from the river. Sometimes, he even used his magical powers to multiply himself—just to confuse everyone! But no matter what he did, the villagers adored him.

"Look at that Krishna!" they would say with a chuckle. "Always up to something, but how can we be angry at him when he brings us so much joy!"

Even the cows in Vrindavan loved Krishna. Whenever he played his flute, the cows would stop whatever they were doing and gather around him, swaying to the sweet music. Birds chirped, the river hummed, and the whole village seemed happier whenever Krishna was near.

Caught in the Act – A Lesson from Mother Yashoda

One day, Krishna's mother decided it was time to teach him a lesson. "If I don't stop him now," she thought, "he'll eat all the butter in the village!" So, Yashoda carefully hid the butter pots and watched from a corner. Just as she expected, Krishna and his friends sneaked into the kitchen.

This time, Yashoda caught Krishna with his hand deep in the butter pot. "Aha! I've got you!" she said. Krishna grinned, his cheeks puffed up with butter.

Yashoda couldn't help but laugh, but she decided to teach her son a little lesson. She tied him to a mortar, saying, "Now, let's see how you get out of this, little one!" Krishna looked at the rope, gave his mother a playful wink, and—poof! The rope fell off.

Instead of running away, Krishna gave his mother a big hug and said, "Don't worry, Mother. I'll always share the butter with you."

The Joy of Sharing and Kindness

Despite his pranks, Krishna's heart was filled with kindness and love. He wasn't selfish—he always shared the butter with his friends. He even fed the hungry animals in the village. Krishna's mischief wasn't about stealing—it was about spreading happiness.

This story teaches us that joy multiplies when it's shared. Krishna's love for butter wasn't just about eating something delicious—it was about bringing people together. Through his playful antics, he showed that life is better when we laugh, play, and share with others.

A Lesson in Joy and Kindness

Krishna's playful spirit and loving nature made him a favorite, not just in Vrindavan but all over the world. People still tell stories of Krishna's childhood adventures to remind us of the importance of joy, friendship, and kindness.

During festivals like Janmashtami, which celebrates Krishna's birth, people remember his love for butter by breaking pots filled with yogurt and sweets. Children dress up as Krishna, and everyone sings songs and dances, celebrating the joy he brought to the world.

The Message of Krishna's Adventures

Krishna's playful adventures teach us that joy and kindness can turn even the simplest moments into magical ones. He reminds us that life doesn't have to be perfect to be beautiful. Sometimes, it's the little things—like sharing butter with friends, playing music, or laughing together—that create the best memories.

Even when Krishna played tricks and got into trouble, his heart was always in the right place. His pranks weren't meant to hurt anyone—they were his way of spreading happiness. And that's an important lesson for all of us: Happiness grows when we share it with others. A small act of kindness, like helping a friend with homework or cheering someone up, can make a big difference.

Facing Life with a Smile and an Open Heart

Another valuable lesson from Krishna's life is the importance of embracing life with an open heart. He never let obstacles or challenges take away his playful spirit. Even when things were tough, Krishna faced them with a smile, using his cleverness and kindness to overcome them. This teaches us that life will always have ups and downs, but if we stay positive and kind, we can turn even hard times into opportunities to learn and grow.

Krishna's adventures also show us that it's okay to make mistakes. Everyone gets into trouble sometimes—just like Krishna did with his butter-stealing pranks! What matters is how we learn from those mistakes and make things right. Life is about having fun, learning along the way, and always trying to do our best.

The Power of Friendship and Community

Krishna's story wouldn't be complete without his friends and the people of Vrindavan. Whether he was stealing butter or playing music, Krishna always included others in his fun. He didn't enjoy life alone—he made sure to spread joy wherever he went, whether it was among his friends, animals, or villagers. His adventures remind us how important it is to build strong friendships and cherish the people around us.

We all need friends to laugh with, play with, and share life's moments—both the good ones and the tough ones. Like Krishna, we can be good friends by including others in our joy and helping them when they need it. Friendship isn't just about having fun; it's also about being there for one another, sharing, and lifting each other up.

Life is an Adventure Meant to Be Enjoyed

Krishna's adventures remind us that life isn't just about getting everything right or being perfect—it's about making the most of every moment and enjoying the journey. When we find joy in small things, like music, nature, or a kind gesture, life feels fuller and more exciting. It's not about waiting for the perfect day to come—it's about making today joyful by spreading happiness wherever we go.

Whenever you feel overwhelmed or stuck, remember Krishna and his butter thieves. Imagine how he would find a way to make even a simple chore fun or turn a quiet day into a festival. Like Krishna, we all have the power to bring light to the world around us, one smile and one kind act at a time.

CHAPTER 5:
THE LEGEND OF SAVITRI AND SATYAVAN - A TALE OF LOVE AND DEVOTION

A long time ago, in a grand palace surrounded by gardens and forests, there lived a beautiful princess named Savitri. She was not only beautiful but also known for her kind heart, sharp mind, and unshakable determination. Even though she could have had anything she wished for, Savitri didn't care for riches or luxury—what she truly believed in was love and doing what was right.

One day, Savitri's parents told her, "It is time for you to choose a husband." But Savitri was no ordinary princess—she wanted to find someone she loved. So, with her parents' blessing, she set off on a journey, traveling through forests, villages, and mountains, looking for someone to share her life with.

After many days, she came across a quiet forest where she saw a kind young man named Satyavan chopping wood. Satyavan wasn't a prince. He lived a simple life in the forest with his parents, but he had a heart full of kindness and a smile that could warm anyone's heart. As soon as Savitri saw him, she knew he was the one she wanted to marry.

A Difficult Decision

Savitri hurried back to the palace and told her parents, "I have found the person I wish to marry. His name is Satyavan, and he lives in the forest."

But to Savitri's surprise, the wise sage Narada—who was visiting her father's court—had some bad news. "Satyavan is a good man," Narada said. "But there is a terrible truth. He is destined to live for only one more year. If Savitri marries him, she will soon face heartbreak."

Everyone in the palace was shocked. Her parents begged her, "Choose someone else, Savitri! You are a princess—you shouldn't have to go through such sorrow."

But Savitri remained calm. "I have made my choice," she said firmly. "I will marry Satyavan, and I will love him with all my heart."

Her parents finally gave in, realizing that Savitri's love was too strong to be swayed. Soon after, Savitri married Satyavan, and the two began their life together in the forest.

A Year of Love and Happiness

Savitri and Satyavan lived a simple but happy life in the forest. Every day, they woke up to the songs of birds and worked side by side, gathering fruits and wood. They didn't need fancy clothes or a grand palace—their love was enough to make every day special.

But as the months passed, Savitri couldn't forget the warning she had received. She knew that the day would come when Satyavan's life would end. Her heart ached at the thought, but she didn't let fear take over. Instead, she decided that she would do everything in her power to protect him.

Finally, the day that Narada had predicted arrived. Savitri knew that something terrible was about to happen, but she stayed close to Satyavan, determined not to let him out of her sight.

"Savitri, I'm going to the forest to collect firewood," Satyavan said, unaware of what lay ahead. "I'll come with you," Savitri replied with a soft smile.

As they walked deeper into the forest, Satyavan suddenly felt tired. "I think I need to rest for a moment," he said, sitting beneath a large tree. Before Savitri could say anything, Satyavan closed his eyes and fell into a deep sleep.

Suddenly, the air grew cold, and a shadow appeared before Savitri. It was Yama, the god of death, holding a noose in his hand. "Satyavan's time on Earth is over," Yama said calmly. "I have come to take him away."

Savitri's Clever Plan

Savitri's heart raced, but she refused to give in to fear. She knew she had to do something—and fast! As Yama took Satyavan's soul and began to walk away, Savitri followed him through the forest.

"Why are you following me, Savitri?" Yama asked, turning to face her. "Your husband's time has come. You cannot change fate."

"I know, Lord Yama," Savitri replied. "But I cannot leave my husband. I promised to be by his side, no matter what."

Yama was impressed by Savitri's loyalty, but he continued walking. "Go back, Princess," he said. "There is nothing you can do for him now."

But Savitri wasn't ready to give up. She knew she couldn't fight Yama with strength, but she had a clever idea. "Lord Yama," she said sweetly, "may I ask you a question? You are wise and powerful, and I would love to hear your thoughts."

Yama was curious. "Very well," he said. "Ask your question."

And so, as they walked, Savitri kept Yama busy with clever conversations. She asked him about life, death, and the nature of the soul. Yama was so impressed by her wisdom and calmness that he couldn't help but enjoy their talk. With every step, Savitri grew more determined. She knew that if she could keep Yama talking, she might find a way to save Satyavan.

The Power of Love and Determination

After walking for what seemed like hours, Yama finally stopped. "Savitri," he said with admiration, "you are no ordinary woman. Your wisdom, courage, and devotion are remarkable. I will grant you one wish—anything you want except the life of your husband."

Savitri thought for a moment, and then she smiled. "Thank you, Lord Yama. If it pleases you, I wish for Satyavan's parents to regain their lost kingdom and live in happiness."

Yama nodded. "So be it," he said, continuing on his way.

But Savitri didn't leave. She kept following him, never giving up. "Why are you still following me?" Yama asked.

"I promised to stay by my husband's side," Savitri replied.

Yama was even more impressed by her devotion. "You are truly extraordinary," he said. "I will grant you another wish—anything you want, except Satyavan's life."

Savitri smiled again. "Then I wish for my husband and me to have children so his family may continue to grow."

Yama agreed, saying, "So be it." But as soon as the words left his lips, he realized that he had been outsmarted. For how could Savitri and Satyavan have children if Satyavan's life ended that day?

Yama smiled, acknowledging Savitri's cleverness. "You have won, Savitri," he said. "Your love and determination have moved me. I return your husband's life to you. May you both live long and happy lives."

The Return of Satyavan

In an instant, Satyavan's soul was returned to his body. He opened his eyes under the tree, confused but healthy. "What happened?" he asked, rubbing his eyes.

Savitri smiled warmly. "Nothing, my love. Everything is as it should be."

The Message of Savitri's Story

Savitri's story shows us that real strength doesn't always come from physical power—it comes from determination, love, and clever thinking. She didn't need weapons or spells to face Yama, the god of death. Instead, she used her mind and her words to outsmart him. She knew that sometimes, being patient and calm in the face of danger is the most powerful thing of all.

This tale teaches us that true love isn't just about happy moments—it's about standing by the people we care about even when things are difficult. Savitri could have chosen an easier path, but her heart wouldn't let her. She loved Satyavan not just in good times but also when the future seemed uncertain. And in the end, it was her unwavering loyalty that gave her the strength to change destiny.

Bravery Comes in Many Forms

Savitri's courage wasn't the kind you see in warriors or heroes fighting battles—it was a quieter, steadfast courage. She faced one of the greatest fears anyone could imagine—losing someone she loved—and yet she didn't give up. Savitri teaches us that being brave doesn't always mean fighting with strength. Sometimes, it means holding on to hope, staying calm, and finding a way to solve problems with kindness and wisdom.

When we encounter challenges in life, we can all try to be a little like Savitri. Whether it's supporting a friend who's going through a hard time or standing up for what's right, true courage means staying kind, loyal, and determined, even when things seem difficult.

The Power of Promises

Savitri's promise to stay with Satyavan no matter what is another powerful message from this story. Promises are important—they show the people we love that we care about them and that they can rely on us. Savitri's unbreakable promise gave her the courage to follow Yama through the forest and never give up. Even though it seemed impossible, she kept her word and found a way to bring Satyavan back to life.

Love that Transforms and Inspires

Savitri's love for Satyavan wasn't just romantic—it was selfless, pure, and transformational. Through her love and determination, she changed her destiny and brought light back into their lives. This story reminds us that love has the power to transform—it can give us the strength to overcome fear, the courage to face challenges, and the patience to find a solution, no matter how difficult things seem.

Savitri teaches us that real love means wanting the best for the people we care about—even if it means putting their needs ahead of our own. Her story inspires us to be patient, kind, and thoughtful in all our relationships.

Even today, the story of Savitri and Satyavan continues to inspire people. The festival of Vat Savitri is celebrated in India to honor her strength, love, and loyalty. On this day, women pray for the health and happiness of their families and tie sacred threads around trees, symbolizing the unbreakable bond between Savitri and Satyavan.

This festival is not just about remembering an ancient story—it's about celebrating love and devotion in everyday life. It reminds us that no matter what challenges we face, love and loyalty will always help us find a way forward.

Savitri's story shows us that we all have the power to be heroes in our own way—by staying loyal, being kind, and never giving up on the people we love. And just like Savitri, we can all use determination, patience, and clever thinking to overcome life's challenges and make the world a better place.

What's Next?

In the next chapter, we'll meet the clever jackal, a witty animal who uses his brain to outsmart a greedy lion. Get ready for a fun and lively story about brains over brawn that will leave you laughing and inspired!

CHAPTER 6: THE CLEVER JACKAL - FOLKTALES FROM THE JUNGLE

Deep in the heart of the Indian jungle, animals of all shapes and sizes roam under the warm sun. Some are big and powerful, like the mighty elephants and roaring tigers. Others are small and quick, like the nimble monkeys swinging from trees. But in the animal kingdom, being the strongest isn't always enough. Sometimes, the smartest animal wins the day.

This is the story of a clever jackal and a greedy lion, a tale that shows us how intelligence and quick thinking can outsmart brute strength. The animals of the jungle have many stories to tell, and each one teaches us a valuable lesson. Let's dive into this exciting folktale and discover how the clever jackal saves himself—and the jungle—using nothing but his wits!

The Greedy Lion

Once upon a time, in the middle of the jungle, there lived a fearsome lion. He was the biggest and strongest animal in the forest, and he knew it. Every day, he roared so loudly that the trees shook and the other animals trembled in fear.

The lion believed that because he was the king of the jungle, he could eat as much as he wanted. Every day, he demanded more food from the other animals, and soon, the creatures of the jungle began to worry.

"If the lion keeps eating like this," whispered the deer to the monkeys, "soon there won't be any animals left in the jungle!"

"We must find a way to stop him," said the peacock sadly. "But how? No one is strong enough to stand up to him."

Just when the animals were losing hope, a clever jackal stepped forward with a sly smile. "Don't worry, my friends," he said. "Leave it to me. I'll take care of our greedy king."

The Jackal's Plan

The jackal was small compared to the lion, but he knew something important—brains are often more powerful than brawn. He came up with a clever plan and set off through the forest to meet the lion. When the jackal arrived, the lion was lounging under a tree, licking his paws after his latest meal.

"Greetings, Your Majesty," the jackal said, bowing politely. "I have come to share some important news with you."

The lion raised an eyebrow. "News?" he growled. "It had better be worth my time, little jackal."

"Oh, it is," the jackal replied, hiding a mischievous grin. "I have found another lion living in the jungle! He's just as strong as you and claims to be the real king of the forest."

The lion's eyes narrowed. "What? Another lion? There is only one king of the jungle, and that's me!" he roared. "Where is this imposter? I'll show him who's boss!"

The jackal pretended to look worried. "He lives in a secret place, Your Majesty—a deep well hidden in the heart of the jungle. If you follow me, I can show you where he hides."

The lion, burning with anger, leaped to his feet. "Take me to him!" he snarled. "I'll tear him to pieces!"

The Lion Meets His Match

The clever jackal led the lion deep into the jungle, weaving through trees and bushes until they reached an old stone well. The well was deep and filled with water, but the lion didn't know that.

"Here it is," the jackal whispered, pointing toward the well. "The other lion is hiding inside. If you look down, you'll see him."

The lion leaned over the edge of the well and peered into the water. What do you think he saw? His own reflection! But the lion, being both greedy and proud, didn't realize this. He thought the lion staring back at him was the imposter.

"How dare you try to steal my throne!" the lion roared at the water. The reflection roared back, perfectly mimicking the lion's movements.

Enraged, the lion let out a mighty roar and jumped into the well, thinking he was about to fight his enemy. But instead, he splashed into the cold water and sank to the bottom with a big splash!

The clever jackal peered over the edge of the well, grinning from ear to ear. "Well, well," he chuckled, "it looks like our greedy king has found his match—his own reflection!"

The Jungle Celebrates

With the greedy lion gone, the animals of the jungle were finally free to live in peace. They celebrated by dancing under the moonlight and singing songs of joy. The monkeys swung from the branches, the peacocks spread their colorful feathers, and the elephants trumpeted happily.

As the animals gathered around the clever jackal, they cheered, "You may not be the biggest or the strongest, but you are certainly the smartest! Thank you, clever jackal, for saving us!"

The jackal gave a modest bow and said, "It's not about how big you are or how loud you roar—it's about how wisely you use your mind."

Lessons from the Clever Jackal

The story of the clever jackal teaches us several important lessons.

Intelligence is more powerful than strength: Even though the lion was the strongest animal, the jackal outsmarted him. This shows us that quick thinking and clever ideas can solve even the toughest problems.

Pride and greed can be dangerous: Both were the lion's downfall. He thought he was invincible, but his own reflection fooled him. This teaches us to be humble and fair, no matter how strong or powerful we are.

Bravery comes in many forms: The jackal didn't need to fight the lion with claws or teeth. Instead, he used his courage and cleverness to protect his friends. This shows us that bravery isn't just about fighting—it's about finding smart solutions to problems.

The Charm of Indian Animal Tales

Indian animal tales like the story of the clever jackal are not only fun to read but also filled with valuable life lessons. These folktales are part of India's rich storytelling tradition, where animals take on human traits—they speak, think, and solve problems just like us! Through these stories, children learn important lessons about friendship, kindness, bravery, and the power of intelligence.

Many of these stories come from ancient collections of tales, such as the Panchatantra, a famous book of wisdom filled with stories about animals. Just like the jackal, the characters in these tales often use their brains instead of brawn to solve problems.

These stories remind us that wisdom and kindness are more important than strength and that every creature, no matter how small, has something valuable to teach us.

What We Can Learn from the Jackal's Adventure

Whenever you feel small or unsure, think of the clever jackal. Remember that being smart and thinking quickly can help you overcome even the biggest challenges. If you ever face a problem that seems too big to handle, don't give up! Take a moment to think it through—just like the jackal did—and you might find a clever solution hiding in plain sight.

And whenever you see someone being greedy or acting unfairly, remember the jackal's story. It teaches us that pride and selfishness can lead to trouble, but kindness, fairness, and cleverness will always help us find the right path.

CHAPTER 7: ARJUNA AND THE MAGIC BOW - HEROES FROM THE MAHABHARATA

Long ago, in the kingdom of Panchala, a great king named Drupada had a beautiful daughter named Draupadi. She was known throughout the land for her wisdom, kindness, and beauty. Many brave warriors dreamed of marrying her, but King Drupada wanted to find the most worthy husband for his daughter.

One day, the king announced a grand competition. "The warrior who wins this challenge will marry Draupadi," he declared. The news spread like wildfire across the land, and soon, kings and princes from far and wide gathered to prove their strength and skill.

But this wasn't going to be an easy contest. To win Draupadi's hand, the competitors had to master a magical bow and perform an impossible task!

The Impossible Challenge

At the heart of the competition stood a huge golden bow, unlike anything the warriors had ever seen. The bow was said to contain ancient magic, making it incredibly heavy and difficult to use. Along with the bow, there was a spinning fish mounted high on a pole, far above the heads of the crowd. The fish had a shiny, mirrored surface, and it twirled rapidly, making it difficult to aim at.

The task was simple to explain but nearly impossible to complete:

The warrior must string the bow, then shoot an arrow into the spinning fish's eye—without looking directly at it! Instead, they could only aim by looking at the fish's reflection in a bowl of water below.

One by one, the warriors tried their luck. But the magic bow was so heavy that most of them couldn't even lift it! Those who did manage to lift it couldn't string it, and their arms trembled under its weight. Others missed the fish entirely, frustrated by how it spun so quickly.

As the competition continued, the crowd began to lose hope. Was there anyone worthy of completing this challenge?

Enter Arjuna – The Prince in Disguise

Among the crowd stood a young man dressed as a humble traveler. He didn't wear the fine clothes of a prince or the armor of a warrior, but there was something special about him. His name was Arjuna, a skilled archer and one of the greatest heroes of the Mahabharata.

Arjuna was a Pandava prince, but he and his brothers had been living in exile, disguised as simple travelers to avoid danger. Though Arjuna's clothes were plain, he carried with him a sharp mind and a heart full of courage. He had spent years mastering the art of archery, training with the best teachers and practicing every single day. The magic bow was no ordinary weapon, but Arjuna was no ordinary archer.

How Arjuna Mastered the Magic Bow

Arjuna stepped forward, and the crowd fell silent. The other warriors sneered, whispering, "How can this simple traveler succeed when mighty kings have failed?"

But Arjuna didn't let their doubts distract him. His teacher, Dronacharya, had always taught him that the key to success was focus and skill. He took a deep breath and cleared his mind. It didn't matter how heavy the bow was or how quickly the fish spun. What mattered was that he believed in his training.

With steady hands, Arjuna lifted the heavy bow as if it weighed nothing. The crowd gasped in surprise! With grace and precision, Arjuna strung the bow, pulling the string back until it hummed like music. The other warriors watched on in disbelief.

Next came the most difficult part. Arjuna knelt by the bowl of water and stared into the reflection of the spinning fish. The fish above whirled rapidly, but Arjuna's gaze remained steady. He blocked out all distractions, focusing only on the reflection.

In a swift motion, Arjuna drew an arrow from his quiver, placed it on the bowstring, and pulled it back. The crowd held their breath, their eyes wide with anticipation. Whoosh! The arrow flew through the air like lightning.

With perfect precision, the arrow struck the fish's eye, stopping it mid-spin. A cheer erupted from the crowd—Arjuna had done the impossible!

Draupadi Chooses Her Hero

As the crowd celebrated, Draupadi stepped forward, her eyes shining with joy. She knew that Arjuna was no ordinary traveler. His skill, focus, and humility had proven that he was a true hero. In her heart, she knew that this was the man she had been waiting for.

With a graceful bow, Draupadi placed a flower garland around Arjuna's neck, choosing him as her husband. The other warriors grumbled in frustration, but the people of Panchala cheered, knowing that Arjuna had earned his victory through skill and hard work.

Arjuna's brothers, the Pandavas, were thrilled by his success. Even the gods smiled down on the young hero, proud of his mastery and determination. Arjuna's victory wasn't just a personal achievement—it was the beginning of a great story filled with adventure, friendship, and challenges.

The Importance of Skill and Focus

The story of Arjuna and the magic bow teaches us that true strength comes from skill, focus, and practice. While many warriors had tried to win the challenge with brute force, it was Arjuna's calm mind and steady hand that led him to victory.

Arjuna reminds us that talent alone isn't enough—we must practice, stay focused, and believe in ourselves. Whether it's learning a new skill, playing a sport, or studying for a test, success comes when we work hard and stay focused.

This story also shows us that it's not always the loudest or the strongest who win. Sometimes, it's the quiet and determined ones—the ones who stay focused and keep trying, even when things get tough—who achieve the greatest victories.

Lessons from Arjuna's Story

Even thousands of years later, Arjuna's story from the Mahabharata continues to inspire people. He is remembered not only as a skilled archer but also as a wise warrior who fought with integrity and honor. His most famous moment came during the battle of Kurukshetra, where he was guided by Lord Krishna, who taught him the importance of duty, inner strength, and self-belief through the teachings of the Bhagavad Gita.

Arjuna's legacy reminds us that the real battle is often within ourselves—between doubt and confidence, between fear and courage. He teaches us to trust our abilities and keep striving for excellence, even when the journey feels tough.

Becoming Your Own Hero

Arjuna's story shows us that being a hero isn't just about strength—it's about staying focused, believing in yourself, and practicing your craft with dedication. Whether you're learning a new skill, playing a sport, or working toward a goal, you can be your own hero by following Arjuna's example.

Remember:

Keep practicing every day, even when it feels hard.
Stay calm and focus on your own progress.
Trust yourself, even if others doubt you.
Be humble—kindness is what makes a true hero.

Arjuna's story reminds us that every one of us has the potential for greatness. With patience, dedication, and focus, we can achieve things we once thought impossible—just like Arjuna did with the magic bow.

A Story That Teaches Us for Generations

From ancient times to today, Arjuna's journey has been told in homes, temples, and schools to inspire people to work hard and pursue their dreams. His story lives on in the lessons we learn from it—about focus, perseverance, and humility.

Every time you feel challenged or unsure of yourself, remember Arjuna standing calmly in front of the spinning fish, blocking out the noise around him and focusing only on the task at hand. You have the same strength within you—you just need to believe it.

So, take aim at your dreams, practice every day, and never give up.

CHAPTER 8: HOLIKA AND PRAHLAD - THE ORIGINS OF HOLI

Long ago, in a grand kingdom, there lived a young boy named Prahlad. Prahlad wasn't just an ordinary boy—he had a pure heart and unshakable faith in the goodness of the world. But this belief would soon put him in danger, for Prahlad's father was Hiranyakashipu, a powerful king with a heart filled with pride and anger.

Hiranyakashipu thought he was the greatest being to ever exist. He believed he was stronger than the gods and demanded that everyone in his kingdom worship him as one. But little Prahlad had his own beliefs. He knew deep down that Lord Vishnu, the protector of the world, was the true source of kindness, wisdom, and strength. No matter how much his father demanded, Prahlad refused to worship him.

Hiranyakashipu's anger grew with every passing day. "How dare my own son go against my orders!" he roared. He tried everything to make Prahlad change his mind, but the boy remained calm and stayed true to his beliefs.

This made Hiranyakashipu furious. He decided to punish Prahlad once and for all. And for that, he turned to Holika, his sister.

Holika's Fiery Plan

Now, Holika wasn't just Hiranyakashipu's sister—she had magical powers. She wore a cloak that protected her from fire, which made her feel invincible. "With this cloak, I can walk through flames and not be harmed," she boasted.

Hiranyakashipu came up with a terrible plan. "Holika," he said, "you will take Prahlad with you into a blazing fire. Your cloak will protect you, and

Prahlad will be burned. That will teach him to disobey me."

Holika smiled wickedly, confident that her cloak would keep her safe. A huge bonfire was prepared in the middle of the kingdom. The fire roared and crackled, sending sparks high into the sky. The villagers watched on with heavy hearts, afraid for the young boy.

Prahlad's Courage and Holika's Defeat

Holika sat on the pyre with Prahlad on her lap, ready to carry out her brother's plan. But Prahlad showed no fear. He closed his eyes and prayed to Lord Vishnu, trusting that goodness would protect him. "Whatever happens, I will remain faithful," Prahlad whispered.

As the fire blazed around them, something unexpected happened. The magical cloak slipped off Holika's shoulders and wrapped itself around Prahlad! Holika's magic had betrayed her because her powers could only protect someone with a pure heart—and that someone was Prahlad.

While Prahlad sat unharmed, Holika was consumed by the flames. The villagers gasped in amazement. Evil had been defeated by the power of faith and goodness! The bonfire roared as a reminder that good will always triumph over evil.

The Triumph of Good Over Evil

When Hiranyakashipu learned what had happened, he couldn't believe his eyes. His own plan had backfired, and his sister had been defeated by the very fire she trusted. Even though he had tried everything to break Prahlad's spirit, the boy's courage and faith had won.

Prahlad's story teaches us that even when things seem scary, staying true to what we believe in can help us overcome any challenge. Kindness, honesty, and courage are stronger than fear and anger, just like the fire was powerless against Prahlad's pure heart.

The Origins of Holi – A Celebration of Colors and Joy

The story of Holika and Prahlad is the reason why people celebrate the festival of Holi. Holi marks the triumph of good over evil, reminding us that even in the darkest times, kindness, courage, and truth will shine through.

Every year, before Holi begins, people gather to light huge bonfires—just like the one that consumed Holika. They throw grains, coconuts, and wood into the fire as offerings, remembering how good triumphed over evil that day. This part of the festival is called Holika Dahan, and it marks the beginning of Holi.

A Festival of Colors and Joy

The next day, the real fun of Holi begins! It's known as the Festival of Colors, and people celebrate by throwing bright-colored powders and water at each other. Children run through the streets, laughing and playing, covering their friends and family in colors of red, blue, yellow, and green. No one is spared on Holi!

Why do people throw colors during Holi? The colors symbolize joy, happiness, and unity. On this special day, everyone forgets their differences and comes together in celebration.

People sing, dance, and enjoy sweet treats like gujiyas and laddoos, making the day even more special. Families and friends gather to celebrate love, friendship, and new beginnings, just like Prahlad's victory marked a fresh start for the kingdom.

The Meaning of Holi for Us Today

The story of Holika and Prahlad isn't just about fire and colors—it carries an important message. It teaches us to stay true to our beliefs, even when things get tough. Life can sometimes feel like a difficult journey, just like Prahlad's, but if we hold on to kindness, courage, and honesty, we can overcome any challenge.

Holi also reminds us that joy is meant to be shared. The colors we throw on each other during the festival symbolize the happiness we spread when we are kind and open-hearted. Just like the villagers celebrated Prahlad's victory, we can celebrate the good things in our own lives by sharing laughter, love, and kindness with others.

What We Can Learn from Prahlad's Story

Prahlad's story gives us some valuable lessons that we can use every day:

Stay True to Yourself: Even when people try to pressure you, believe in what's right and stay true to yourself, just like Prahlad did.

Courage Over Fear: It's okay to feel scared sometimes, but bravery comes from doing the right thing, even when it's hard.

Kindness Always Wins: Holi teaches us that being kind and honest will always triumph over greed, anger, or fear.

Celebrate with Joy: Life is full of colors and surprises—enjoy every moment and spread happiness wherever you go!

A Celebration to Remember

Holi isn't just about colors and fun—it's about starting fresh and celebrating the joy of being together. Every year, people come together to forgive old grudges and spread happiness. It's a time when we let go of what's gone and look forward to the future with open hearts.

The colorful powders we throw during Holi represent all the different emotions and experiences that make life beautiful—joy, love, and even challenges. When we mix and splash colors on one another, we remind ourselves that life is meant to be celebrated in all its forms.

Holi also teaches us to find joy in the little moments, just as Prahlad found strength in his faith, even during difficult times. Whether it's laughing with friends, dancing to music, or enjoying a sweet treat, Holi reminds us that the most meaningful moments in life come from spending time with those we care about.

Goodness Always Wins

The story of Prahlad and Holika reminds us that, no matter how powerful evil may seem, goodness will always triumph in the end. When we stay kind and courageous, we become part of that victory—just like Prahlad. The bonfires during Holika Dahan are more than just flames; they represent the burning away of negativity, leaving room for hope, joy, and new beginnings.

So, the next time you feel overwhelmed or unsure, think of Prahlad's courage. Good things always find a way through difficult times—sometimes, all we need is a little patience and belief in ourselves.

What Holi Teaches Us About Life

Find Joy in Every Day: Just like Holi's colors, life is filled with moments of joy waiting to be experienced. Look for reasons to smile, even on ordinary days.

Make Time for Laughter and Fun: Holi teaches us to celebrate life's happy moments with those we care about. It's a reminder that spending time with friends and family is what makes life meaningful.

Spread Kindness Like Color: When we throw bright colors on others during Holi, it's a way of sharing happiness. Kindness works the same way—the more you share it, the more it spreads.

New Beginnings Are Always Possible: Holi marks a fresh start, showing us that it's never too late to begin again. If something didn't go right yesterday, today is a new chance to make it better.

So, the next time you celebrate Holi, remember the story of Prahlad's courage and Holika's defeat. Let it remind you that life will always bring challenges, but goodness, kindness, and determination will always win. Use Holi as a time to reconnect with friends, forgive old hurts, and spread joy wherever you go.

CHAPTER 9: THE CHURNING OF THE OCEAN - THE QUEST FOR IMMORTALITY

A long time ago, the gods (devas) and demons (asuras) were in constant battle. The gods were good-hearted and kind, but the demons were powerful and always causing trouble. One day, the gods faced a big problem: they were losing their strength and power. Without their energy, they wouldn't be able to protect the world from evil.

The gods needed something to make them strong again—Amrit, the nectar of immortality. Whoever drank Amrit would become immortal and never grow weak. But there was only one way to find it: by churning the ocean of milk, a vast ocean full of magical treasures hidden beneath its surface.

But there was a catch. Churning the ocean wasn't something the gods could do alone. They needed the help of their enemies—the demons!

A Tricky Partnership

The gods were worried. How could they trust the demons to help? After all, the demons loved causing mischief and didn't care much for rules. But the gods knew they had no choice. They decided to make a deal:

"If you help us churn the ocean," the gods told the demons, "you will get a share of the treasures that come out of it—including the Amrit."

The demons agreed, their eyes gleaming with greed. "We'll help," they said, secretly planning to keep all the treasures for themselves.

The Mighty Mount Mandara and the Snake King

To churn the ocean, the gods and demons needed a huge churning stick and a long rope. They chose Mount Mandara, a mighty mountain, as the stick.

But how would they churn the ocean with a mountain?

"We'll need a giant rope to spin the mountain," the gods said. And for the rope, they turned to Vasuki, the great king of snakes. Vasuki agreed to help, curling his enormous body around the mountain to act as the rope.

With everything ready, the gods grabbed one end of the snake, and the demons took the other. Together, they pulled the snake back and forth, spinning the mountain like a giant churn in the middle of the ocean. The water swirled and bubbled as they worked, and the ocean began to release its hidden treasures.

The Treasures of the Ocean

As the gods and demons churned the ocean, many amazing treasures rose from the depths. Every time the water bubbled, something magical appeared!

Kamadhenu, a sacred cow, appeared, bringing good fortune and blessings.

Kalpavriksha, the wish-fulfilling tree, sprouted from the ocean, capable of granting any desire.

Goddess Lakshmi, the goddess of wealth and prosperity, emerged from the waves in all her beauty, bringing happiness wherever she went.

The gods and demons were thrilled by all of these treasures—but they knew they had to keep going. The nectar of immortality was still hidden deep within the ocean, and they had to be patient.

A Challenge Arises – Poison from the Ocean

Just when it seemed like everything was going smoothly, something terrible happened. Instead of a treasure, a deadly black poison called Halahala rose to the surface. It was so powerful that it could destroy the world if it spread!

The gods and demons panicked. "What do we do?" they cried.

At that moment, Lord Shiva, the powerful god of destruction, came to their rescue. Without hesitation, Shiva drank the poison to save everyone. But instead of swallowing it, he held the poison in his throat, which turned his neck blue. From that day on, Shiva became known as Neelkanth, the blue-throated one, for his bravery.

The gods and demons were grateful, but they knew they had to keep churning the ocean if they wanted to find the Amrit.

The Nectar of Immortality – Amrit Appears!

After much hard work, the gods and demons finally saw a golden pot. It was filled with Amrit, the nectar of immortality! The gods rejoiced, knowing that this nectar would restore their strength and protect the world from evil.

But the demons had other ideas. "This nectar belongs to us!" they shouted, grabbing the pot.

Just then, Lord Vishnu appeared, disguised as a beautiful woman named Mohini. With her charm and cleverness, Mohini tricked the demons into handing over the pot. She then gave the nectar to the gods, ensuring that the forces of good would remain strong.

The Power of Teamwork and Patience

The story of the Churning of the Ocean teaches us some important lessons:

Teamwork Makes Big Tasks Possible: The gods and demons may have been enemies, but they had to work together to achieve their goal. This shows us that sometimes, even people with differences need to come together and cooperate to accomplish great things.

Patience Pays Off: Churning the ocean wasn't easy—it took time, effort, and patience. Good things don't always happen right away, but if we keep working and stay patient, we can achieve our goals.

Challenges are Part of the Journey: Just like the gods and demons faced the danger of Halahala, we all face challenges on the way to our goals. But with courage and the right help, we can overcome anything.

Smart Thinking Saves the Day: When the demons tried to take the Amrit, Vishnu's clever disguise as Mohini saved the day. This reminds us that being smart and thinking creatively can solve even the trickiest problems.

A Story that Teaches Us for Life

The Churning of the Ocean is more than just an exciting story—it teaches us that life is full of ups and downs. Just like the gods and demons had to keep working through challenges, we, too, must stay focused and patient. Whether it's when learning a new skill, making friends, or solving problems, teamwork, patience, and clever thinking can help us achieve great things.

And most importantly, the story reminds us that goodness and kindness will always win in the end—just like the gods succeeded in their quest for Amrit.

CHAPTER 10: THE NAGA AND THE WISE FARMER - MYTHICAL SERPENTS OF INDIA

A long time ago, in a quiet village surrounded by green fields and tall trees, there lived a wise and kind farmer named Hariram. Every day, Hariram worked hard, planting seeds, tending to his crops, and caring for the animals. But unlike some other farmers, Hariram had a special quality—he was kind not only to people but also to nature.

He never cut down trees without reason, and he always made sure to leave some fruit on the branches for the birds. "The land takes care of us," he would say, "so we must take care of the land in return." The other villagers thought he was a little strange, but Hariram didn't mind. He believed in kindness above all else.

The Naga in the Farmer's Field

One sunny afternoon, as Hariram was plowing his field, he noticed a large, shimmering serpent lay coiled near a tree stump. The snake's scales glimmered in the sunlight, and it looked tired and weak as if it had been injured.

The villagers believed that serpents, or Nagas, were not ordinary creatures. Nagas were mystical beings—half-human, half-serpent—who lived underground or in water, guarding hidden treasures. Some villagers feared them, thinking they were dangerous, but Hariram didn't believe in fear. He saw a creature in need of help, and that was all that mattered.

"Poor thing," Hariram murmured as he carefully approached the serpent. "You must be hurt." The serpent's golden eyes blinked slowly as if it could sense the farmer's kindness. Without hesitation,

Hariram gave the serpent some water from his pot and gently covered it with soft leaves to keep it cool.

"There now," Hariram whispered. "You'll feel better soon."

The serpent looked up at him, and Hariram noticed something strange—the serpent's eyes were filled with gratitude, almost as if it understood his kindness.

A Surprising Visitor

The next morning, Hariram woke up to a surprise. A beautiful young man with bright eyes and golden jewelry stood at his doorstep. The man was unlike anyone Hariram had ever seen. His clothes shimmered like water in the sunlight, and he had a calm, wise expression on his face.

"Who are you?" Hariram asked, astonished.

"I am Takshaka, the Naga you saved," the young man said with a warm smile. "Because of your kindness, I was able to recover from my injury. You didn't fear me, and you treated me with care. For that, I am grateful."

Hariram was speechless. He had heard stories about the magical Nagas but never thought he would meet one himself!

"To thank you," Takshaka continued, "I wish to bless you. From today onward, your farm will prosper like never before. Your crops will grow strong, your animals will flourish, and your home will always be filled with happiness."

The Blessing of the Naga

True to Takshaka's word, Hariram's farm flourished like never before. His fields overflowed with golden wheat, his fruit trees drooped under the weight of sweet mangoes, and his animals became healthier and stronger. No matter how hard the weather or how difficult the season, Hariram's crops always thrived.

The other villagers noticed Hariram's good fortune and asked, "What is your secret, Hariram? How do your crops grow so well?"

Hariram smiled and said, "There is no secret. Kindness is like a seed. If you plant it, it will grow into something wonderful." But the villagers didn't understand. They thought he was just being modest.

The Test of Kindness

One day, a curious neighbor named Bhola decided to visit Hariram's farm. Bhola wasn't a bad person, but he was a little jealous of Hariram's success. "If

Hariram has found a magical way to grow his crops," Bhola thought, "I'll find out what it is."

When Bhola arrived, he noticed something unusual near the edge of the farm—a small silver bowl filled with milk. Every morning, Hariram placed the bowl by the old tree stump where he had first found the injured serpent.

"Why do you leave milk here every day?" Bhola asked, puzzled.

Hariram smiled. "I leave it as a gift for my friend, Takshaka, the Naga I saved. It's my way of thanking him for the blessings he has given me."

Bhola laughed. "A serpent? Blessing a farm? That's just a silly story!"

Despite Hariram's warning, Bhola knocked over the bowl of milk and kicked it away. "There's no such thing as magic serpents," he scoffed.

The Naga's Lesson

That evening, Takshaka appeared before Hariram once more, his face calm but serious. "Your kindness has not gone unnoticed, Hariram," he said. "But there are those who doubt the value of it, like your neighbor. It is time they learn the importance of respect—for both nature and creatures like us."

The next day, something strange happened. Bhola's crops began to wither, and his well ran dry. No matter how hard he worked, nothing seemed to grow. The other villagers whispered, "Maybe it was unwise to mock the Naga's blessings."

Feeling sorry for Bhola, Hariram decided to help. He visited Bhola's farm, bringing seeds and water, and even helped him plant new crops. "You see," Hariram said gently, "kindness isn't just for magical creatures—it's for everyone. When we take care of others, life takes care of us in return."

Bhola finally understood. He apologized to Takshaka and to Hariram for his actions. From that day on, Bhola promised to treat both people and nature with kindness, just as Hariram had done.

The Importance of Kindness to People and Nature

The story of the Naga and the Wise Farmer teaches us some important lessons:

Kindness Always Comes Back: Hariram's kindness toward the injured Naga brought him prosperity. The story reminds us that kindness is never wasted—when we do good things, life often rewards us in unexpected ways.

Respect Nature and All Living Creatures: Just like Hariram, we must learn to treat animals and the environment with care and respect. Nature provides us with everything we need—food, water, and shelter—so it's important to give back by taking care of the land and all creatures.

Believe in the Power of Goodness: Bhola learned the hard way that mocking others and ignoring kindness leads to trouble. When we act with kindness, even towards those who are different from us, good things happen. It's not just magic—it's a lesson that applies to real life, too.

Helping Others Brings Joy: Hariram didn't just keep his good fortune to himself—he helped his neighbor when Bhola needed it. Sharing what we have makes the world a better place for everyone.

A Friendship That Lasts Forever

Hariram continued to offer milk to Takshaka, the Naga, every day. Even though Takshaka rarely appeared, Hariram knew that the Naga's blessings were always with him. His farm remained lush and full of life, and his heart was light with happiness. The other villagers also learned to care for the land and treat animals with respect, knowing that kindness connects us all—humans, animals, and nature alike.

And so, the legend of the Naga and the Wise Farmer was passed down from generation to generation. Children heard the story and learned that kindness is the most magical power of all, one that can change lives and make the world a more beautiful place.

CHAPTER 11:
THE SEVEN SISTERS AND THE STARRY SKY

A long time ago, in the green hills of northeastern India, there lived seven sisters who loved each other dearly. They were known throughout their village for their beauty, kindness, and playful spirits. The sisters did everything together—whether it was singing songs, gathering flowers, or playing by the river. Their bond was so strong that no one could imagine them ever being apart.

Each evening, they would sit under the night sky, telling stories and watching the stars twinkle above. They dreamed of far-off lands and magical worlds beyond the stars, always wondering what it would be like to live among them. Little did they know that one day, their dream would come true—but not in the way they had imagined.

Trouble Comes to the Village

One summer, a great drought came to the land. The rivers ran dry, and the crops withered. The people in the village began to worry—without water and food, how would they survive?

The seven sisters felt the struggle deeply. They hated seeing their family and neighbors go hungry. One evening, as they sat under the stars, they made a promise to each other: "We will do whatever it takes to help our family and village survive."

A Difficult Decision

The days grew hotter, and the drought worsened. There was almost no food left, and the sisters knew they had to act. They thought and thought until the eldest sister had an idea. "If we offer ourselves as a sacrifice to the gods, maybe they will send rain to save the village," she said.

The younger sisters gasped. "But if we leave, we'll be apart forever!"

The eldest sister smiled sadly. "Sometimes, we must make hard choices to protect those we love," she whispered. The sisters hugged each other tightly, knowing that their bond would last, even if they were separated.

With heavy hearts, they went to the highest hilltop near their village. They closed their eyes, held hands, and offered themselves to the heavens, praying that the gods would send rain to save their people.

A Gift from the Gods

The gods, touched by the sisters' selfless sacrifice, decided to reward them. They transformed the seven sisters into stars and placed them high in the night sky, where they would shine brightly for all eternity. From that day forward, the stars of the seven sisters—what we now call the Pleiades constellation—sparkled in the heavens, a reminder of family, love, and sacrifice.

Soon after the sisters became stars, rain fell. The rivers filled with water, the crops flourished, and the village was saved. The people rejoiced, grateful for the sudden miracle—but only the sisters' family knew the true story behind the rain.

A Family Reunited in the Sky

Though the seven sisters had left the Earth, they were never truly apart. Every night, they shone together in the sky, closer than ever. People say that when the wind blows through the trees at night, you can hear the sisters singing softly, just as they used to in the fields and by the river. And when you look up at the sky and see the seven bright stars twinkling, it's like seeing their laughter sparkling across the heavens.

The Wonder of the Stars and Constellations

The story of the seven sisters is just one of many legends about the stars. Across the world, different cultures tell tales about constellations, each one adding magic and meaning to the night sky. In northeastern India, the story of the seven sisters teaches us about family, love, and the beauty of sacrifice.

The Pleiades constellation, which looks like a small cluster of stars, has inspired stories in many cultures. Some say the stars represent siblings, others say they are a group of birds flying together. No matter where you are in the world, the stars remind us that we are connected, just like the seven sisters.

How the Stars Teach Us About Life

The story of the seven sisters teaches us some important lessons:

Family Comes First: Just like the sisters sacrificed for their family, taking care of the people we love is one of the most important things we can do.

Even When We're Apart, We're Still Connected: The seven sisters became stars, but they stayed together in the sky. Love and family bonds can't be broken, no matter the distance—whether we are across the world or among the stars.

Kindness Can Change the World: The sisters' selflessness brought rain to the village. Even small acts of kindness can create big changes—just like the stars that light up the dark sky.

Look for Magic Everywhere: The stars in the night sky remind us that there is always wonder and beauty, even on the darkest nights. Every star has a story, and every story has a lesson.

The Sky Is Full of Stories

The stars above are like a storybook in the sky, filled with tales of adventure, sacrifice, and love. If you ever feel lonely, look up at the stars and remember the seven sisters. Their light shines as a reminder that no matter how difficult life becomes, love and kindness will always find a way to shine through.

CHAPTER 12: THE STORY OF BUDDHA - A PRINCE WHO FOUND PEACE

A long time ago, in the ancient city of Kapilavastu, there was a prince named Siddhartha Gautama. Siddhartha had everything a boy could dream of—golden palaces, delicious food, fancy clothes, and even the most beautiful gardens to play in. His father, the king, made sure that Siddhartha was always happy. The king believed that if Siddhartha never faced sadness or difficulty, he would grow up to be a great ruler.

So, the king built high walls around the palace, keeping Siddhartha safe from the world outside. There was always music, laughter, and celebrations in the palace, and no one was ever allowed to speak about sickness, old age, or sadness in front of the prince.

But Siddhartha was curious by nature. He often wondered what life outside the palace was like. "Is the world beyond these walls as perfect as the palace?" he asked himself.

One day, Siddhartha decided to find out. Little did he know that his adventure outside the palace would change his life—and the world—forever.

Siddhartha's First Journey Beyond the Palace

With the help of his trusted charioteer, Channa, Siddhartha slipped out of the palace gates one night. What he saw amazed and troubled him. For the first time in his life, Siddhartha saw things he had never imagined:

An old man with wrinkles and a hunched back, struggling to walk.

A sick man lying on the ground, moaning in pain.

A funeral procession, where people were crying for someone who had passed away.

Siddhartha's heart felt heavy. "What is this?" he asked Channa. "Why are these people suffering?"

Channa explained, "This is the way of life, my prince. Everyone grows old, falls ill, and one day, all living beings must leave this world."

Siddhartha felt true sadness for the first time. How could people be happy if life was filled with pain and sorrow?

Meeting a Wise Monk

On another journey, Siddhartha saw something that gave him hope. He noticed a calm and peaceful monk walking quietly along the road. The monk looked happy and content, even though he had nothing but a simple robe and a begging bowl.

Siddhartha turned to Channa and asked, "How is this man so peaceful, even when he has no wealth or comfort?"

Channa replied, "This is a monk, my prince. Monks seek peace by giving up worldly things and finding happiness within themselves."

This moment stayed with Siddhartha. He realized that wealth and power could not bring true happiness. He knew he had to leave the palace and find the truth for himself—the truth about how to end suffering and live in peace.

The Prince Leaves the Palace

One night, while everyone was asleep, Siddhartha made a brave decision. He kissed his sleeping wife and newborn son goodbye and quietly left the palace on his horse, Kanthaka, with Channa by his side. He gave up his life as a prince and set off into the world, dressed in simple clothes, determined to find the answers to life's greatest questions.

For many years, Siddhartha traveled from place to place, meeting wise teachers and learning their ways. He lived like a monk, eating very little, meditating, and searching for wisdom. But no matter what he tried, he still felt that something was missing.

One day, he realized that extreme hardship wasn't the answer either. "Happiness lies somewhere in the middle, not in wealth or in suffering," he thought. This idea became known as the Middle Path—a way of living in balance, avoiding both too much comfort and too much pain.

Siddhartha Finds Enlightenment

One evening, Siddhartha sat under a large Bodhi tree, determined to meditate until he found the truth. The night was peaceful, but his mind was filled with distractions—thoughts of fear, desire, and doubt tried to pull him away from his goal. But Siddhartha stayed calm and focused, breathing slowly and quietly, letting go of all his worries.

As the sun rose, Siddhartha opened his eyes and smiled. He had finally found what he was searching for—Enlightenment, or the complete understanding of life. From that moment on, Siddhartha became known as Buddha, which means "The Awakened One."

Buddha had discovered that the key to ending suffering was kindness, peace, and wisdom. He knew that he needed to share his teachings with the world so that everyone could find the same happiness he had.

Buddha's Teachings – The Path to Peace

Buddha spent the rest of his life traveling from village to village, teaching people the lessons he had learned. His teachings were simple, but they held great wisdom. Here are some of the most important lessons Buddha shared:

Be Kind to All Living Beings: Buddha taught that we should treat all creatures with kindness, whether they are people, animals, or even the smallest insects. When we are kind, we create a more peaceful world.

Find Peace Within Yourself: True happiness comes from within. Buddha explained that we can't rely on things like money or possessions to make us happy. Instead, we need to find peace in our hearts through kindness and meditation.

Be Present in the Moment: Buddha encouraged people to focus on the present instead of worrying about the past or future. When we appreciate what we have right now, life becomes more joyful.

Practice the Middle Path: Buddha's Middle Path teaches us to live with balance—not too much, not too little. Whether it's eating, working, or playing, we need to find a middle ground to stay healthy and happy.

Let Go of Anger and Hatred: Buddha believed that anger only creates more suffering. Instead, he taught people to forgive others and let go of negative feelings, making room for peace and joy.

The Impact of Buddha's Teachings on the World

Buddha's message of kindness, peace, and wisdom spread far and wide. Over time, people from different parts of the world followed his teachings, and Buddhism became one of the world's most peaceful religions. Temples, statues, and monasteries were built in his honor, and people gathered to meditate and learn from his teachings.

Even today, thousands of years later, Buddha's wisdom continues to inspire people. His teachings remind us that life is not about wealth or power—it's about being kind, staying calm, and finding happiness within ourselves.

Meditation—a practice that Buddha encouraged—has become popular around the world. People of all ages sit quietly to breathe and calm their minds, just as Buddha did under the Bodhi tree. Whether they are children learning to be kind or adults finding peace in difficult times, Buddha's lessons continue to guide people toward a life of happiness and balance.

A Legacy of Kindness and Peace

Buddha's story teaches us that we all have the power to change the world—not by becoming rich or powerful, but by being kind, wise, and peaceful. His journey shows us that true happiness comes from helping others and treating all living beings with respect.

Even though Buddha was born a prince, his greatest treasure was the peace he found within himself. And the best part is that we don't need to be royalty to follow Buddha's path—anyone can practice kindness, patience, and wisdom every day.

What We Can Learn from Buddha's Story

Buddha's wisdom isn't just for ancient times—it's something we can use every day. Here are a few easy ways to bring Buddha's teachings into your life:

Take a moment to breathe: If you feel worried or upset, pause and take a few deep breaths. This can help you feel calm, just like Buddha during his meditation.

Be kind to yourself and others: Treat yourself with the same kindness you would give to a friend.

And remember—every act of kindness counts, no matter how small.

Practice gratitude: Every night, try to think of three things you are thankful for. It could be as simple as a fun conversation with a friend or a sunny day.

Enjoy the moment: When you're playing or spending time with family, put away distractions and enjoy the moment fully—just like savoring every bite of your favorite snack!

Find your own Middle Path: Whether it's balancing time between homework and play or choosing a healthy snack over too many sweets, finding balance will help you feel your best.

Buddha's Message Lives On

Buddha's story may be thousands of years old, but his message is just as powerful today. His teachings remind us that happiness comes from within, not from what we own or achieve. We learn that kindness, balance, and inner peace can help us through life's challenges and bring joy to those around us.

So, the next time you feel overwhelmed or unsure, remember Buddha sitting calmly under the Bodhi tree. Take a deep breath, look for kindness around you, and know that peace is always within your reach.

CHAPTER 13: THE BIRTH OF DURGA - THE GODDESS OF POWER

Once upon a time, a powerful demon named Mahishasura sought to become unstoppable. He prayed and performed penances for many years until Lord Brahma, the god of creation, appeared before him. Mahishasura asked for a boon: "Grant me that no man or god can ever defeat me!"

Brahma granted his wish, and Mahishasura grew arrogant. He believed no one could stop him and declared himself ruler of the heavens and Earth. With his army of demons, Mahishasura attacked the gods and took over Indra's throne, the seat of the king of gods.

The gods tried to fight back, but Mahishasura's strength was unmatched. Defeated, they fled from the heavens, wondering how they could defeat an unbeatable demon. They needed a hero—someone powerful and unstoppable—to save the world from Mahishasura's reign of terror.

The Creation of Durga

The gods realized that only a force greater than any man or god could defeat Mahishasura. So, they decided to create a goddess, someone more powerful than all of them combined.

With all their energy and strength, the gods united their powers, each contributing a part of themselves to create a mighty warrior: Durga, the goddess of power and courage.

Shiva gave her a trident.
Vishnu gifted her a discus.
Agni gave her the power of fire.
Indra offered her a thunderbolt, and Varuna gave her a powerful bow and arrows.

Durga emerged, shining with the brilliance of a thousand suns, riding a lion as her mighty companion. Her many hands carried weapons from all the gods, and her presence radiated strength, courage, and grace. The gods rejoiced, knowing that Mahishasura's end had arrived.

Durga's Fierce Battle

Durga rode toward Mahishasura's palace on her fearless lion. The demon laughed when he saw her. "Do you think you can defeat me? I am invincible!"

he roared, transforming into a giant buffalo. But Durga was calm. She stood tall, ready to fight.

For nine days and nine nights, Durga and Mahishasura's army battled fiercely. Mahishasura changed forms many times—first, a lion, then an elephant, then a warrior—but Durga fought him with courage, using all the weapons given to her by the gods. She remained unshaken, slashing through demons with her sword, sending thunderbolts from her hands, and hurling flames from her trident.

Finally, on the tenth day, Mahishasura took his buffalo form once more, believing he could still overpower Durga. But this time, Durga's lion pounced on him, pinning him to the ground. With a single, powerful thrust, Durga plunged her trident into his heart, ending the reign of the demon once and for all.

Victory of Good Over Evil – The Origin of Navratri and Durga Puja

The gods and goddesses celebrated Durga's victory with great joy. They praised her strength, bravery, and unyielding spirit. Durga had saved the world, restoring peace and harmony.

To honor her victory, people celebrate the festival of Navratri (which means "Nine Nights"). During these nine nights, people pray, dance, and sing, remembering Durga's battle against Mahishasura. On the tenth day, known as Vijayadashami or Dussehra, people mark the final victory of good over evil.

In many parts of India, the festival of Durga Puja is also celebrated. Beautiful statues of Goddess Durga are made, showing her riding her lion and slaying Mahishasura. Families come together to offer prayers, enjoy delicious food, and participate in grand processions to immerse the statues in rivers or oceans. The celebrations remind everyone that no matter how strong evil may seem, goodness and courage will always win in the end.

Lessons from Durga's Story – The Power of Courage and Standing Up for What's Right

Durga's story is more than just an exciting battle—it teaches us important lessons about life:

Courage is Stronger than Fear: Durga didn't let fear stop her from facing the powerful Mahishasura. Bravery means standing up for what's right, even when things seem scary.

Everyone Has a Role to Play: Just as the gods gave their powers to Durga, we all have unique strengths that can help others. When we work together, we can overcome any challenge.

Goodness Always Wins in the End: Mahishasura seemed invincible, but evil never lasts. With patience and perseverance, good always triumphs, just like Durga's victory on the tenth day.

Believe in Yourself: Durga fought fiercely because she believed in her strength and purpose. Believing in yourself is the first step to conquering challenges, no matter how big they seem.

Celebrate Life's Victories: Festivals like Navratri and Durga Puja remind us to celebrate the victories, big and small, in our own lives. It's important to pause, reflect, and appreciate the good things we achieve, just like the gods celebrated Durga's victory.

The Spirit of Durga in Everyday Life

Even today, the story of Goddess Durga inspires people. She reminds us to be brave, kind, and confident, no matter what challenges we might face. Whenever you feel afraid or unsure, remember Durga—her strength lives inside everyone. We all have the power to face difficulties and stand up for what's right, just like she did.

So, the next time you celebrate Navratri or Durga Puja, think of Durga's mighty lion, her shining weapons, and her fierce battle with Mahishasura. Feel the courage inside you—because you, too, have the power to make the world a better place.

And just like Durga, you can be a hero in your own life by being brave, standing up for kindness, and helping others along the way.

CHAPTER 14: THE LEGEND OF THE BAMBOO PRINCESS - A FOLKTALE FROM ASSAM

Long ago, in a beautiful forest in the region of Assam, there lived an old woodcutter and his wife. They had no children but lived a peaceful life surrounded by tall bamboo groves. One day, while the woodcutter was out cutting bamboo, he saw something extraordinary—one of the bamboo stalks glowed like a golden flame. Curious, he cut the glowing stalk, and to his amazement, he found a tiny baby girl inside the hollow shoot!

The woodcutter gently picked up the baby. "She is a gift from the gods," he whispered, his heart filled with joy. The old couple took the baby home and raised her as their daughter, naming her Banon, meaning 'forest girl.' Soon, she became the most beautiful child in the village.

The Princess Grows Up – Her Beauty and Wisdom Enchant Everyone

Banon wasn't just beautiful—she was kind, gentle, and wise beyond her years. As she grew, everyone in the village marveled at her charm.

Although Banon came from humble beginnings, many princes and noblemen heard stories of her beauty and came from far and wide, hoping to marry her. But Banon remained humble. She said to her parents, "I am happy here with you. I do not wish for a grand palace or riches." Her words filled her parents' hearts with pride, but deep down, they wondered where their mysterious daughter had truly come from.

A Magical Journey – The Princess Reveals Her Celestial Origins

As time passed, Banon grew even more beautiful and wise, but she felt more restless. It was as if a part of her soul longed for something far away, something beyond the forests and hills of Assam. One evening, as the moonlight bathed the bamboo grove in a silvery glow, Banon sat quietly with her parents. She turned to them and said, "It is time for me to reveal the truth."

The woodcutter and his wife looked at her, puzzled. Banon's eyes sparkled with both sadness and joy as she continued, "I am not from this world. I was sent here from the heavens to learn the ways of human life, to understand love, kindness, and wisdom. But now, the time has come for me to return to the celestial world."

Her parents were heartbroken. "But you are our daughter," the woodcutter said. "We love you dearly. How can we let you go?"

Banon took their hands in hers and said gently, "I will always love you, but every journey must come to an end. My time here was a gift, just as my time with you was a blessing. It is now time for a new beginning."

The next morning, Banon walked to the bamboo grove where she was born. A bright light shone down from the sky, and Banon smiled one last time at her parents. "Goodbye," she whispered as she rose gracefully into the heavens.

INDIAN LEGENDS FOR KIDS

The Lesson of Acceptance – A Story About Letting Go and Celebrating New Beginnings

The woodcutter and his wife were sad to see Banon leave, but they knew her journey was meant to take her elsewhere. They returned to their home, grateful for the time they had spent with her. Even though Banon was no longer with them, her spirit remained in their hearts, filling their lives with the joy and love she had shared.

The people of the village remembered Banon's kindness and wisdom long after she returned to the heavens. They spoke of her with fondness and admiration, knowing that her story was not just about loss but about acceptance and gratitude.

Letting go of what we love can be hard, but Banon's story teaches us that every ending is also a new beginning. Just as the bamboo grove continued to grow strong and tall after her departure, life moves forward—bringing new adventures and opportunities.

A Story that Teaches Us for Life

The story of the Bamboo Princess teaches us that everything in life has a time and place. Just as the bamboo grows and bends with the wind, we, too, must learn to accept change and embrace new beginnings.

Embrace the Present: Banon's parents enjoyed every moment with her, knowing that life is made up of beautiful, fleeting moments. When we appreciate what we have, we live happier lives.

Letting Go is Part of Love: Banon's story reminds us that sometimes we must let go of the people or things we love. Letting go doesn't mean forgetting—it means allowing new journeys to begin.

Celebrate New Beginnings: The bamboo grove thrived even after Banon left, just as life brings new opportunities after change. Every ending is a chance for a new beginning.

A Story for All Generations

Even today, the Bamboo Princess lives on in the hearts of people who hear her story. In the bamboo groves of Assam, some say you can feel her presence in the breeze that whispers through the leaves. Her story teaches us that life is a journey filled with love, change, and growth.

Whenever you face a change or a goodbye, remember the Bamboo Princess. Her journey reminds us that every farewell brings a new adventure, and every change brings a chance to grow.

CHAPTER 15:
THE TALE OF KING HARISHCHANDRA - THE VALUE OF HONESTY

Long ago, in a beautiful kingdom, there ruled a wise and just king named Harishchandra. He was known throughout the land for his truthfulness and unwavering commitment to honesty. His people loved him, and neighboring kingdoms admired his fairness and kindness. "A promise is a sacred bond," the king often said, "and the truth is a light that must never be dimmed."

But Harishchandra's dedication to truth was soon put to the ultimate test—one that would challenge not just his words but his heart and soul.

A Difficult Test – The King Loses His Kingdom but Refuses to Break His Promise

One day, the mighty sage Vishwamitra decided to test King Harishchandra's honesty. The sage appeared before the king and said, "I need your help, O noble king. Will you promise to grant me anything I ask?"

Without hesitation, Harishchandra agreed. "Anything you wish, I shall grant."

The sage smiled and said, "I want your kingdom."

The king's courtiers gasped. Giving away the entire kingdom would leave Harishchandra with nothing—no wealth, no throne, and no power. But the king remained calm. "I have given my word," Harishchandra said. "The kingdom is yours."

True to his word, Harishchandra handed over his crown and his palace. He, his wife Shaivya, and their young son Rohitashva left the kingdom with nothing but the clothes on their backs. Despite losing everything, the king knew in his heart that keeping a promise was more valuable than any throne.

A Life of Hardship – Harishchandra Works as a Humble Servant

With no palace to live in and no riches to their name, Harishchandra and his family wandered from place to place. Eventually, they reached the holy city of Kashi (now known as Varanasi). Here, Harishchandra took a job as a servant in a cremation ground, working for the chief of the grounds. His job was to prepare funeral pyres and collect fees from grieving families. It was a difficult and sorrowful job, but Harishchandra performed it with dedication and honesty.

Meanwhile, his wife, Shaivya, worked as a maid, trying to earn enough to feed their little son. Despite their hardships, the family never complained.

One day, tragedy struck. Their beloved son Rohitashva fell ill and passed away. With heavy hearts, Harishchandra and Shaivya brought their son to the cremation ground, where Harishchandra worked. But when Shaivya asked to perform the last rites for their son, the chief of the cremation ground demanded a fee for the funeral pyre—the same fee that Harishchandra was required to collect from others.

Though it pained him deeply, Harishchandra did not break the rules. "A promise is a promise," he told his wife. "We must follow the laws, even in the hardest of times." With no money to pay the fee, Shaivya offered her own sari as payment. Harishchandra accepted it with tears in his eyes, for honesty and duty came before even his personal sorrow.

The Gods Reward His Honesty – His Kingdom and Family are Restored

As Harishchandra lit the funeral pyre for his son, the gods in heaven watched his unwavering commitment to truth and righteousness. Lord Vishnu and the sage Vishwamitra appeared before the king, moved by his strength and honesty.

"O noble king," they said, "your truthfulness and devotion have passed every test. You have remained honest, even in the face of great hardship."

With a wave of Vishwamitra's hand, Rohitashva was brought back to life, and the chief of the cremation ground bowed before the king. "You are the greatest of kings," he said, "and your truth is more valuable than any treasure."

The gods restored Harishchandra's kingdom and riches, returning him, Shaivya, and Rohitashva to their former lives. The people of the kingdom rejoiced to have their beloved king back on the throne. But more than anything, they admired him for his unshakeable honesty and the way he had honored his promises.

The Power of Truth – The Lesson That Honesty is the Greatest Virtue

The story of King Harishchandra teaches us that honesty is one of the greatest virtues a person can have. Even when life became incredibly difficult, Harishchandra never gave up his commitment to truth. His story reminds us that:

Promises Are Sacred: When we make a promise, it's important to keep our word, no matter how hard it may seem. Trust is built on honesty.

Truth Requires Courage: Harishchandra showed that being truthful isn't always easy, but it is always the right thing to do. Sometimes, telling the truth means making sacrifices, but it also brings great rewards.

Hard Work with Honesty Brings Respect: Even when Harishchandra worked in the cremation ground, he performed his duties with honor and respect. When we work honestly, no task is too small or unimportant.

Stay True in Tough Times: Harishchandra's story shows us that even when life feels unfair, staying honest and kind is the path to real happiness.

Honesty Brings Lasting Rewards: Just as the gods restored Harishchandra's family and kingdom, truth and honesty always bring peace and happiness in the end, even if the journey feels difficult at times.

The Spirit of Harishchandra's Story in Everyday Life

The tale of King Harishchandra is still told across India today, reminding children and adults alike of the power of truth. Schools, temples, and families share this story to inspire honesty, integrity, and kindness.

Whenever you are tempted to tell a lie or break a promise, remember King Harishchandra. Even when he lost everything, he held on to his honesty. His story teaches us that it's better to lose things than to lose trust—because truth is the greatest treasure we can have.

The next time you make a promise, think of Harishchandra and his journey. Be honest in your words and actions—and know that truth always shines the brightest, even in difficult times.

CHAPTER 16: PARVATI AND SHIVA - A LOVE STORY OF THE MOUNTAINS

High in the Himalayan mountains, in a kingdom surrounded by snow-capped peaks, there lived Parvati, a princess filled with kindness and determination. From a young age, Parvati had heard stories of Lord Shiva, the great god of destruction and meditation. Shiva lived alone on Mount Kailash, lost in deep meditation, far from the world's distractions.

Parvati was drawn to Shiva's wisdom and strength. Though he seemed distant and uninterested in worldly matters, Parvati decided she would win his heart.

Determined to show her love, Parvati lived a life of simplicity and devotion, just as Shiva did. She wore plain clothes, gave up the comforts of palace life, and performed austerities—sitting for hours in meditation, just like Shiva. Day after day, she prayed and meditated, her love for Shiva growing stronger with each passing moment.

Shiva, at first, was unmoved by her efforts. He had renounced love and attachment, believing that his only purpose was to meditate and help the world through his wisdom. But Parvati's persistence and kindness softened his heart over time. He saw her pure devotion and realized that her love was as strong as the mountains themselves. Shiva finally opened his heart to Parvati, recognizing her as his equal and partner.

Shiva and Parvati's Marriage – The Union of the Cosmic Couple

When Shiva accepted Parvati's love, the heavens rejoiced, and all the gods celebrated their union. Their marriage was not just the coming together of two beings—it symbolized the balance of opposites in the universe. Shiva represented detachment and power, while Parvati embodied love, warmth, and creation. Together, they brought harmony to the cosmos.

The gods arranged a grand wedding on Mount Kailash, inviting all beings—humans, gods, animals, and celestials. Shiva arrived dressed as a wild ascetic, with snakes coiled around his neck and ash covering his body. Parvati, in contrast, wore a radiant wedding dress, glowing like the moon. But Parvati loved Shiva for who he was and saw his inner beauty beyond his rugged appearance.

The divine couple's love for each other grew deeper with time, and they made Mount Kailash their home, living peacefully in the mountains, far from the distractions of the world.

The Birth of Ganesha and Kartikeya – Their Legendary Children

Shiva and Parvati's union brought not just balance to the universe, but also new life and joy. They had two legendary children, each with their own unique story and powers.

Ganesha: One day, while Shiva was away, Parvati decided to create a child from her own essence. Using sandalwood paste, she shaped a boy and breathed life into him. This boy was Ganesha, the elephant-headed god of wisdom, knowledge, and beginnings. However, when Shiva returned and didn't recognize Ganesha, a misunderstanding led to a battle, and Ganesha lost his head. To console Parvati, Shiva replaced Ganesha's head with that of an elephant, and he blessed him to be worshiped before all new beginnings.

Kartikeya: Parvati and Shiva's second son was Kartikeya, also known as Skanda or Murugan. He grew up to become a mighty warrior and the commander of the celestial armies. Kartikeya is honored as a symbol of bravery and strength. His adventures inspire people to face challenges with courage and determination.

With their children, Shiva and Parvati's family was complete. Their life together became a reminder that love, family, and devotion create lasting happiness.

Lessons from Parvati and Shiva – The Importance of Love, Patience, and Family

The story of Parvati and Shiva offers us many valuable lessons:

Love Requires Patience and Dedication: Parvati's love for Shiva was not easy to earn—she had to be patient, determined, and sincere. Her story teaches us that true love requires effort, but the rewards are worth it.

Acceptance is the Heart of Love: Parvati accepted Shiva as he was without trying to change him, and Shiva learned to open his heart to her love. This teaches us that loving someone means accepting them as they are, with all their strengths and imperfections.

Balance Brings Harmony: Shiva and Parvati's union symbolizes the balance between opposites—strength and gentleness, detachment and love. Their story reminds us that balance is key to a peaceful life.

Family is a Source of Strength: The love between Parvati, Shiva, and their children shows us that family bonds give us joy and strength, helping us face life's challenges together.

Beginnings Are Sacred: The birth of Ganesha teaches us that every new beginning should be welcomed with joy and wisdom. Just as Ganesha is worshiped before any important event, we, too, can approach new challenges with an open heart and a clear mind.

A Love That Transcends Time

Even today, Shiva and Parvati's love story is celebrated throughout India. Their relationship is a symbol of devotion, patience, and harmony, reminding people to value love and family. During festivals like Mahashivaratri, people honor their union, offering prayers for love, peace, and balance in their own lives.

The story of Parvati and Shiva teaches us that love is about more than just grand gestures—it is built through small acts of kindness, patience, and understanding. And just like Parvati, when we are patient and loving, we can bring light and joy into the lives of those around us.

In the end, the story of Shiva and Parvati shows us that true love isn't just about romance—it's about acceptance, partnership, and finding joy in life's little moments. Their story reminds us that with love, anything is possible—whether it's balancing a busy life, facing challenges together, or raising a family with joy and laughter.

CONCLUSION

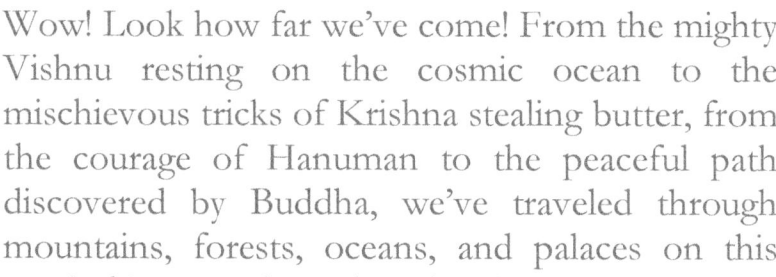

Wow! Look how far we've come! From the mighty Vishnu resting on the cosmic ocean to the mischievous tricks of Krishna stealing butter, from the courage of Hanuman to the peaceful path discovered by Buddha, we've traveled through mountains, forests, oceans, and palaces on this magical journey through India's legends.

These stories are like time machines, taking us to ancient worlds full of heroes, gods, talking animals, and life-changing adventures. They aren't just fun tales to read; they are filled with wisdom that teaches us how to be brave, kind, and thoughtful in our everyday lives. And the best part? These legends remind us that everyone has a special power inside them.

What Can We Learn from These Legends?

Indian legends are more than just exciting stories—they help us understand important lessons about life, family, and friendship. Let's take a moment to reflect on what these ancient tales can teach us today:

Stay True to Yourself: Just like Prahlad stood by his beliefs, even when things got tough, we can learn to stand up for what's right, no matter what others say.

Courage is More Than Strength: The clever jackal didn't need muscles to outsmart the lion—he used his brain! These stories teach us that thinking smart is just as

important as being strong.

Kindness Always Wins: Whether it's Savitri's love that brings Satyavan back or the wise farmer saving the Naga, these stories show us that kindness to others—and to nature—always leads to good things.

The Power of Teamwork: The gods and demons worked together to churn the ocean and find the nectar of immortality. We learn that big tasks become easier when we cooperate and work as a team.

Life is Full of Adventures: Krishna's butter-stealing fun and the seven sisters becoming stars remind us that life is meant to be enjoyed, with all its colors, surprises, and magic.

These lessons, hidden within the stories of gods, heroes, and mythical creatures, are as useful today as they were thousands of years ago. They remind us that kindness, bravery, and wisdom are timeless treasures.

The Magic Never Ends

Even though we've reached the end of this book, the magic of Indian legends doesn't stop here. There are so many more stories waiting to be discovered! Did you know there are more exciting tales from the Mahabharata and the Ramayana? Or that there are countless folktales from different parts of India, filled with talking animals, magical forests, and clever heroes?

Indian legends are like a treasure chest—each time you open it, you find something new. Some stories will make you laugh, some will make you think, and some might even inspire you to be braver or kinder in your own life. The more you explore, the more you'll discover how stories connect people across time and places.

How You Can Explore More Stories

There are many ways to keep the adventure going. Here are some fun ideas to help you explore more legends:

Talk to Family and Friends: Ask your parents, grandparents, or teachers if they know any Indian legends or folktales. Many of the best stories are passed down through families—and who knows? You might discover a tale no one else knows!

Visit a Library or Temple: Libraries are full of books about mythology and ancient stories. You can also visit temples and ask about the gods and heroes worshipped there—many temples have their own stories, too!

Draw Your Favorite Characters: Try drawing Krishna, Hanuman, or the Naga! Imagine what these characters might look like if they were in today's world. What would they wear? What adventures would they have?

Write Your Own Story: If you could make up your own legend, what would it be about? Maybe you'll create a new hero or a magical creature that saves the day! Writing your own stories helps you imagine new worlds and share your ideas with others.

Learn About the Night Sky: The story of the seven sisters reminds us that the stars are filled with stories from many cultures. Explore constellations and discover how people from all over the world saw magic in the stars.

Be Your Own Hero

One of the most important lessons from these legends is that anyone can be a hero—just like you! You don't need to lift mountains or shoot arrows at spinning fish. Being a hero means helping others, standing up for what's right, and being kind, even when it's not easy. Whether you're cheering up a friend, helping your parents, or taking care of nature, you're making the world a better place—just like the heroes in these stories.

And remember, heroes also have fun along the way! Life is full of adventures, big and small. Sometimes, being playful like Krishna or wise like Buddha will help you enjoy the journey, no matter where it takes you.

The World of Legends Awaits!

The world is filled with stories waiting to be discovered—not just from India but from every corner of the globe. As you grow, you'll find more legends and myths from different cultures. Each one will teach you something new and exciting about life, just like the Indian legends you've explored in this book.

So, keep your heart open, your mind curious, and your imagination ready—because every story is an adventure waiting to happen. And who knows? Maybe one day, you'll write your own legend that will inspire others.

Thank You for Joining the Journey!

We hope you've had as much fun reading these stories as we've had sharing them! Legends are gifts from the past, filled with lessons and magic that never grow old. They connect us to each other and remind us that we all have the power to make the world a better place, one act of kindness, courage, or creativity at a time.

The adventure doesn't end here—it's just the beginning! So, go out into the world, be curious, and create your own stories along the way. Just like the gods, heroes, and animals in these legends, you have a special place in the world—and your story is one worth telling.

What's Next?

Thank you for joining us on this incredible journey through the legends of India! Now that you've finished the book, it's your turn to become a storyteller. What story will you tell next? Will you write about a clever fox, a brave child, or a magical creature no one has ever heard of before?

Whatever your next adventure is, keep exploring, learning, and imagining. The world is full of stories—and the best ones are yet to come.

BONUS: ACTIVITIES

Let's dive into some exciting activities inspired by these wonderful legends! These fun tasks will help you connect with the stories, learn new things, and unleash your creativity. Whether you enjoy drawing, writing, acting, or exploring nature, there's something here for everyone. Get ready to bring these legends to life!

1. Create Your Own Constellation

Inspired by: The Seven Sisters and the Starry Sky

What to Do:

- Go outside on a clear night and look at the stars.
- Imagine your own constellation—maybe a hero, an animal, or something magical!
- Use stars on paper or stickers to map out your new constellation.
- Write a short story about what your constellation represents and how it got there.

2. Act Out a Scene from a Legend

Inspired by: The Adventures of Hanuman or Krishna and the Butter Thieves

What to Do:

Gather friends or family and pick your favorite legend to act out.

- Choose roles—who will play the heroes, gods, or animals?
- Create simple props using household items (like a crown or a cardboard bow).
- Perform your play for others! Don't forget to add fun sound effects.

3. Design Your Own Magic Bow

Inspired by: Arjuna and the Magic Bow

What to Do:

- Draw a picture of a magic bow that only a hero like you could use.
- Decorate your bow with symbols and colors representing strength and wisdom.
- Give your bow a name and describe what magical powers it has. Does it grant

courage, shoot flaming arrows, or summon animals to help in battle?

4. Write a Letter to Buddha

Inspired by: The Story of Buddha – A Prince Who Found Peace

What to Do:

- Imagine you are living in Buddha's time. Write a letter asking for advice on how to stay calm, be kind, or solve a problem.
- Use your imagination—what kind of advice would Buddha give you? How would it change your life?

5. Make a Nature Offering for the Naga

Inspired by: The Naga and the Wise Farmer

What to Do:

- Go outside and collect small natural items like flowers, leaves, or smooth stones.
- Arrange them as an offering for nature, just like the farmer offered milk to the Naga.
- Write down how you can take care of nature and the animals around you every day.

6. Create a Festival of Colors at Home

Inspired by: The Origins of Holi

What to Do:

- Gather some colored powders (you can use eco-friendly powders or colored chalk dust).
- Plan a mini Holi celebration with family or friends. Throw colors, dance, and share sweets.
- Write down what you are thankful for and who you will forgive, just like people do during Holi.

7. Meditate Like Buddha

Inspired by: The Story of Buddha

What to Do:

- Find a quiet spot to sit comfortably.
- Close your eyes, take a few deep breaths, and listen to your breath going in and out.
- Try to sit still and peacefully for five minutes. If thoughts pop into your mind, just let them go.
- How do you feel afterward? Can you notice a little bit of calm inside?

INDIAN LEGENDS FOR KIDS

BONUS: FACTS

Here are some fascinating facts about the stories, gods, and heroes you've discovered in this book.

1. The Churning of the Ocean Was an Ancient Team Effort

In the legend, gods and demons—usually enemies—had to work together to churn the ocean and find Amrit, the nectar of immortality.

Vasuki, the giant serpent, acted as the rope, while Mount Mandara became the churning stick.

2. Holi is Celebrated with Over 200,000 Kilograms of Colors!

The Festival of Holi is not just celebrated in India but in countries all around the world.

During Holi, people throw bright-colored powders to represent joy, unity, and the victory of good over evil.

3. Buddha's Teachings Inspire Millions Worldwide

Buddhism, the religion based on Buddha's teachings, is followed by millions of people across the globe.

Buddha's Middle Path is a way of living that teaches balance—neither too much nor too little of anything.

4. Krishna's Butter Thieves are Celebrated in Festivals

Krishna's childhood love for butter is remembered during the festival of Janmashtami, where children try to break clay pots filled with yogurt and butter, just like Krishna did!

5. Hanuman's Name Means "The One with a Jaw Like a Thunderbolt"

In Sanskrit, "Hanuman" means one with a strong jaw. According to legend, as a child, he tried to swallow the sun, mistaking it for a ripe mango!

6. Arjuna's Bow, Gandiva, Was a Gift from the Gods

Arjuna's legendary bow, Gandiva, was a gift from the god Agni, the fire god. The bow had the power to make any warrior invincible.

7. The Seven Sisters Exist in Many Cultures

The Pleiades, also known as the Seven Sisters, appear in many cultures around the world. In Greece, they are seen as nymphs, and in Japan, they are called Subaru.

In northeastern India, the Seven Sisters are remembered as a symbol of family, love, and sacrifice.

8. The Naga are Guardians of Water and Wealth

Nagas are often believed to guard rivers, lakes, and hidden treasures. They appear not only in Indian mythology but also in stories from Thailand, Cambodia, and Laos.

9. Temples Dedicated to Heroes and Gods

Many temples in India are dedicated to heroes and gods from legends. For example, there are Hanuman temples where people go to pray for strength and courage.

In temples dedicated to Ganesha, people pray before starting new projects, asking for wisdom and success.

10. The Ramayana and Mahabharata are Epic Poems

The Mahabharata is one of the longest poems ever written, with over 100,000 verses!

The Ramayana tells the story of Rama and his adventures to rescue Sita from the demon king Ravana. Both stories continue to inspire people to this day.

11. The Lotus Flower Symbol in Indian Legends

The lotus flower is a symbol of purity and wisdom. It is said that the god Brahma was born from a lotus flower that sprouted from Vishnu's navel.

And that's just the beginning!

These legends and facts are just a glimpse of the rich culture and wisdom found in Indian stories. As you explore more, you'll discover that every legend teaches something valuable and brings a little more magic into your life.

Enjoy the journey, keep asking questions, and don't stop exploring—because every story has a lesson, and every adventure begins with curiosity!

REFERENCES

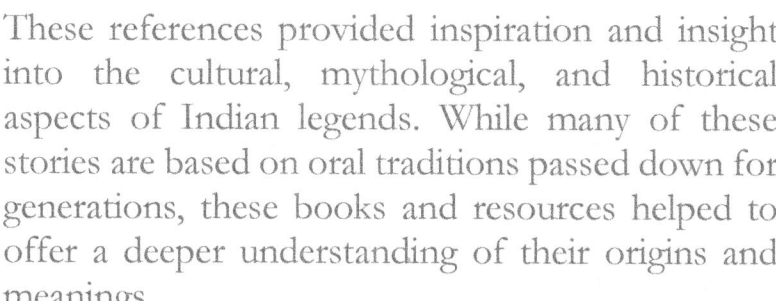

These references provided inspiration and insight into the cultural, mythological, and historical aspects of Indian legends. While many of these stories are based on oral traditions passed down for generations, these books and resources helped to offer a deeper understanding of their origins and meanings.

- Chopra, D. (2007). Buddha: A Story of Enlightenment. HarperOne.
- Pattanaik, D. (2003). Indian Mythology: Tales, Symbols, and Rituals from the Heart of the Subcontinent. Inner Traditions.
- Valmiki. (Trans. 2018). The Ramayana. Penguin Classics.
- Vyasa. (Trans. 2009). The Mahabharata. Penguin Classics.
- Bhagavad Gita. (Trans. Eknath Easwaran, 2007). Nilgiri Press.
- Ramanujan, A. K. (1991). Folktales from India: A Selection of Oral Tales from Twenty-Two Languages. Pantheon Books.

- Krishna, N. (2014). Sacred Animals of India. Penguin Books India.
- Anderson, J. K. (1982). The Pleiades in Myth and Folklore. Peter Lang Publishing.
- The Art and Meaning of Holi. (n.d.). Encyclopedia Britannica. Retrieved from www.britannica.com
- The Story of Buddha. (n.d.). Access to Insight. Retrieved from www.accesstoinsight.org
- Hindu Mythology and Legends. (n.d.). Hinduwebsite. Retrieved from www.hinduwebsite.com
- Oral traditions from storytellers in the northeastern regions of India.
- Conversations with priests and devotees during temple visits in India.
- Family folklore and oral traditions shared across generations.

JAPANESE LEGENDS FOR KIDS:

SAMURAI, SPIRITS, EMPERORS, MYTHS, MAGIC & MORE FROM JAPAN

TABLE OF CONTENTS

INTRODUCTION: WELCOME TO THE MAGICAL WORLD OF JAPANESE LEGENDS 1

CHAPTER 1: AMATERASU – THE SUN GODDESS AND THE LIGHT OF THE WORLD 9

CHAPTER 2: SUSANOO AND OROCHI – THE EIGHT-HEADED DRAGON 17

CHAPTER 3: URASHIMA TARO – THE FISHERMAN'S ADVENTURE UNDER THE SEA 26

CHAPTER 4: MOMOTARO – THE PEACH BOY'S BRAVE QUEST 34

CHAPTER 5: KAGUYA-HIME – THE BAMBOO PRINCESS FROM THE MOON 43

CHAPTER 6: THE TANUKI – THE SHAPE-SHIFTING RACCOON DOG 50

CHAPTER 7: THE RABBIT ON THE MOON – A STORY OF SELFLESSNESS 58

CHAPTER 8: HACHIKO – THE LOYAL DOG 65

CHAPTER 9: TENGU – THE MYSTERIOUS MOUNTAIN GOBLINS 72

CHAPTER 10: THE CRANE WIFE – A TALE OF LOVE AND SACRIFICE 80

CHAPTER 11: KITSUNE – THE FOX SPIRITS OF JAPAN............87

CHAPTER 12: THE BATTLE OF THE KAPPA – THE MISCHIEVOUS RIVER SPIRITS..95

CHAPTER 13: RAIJIN AND FUJIN – THE GODS OF THUNDER AND WIND 103

CHAPTER 14: JIZO – THE PROTECTOR OF CHILDREN AND TRAVELERS 110

CHAPTER 15: THE SPIDER'S THREAD – A LESSON IN KINDNESS 118

CHAPTER 16: YUKI-ONNA – THE MYSTERIOUS SNOW WOMAN 125

CHAPTER 17: HOICHI THE EARLESS – THE TALE OF A GHOSTLY ENCOUNTER 132

CHAPTER 18: THE TALE OF THE FIREFLIES – A STORY OF LOVE AND LOSS 139

CONCLUSION: THE LESSONS HIDDEN IN THESE LEGENDS 145

BONUS: AND FUN FACTS – EXPLORE THE WORLD OF JAPANESE LEGENDS! 153

FUN FACTS ABOUT JAPANESE LEGENDS 156

REFERENCES 159

INTRODUCTION: WELCOME TO THE MAGICAL WORLD OF JAPANESE LEGENDS

Hello, young adventurer! Are you ready to step into a world filled with magic, mystery, and heroic tales? In this book, we'll explore some of the most exciting stories ever told in the land of Japan. Japanese legends are like treasure chests—each one filled with gods, brave heroes, clever animals, and magical creatures waiting to take you on an unforgettable journey. From the highest mountains to the deepest oceans, these tales will inspire you, make you laugh, and teach you valuable lessons along the way.

What Makes Japanese Legends So Special?

Japan is a country with a rich history, and for thousands of years, people have told these stories to explain the wonders of the world. Have you ever wondered why the sun rises every day or what causes thunder during a storm? The Japanese people told stories to answer these questions and to bring meaning to the world around them. In their myths, the sun is not just a ball of fire in the sky—it's ruled by a beautiful and powerful goddess named Amaterasu! And thunderstorms? Well, they are caused by the loud, drum-beating god Raijin, who plays in the skies.

These stories are full of magic and imagination, but they aren't just about having fun—they're also about learning important life lessons. Long ago, people passed these stories down by word of mouth, teaching children (just like you!) the importance of kindness, bravery, and respect for others.

So, whether it's the tale of a mischievous raccoon dog called Tanuki or a kind fisherman named

Urashima Taro, there's always something meaningful hidden within every adventure. And guess what? You get to uncover it all!

Lessons Hidden in Every Story: Kindness, Bravery, and Respect

Japanese legends are like little treasure maps; each story points you toward a lesson to make you wiser and kinder. Let's take a look at some of the lessons hidden in these ancient tales:

Kindness

In the story of The Crane Wife, a kind man saves an injured bird, and later, the bird returns in disguise to help him in his time of need. This story reminds us that being kind to others, no matter how small, can bring joy and kindness back to us in surprising ways.

Bravery

The story of Momotaro the Peach Boy shows us what true courage looks like. He embarks on an adventure to fight terrifying ogres, even though he's just a boy! His bravery teaches us that we can overcome challenges, no matter how big they seem, if we believe in ourselves.

Respect

One of the most famous Japanese legends is about Amaterasu, the Sun Goddess, and her mischievous brother, Susanoo. Susanoo learns the hard way that being disrespectful can cause trouble, even for mighty gods. But through patience and effort, he earns forgiveness, teaching us the value of treating others with respect.

Meet the Heroes and Magical Creatures!

Get ready to meet all sorts of fascinating characters on your journey through these stories! There are gods who rule the skies, animals with magical powers, and heroes who face impossible challenges.

Gods and Goddesses

Amaterasu, the radiant Sun Goddess, brings light to the world while her brother Susanoo battles sea creatures and dragons. You'll also meet Raijin, the thunder god, who loves to make noise during storms, and his friend Fujin, the god of wind.

Animals with Special Powers

Have you ever heard of a Kitsune? These clever foxes can shape-shift into humans! Some Kitsune are friendly and helpful, while others like to play tricks. And then there's Tanuki, a magical raccoon dog who loves to have fun and make mischief—but always learns a lesson in the end.

Heroes and Brave Adventurers

Not all heroes are gods—some are just ordinary people with extraordinary courage. Meet Urashima Taro, a kind fisherman who takes a magical trip to an underwater palace, and Momotaro, a boy born from a peach, who becomes a hero with the help of his animal friends.

Spooky Spirits and Mischievous Creatures

Watch out for the Tengu, bird-like creatures who live in the mountains. Sometimes, they help people learn important lessons, but other times, they play sneaky tricks. And beware of the Kappa, strange water creatures with bowls on their heads—they might challenge you to a wrestling match if you're not careful!

How to Enjoy These Stories

These legends are keys to discovering a world full of wonder. As you read, try to imagine yourself in the middle of the adventure. What would you do if you found a glowing bamboo stalk with a princess inside? How would you feel if you received a magical box that could change your life forever?

Here are a few fun ways to explore the stories in this book:

Act Them Out

Pretend you are a brave hero like Momotaro or a clever fox like Kitsune. You can even make masks and costumes to bring the stories to life with your family and friends!

Draw Your Favorite Characters

Create your own pictures of the characters you meet. What does Amaterasu look like in your imagination? What about the mischievous Tanuki?

Talk About the Lessons

After reading each story, think about the message hidden inside. What did the hero learn? How can that lesson help you in your life?

Celebrating These Legends Today

Did you know that many of these legends are still celebrated in Japan today? Every year, people gather to honor gods and heroes through festivals called matsuri. During these festivals, you might see colorful parades, hear lively music, and enjoy delicious food. There are even dances and plays that bring the old stories to life!

In some parts of Japan, people visit shrines dedicated to gods like Amaterasu and Susanoo, leaving offerings and saying prayers. Statues of Jizo, the guardian of travelers and children, can be found along roadsides, always wearing little red hats or bibs to protect them.

Even Hachiko, the loyal dog, has his own statue at a train station in Tokyo. People visit it every day to remember his story of love and loyalty.

A Journey Awaits—Are You Ready?

In the pages that follow, you will find adventures big and small, heroes bold and kind, and creatures that will make your imagination soar. Whether you dream of flying with a dragon, chatting with a shape-shifting fox, or uncovering the secrets of the moon princess, this book is your gateway to endless possibilities.

So, grab your backpack of curiosity, put on your shoes of wonder, and get ready to leap into a magical world where anything can happen!

Are you ready to meet the gods, heroes, and creatures of Japan? Let's dive into the first story—The Sun Goddess Amaterasu—and see where this adventure takes us!

CHAPTER 1: AMATERASU - THE SUN GODDESS AND THE LIGHT OF THE WORLD

Long ago, in the magical world of Japan's heavens, there lived a brilliant and kind goddess named Amaterasu. Amaterasu (pronounced ah-MAT-er-A-su) was the Sun Goddess, who made the sun rise every day. Thanks to her, the world was filled with warmth, light, and happiness. Without her, everything would be dark and cold. Everyone loved Amaterasu since she shone brightly, bringing joy to the world below.

But Amaterasu had a brother named Susanoo (pronounced su-SAH-no-oh). And, oh boy, Susanoo could be a handful! He was the God of Storms, known for his wild and mischievous behavior. He would race through the skies with thunderclouds and roaring winds, causing all sorts of trouble. Even though Susanoo and Amaterasu were siblings, they couldn't have been more different—like night and day!

Susanoo's Stormy Trouble

One day, Susanoo was in a very bad mood. He stomped around the heavens, tossing thunder and lightning like toys. He didn't care who he upset—he just wanted to cause mischief. And guess who he decided to annoy? That's right—his sister, Amaterasu!

At first, Amaterasu tried to ignore her brother's nonsense. "He'll get tired of it soon," she thought. But Susanoo didn't stop. He threw a tantrum so wild that the wind howled, trees shook, and rain poured from the sky. Then, as if that wasn't enough, Susanoo barged into Amaterasu's beautiful palace!

Inside her palace, Susanoo did everything he could to get on her nerves. He trampled over her rice fields, smashed her looms where she wove magical cloth, and even tossed mud all over her palace walls.

Amaterasu was furious. "How could Susanoo be so cruel and thoughtless?" she wondered. Hurt and frustrated, she decided she couldn't take it anymore.

Amaterasu Hides in the Cave

Amaterasu felt so upset by her brother's behavior that she hid from the world. "If Susanoo wants to act like a storm, let him live in darkness!" she thought. And with that, she disappeared into a cave, closing the entrance behind her with a giant boulder.

The moment Amaterasu shut herself inside the cave, the world changed. The sun vanished from the sky. Darkness spread across the heavens and the earth. Without Amaterasu's light, people couldn't see where they were going. Flowers withered, birds stopped singing, and the world became cold and gloomy.

Even the other gods were worried. "What do we do without the sun?" they whispered. "If Amaterasu doesn't come out, everything will wither away." It wasn't long before the animals and people began to lose hope. They needed Amaterasu's light more than ever.

The Gods' Plan to Bring Back the Sun

The gods knew they had to do something—and fast! They gathered at the cave entrance, but no matter how much they begged and pleaded, Amaterasu refused to come out. "I don't want to see anyone!" she shouted from behind the boulder.

The gods weren't ready to give up. One of the cleverest gods, Omoikane (pronounced o-mo-ee-KAH-neh), had an idea. "If we can't convince her to come out with words, let's try something unexpected—something fun!"

The gods all agreed it was worth a try. They came up with a wild plan: they would throw the most exciting, funnest party ever—right outside the cave! Maybe, just maybe, Amaterasu would get curious and come out to see what was happening.

The gods gathered everything they needed for their plan: drums, flutes, and even some brightly colored ribbons. They also found Ame-no-Uzume, the Goddess of Laughter and Dance, to lead the celebration. Ame-no-Uzume was known for her silly dances, and if anyone could make a goddess curious enough to leave a cave, it was her!

With everything in place, the gods began their party. Ame-no-Uzume jumped onto an overturned barrel and started dancing wildly. She twirled, stomped, and waved her ribbons in the air. The other gods clapped and cheered, and the sound of drums echoed through the mountains.

The funniest part? Ame-no-Uzume danced so energetically that her clothes started slipping off! The gods roared with laughter, slapping their knees and clapping louder and louder. It was such a ridiculous and joyful sight that even the animals joined in, barking, chirping, and howling with delight.

Amaterasu Peeks Out

Inside the cave, Amaterasu sat quietly in the dark. But as the sounds of laughter and music drifted through the air, she couldn't help but feel curious. "What's going on out there?" she wondered. It sounded like everyone was having the most fun without her!

Finally, Amaterasu couldn't resist. She peeked out from behind the boulder to see what all the noise was about. The gods had been waiting for this moment!

Before Amaterasu could slip back inside, the strongest god, Ame-no-Tajikarao, quickly grabbed the boulder and pulled it away from the entrance.

"Surprise!" shouted the gods. They welcomed Amaterasu back with cheers, music, and bright flowers. As soon as she stepped out of the cave, the sun's light returned to the world. The sky brightened, the flowers bloomed, and birds began to sing once again.

A Lesson for Everyone: Light after Darkness

The gods celebrated Amaterasu's return, and the world rejoiced. Even Susanoo, realizing how much trouble he had caused, apologized to his sister and promised to behave better. Amaterasu forgave him, but she reminded him—and everyone else—that respect and kindness are just as important as bravery.

This story teaches us that, even when we feel hurt or upset, hiding away isn't the answer. Just like Amaterasu found her way back to the light, we too can overcome sadness by joining others, finding joy, and remembering the people who care about us.

Thanks to the gods' clever plan, Amaterasu shines brightly in the sky every day, reminding us that light always follows darkness. No matter how hard things seem, there's always a reason to smile, laugh, and keep going.

What We Can Learn from Amaterasu's Story

Amaterasu's story is a reminder of important lessons that we can use in our own lives.

Kindness and Respect Matter

Susanoo's actions hurt Amaterasu because he didn't respect her space. We should always treat others with kindness and think about how our actions affect them.

Laughter Can Heal

When things feel tough, laughter and joy can help us find light again. Just like Ame-no-Uzume's dance brightened everyone's mood, having fun with friends can make us feel better.

The World Needs Your Light

In the same way that the world needed Amaterasu's sunlight, the people around you need your kindness, joy, and courage. You are just as important as the sun in making the world a brighter place!

And so, thanks to Amaterasu's return, the sun rises each morning to greet us with warmth and light. Every time you see the sun shining in the sky, remember her story—and the joy that comes from laughter, kindness, and forgiveness.

Now that you've met the Sun Goddess, let's continue our journey through more exciting Japanese legends. Get ready to meet new gods, heroes, and magical creatures as we dive deeper into the world of myths!

Are you ready for the next adventure? Let's go!

CHAPTER 2:
SUSANOO AND OROCHI
-THE EIGHT-HEADED DRAGON

Once upon a time, in the vast sky high above the Earth, there lived a wild and unpredictable god named Susanoo. He was known as the God of Storms, with a personality as fierce as thunder and as wild as the wind. Wherever Susanoo went, chaos followed—he brought storms, howling winds, and crashing waves.

Unfortunately, Susanoo's reckless behavior finally got him into trouble with the other gods, especially his sister, Amaterasu, the Sun Goddess. After one too many pranks and tantrums, the gods had enough of his mischief. They decided it was time to send Susanoo away from the heavens.

Falling from the Heavens

Susanoo was banished from the heavens, tossed down from the sky like a shooting star. He tumbled through clouds, whirling winds carrying him all the way to the earth below. When he finally landed, he found himself in a strange land with tall mountains, rushing rivers, and dark forests.

At first, Susanoo sat by a river, feeling grumpy about being kicked out of the heavens. "This is boring," he muttered, tossing stones into the water. "What's a storm god supposed to do down here?"

As Susanoo walked along the riverbank, looking for something interesting to do, he heard something strange—a sound that made him stop in his tracks.

It was the sound of someone crying.

A Family in Distress

Susanoo followed the sound of the crying and soon found a little house near the river. Outside the house sat an old man and an old woman, both weeping. Beside them was a young girl with long black hair, holding her hands over her face and sobbing quietly.

"Why are you all so sad?" Susanoo asked, curious.

The old man wiped his tears and looked up at Susanoo. "We are in great trouble," he said. "Our family is being terrorized by a terrible monster—the eight-headed dragon named Orochi."

"A dragon?" Susanoo's eyes lit up with excitement. "Tell me more!"

The old woman nodded. "Orochi is a massive dragon with eight heads and eight tails. He's bigger than the mountains, and he comes once a year to devour one of our daughters."

Susanoo glanced at the young girl, who was still crying softly. "Is she next?" he whispered.

The old man nodded sadly. "This is our last daughter, Kushinada-hime. We've already lost all seven of our other daughters to Orochi. Now it's her turn, and we have no way to stop the monster."

Susanoo stroked his chin, thinking hard. "What if I could defeat this dragon for you?" he asked.

The family's eyes widened. "You would do that?" the old man asked in disbelief. "But Orochi is gigantic and dangerous!"

Susanoo grinned confidently. "No problem! I've got a clever plan. I'll deal with this dragon, and no one else will have to cry."

A Clever Plan with Sake

Susanoo's mind began to race with ideas. Fighting Orochi (pronounced o-ROH-chee) head-on would be too risky—after all, the dragon had eight heads and eight tails! He needed to outsmart the beast. That's when he had a brilliant idea.

"Do you have any sake to drink?" Susanoo asked the old couple.

The old man nodded. "Yes, we have some sake saved for celebrations—why?"

"I need a lot of it," Susanoo said with a mischievous grin. "We're going to trick Orochi!"

Susanoo explained his plan to the family. First, they gathered eight enormous barrels of sake, each one as big as a bathtub. Then, they found a spot along the river where Orochi was known to appear. There, Susanoo arranged the barrels in a circle, filling each one to the brim with the finest sake.

"When Orochi shows up, he won't be able to resist the smell of the sake," Susanoo explained. "Each of his heads will drink from a different barrel—and when he's too drunk to move, that's when I'll strike!"

The old man and woman nervously agreed to the plan, hoping that Susanoo's clever trick would work.

The Arrival of Orochi

The ground trembled, and the air filled with the sound of something huge slithering toward them. Suddenly, the sky darkened as the enormous dragon Orochi appeared, each of his eight heads twisting and hissing and his scaly tails dragging behind him. The dragon's hungry red eyes glowed, and his many mouths hissed as he approached the family's home.

Orochi's heads sniffed the air—and then they all caught the scent of the sake! The dragon paused, his tongues flickering, tempted by the delicious smell. One by one, each of Orochi's heads dipped down to drink from the barrels.

Gulp! Gulp! Gulp! Orochi's heads drank greedily, slurping up the sake until each of the barrels was empty. The dragon swayed back and forth, dizzy and drunk, his many heads bobbing and wobbling like balloons in the wind.

The Battle with Orochi

Susanoo watched from the shadows, waiting for the perfect moment to pounce. When Orochi's heads all collapsed to the ground, snoring loudly, Susanoo jumped into action!

With a mighty roar, Susanoo leaped onto the dragon's massive body. He drew his sword and began slicing through the dragon's thick, scaly necks, one by one. *Slash! Slash! Slash!*

The battle was fierce, but Orochi was too drunk to fight back. His head wobbled uselessly as Susanoo slashed and hacked until the great dragon lay defeated.

Just as Susanoo was about to put his sword away, something shiny caught his eye.

The Sword Hidden in Orochi's Tail

Susanoo knelt down beside one of Orochi's tails. To his surprise, hidden inside the dragon's thick scales, he found a magnificent sword! It shimmered in the sunlight, its blade sharp and powerful.

"This must be a gift from the gods," Susanoo whispered, holding the sword in his hands. He named the sword Kusanagi, meaning "Grass-Cutting Sword." It was no ordinary weapon—it was a sacred sword with magical powers.

Susanoo knew that the prize sword Kusanagi was a symbol of victory, courage, and clever thinking.

With the dragon defeated and Kusanagi in hand, Susanoo returned to the old man, the old woman, and their daughter, Kushinada-hime. They were overjoyed to see him safe and sound.

"You saved our daughter and defeated the terrible dragon!" the old man exclaimed. "We will forever be grateful to you, brave Susanoo!"

Susanoo smiled proudly, knowing that he had done something good. For once, instead of causing storms and trouble, he had helped others—and it felt amazing!

The family invited Susanoo to stay with them, and he gladly accepted. Over time, Susanoo married the beautiful Kushinada-hime, and they lived happily together.

What We Can Learn from Susanoo's Adventure

Susanoo's battle with the eight-headed dragon Orochi teaches us some important lessons.

Cleverness Wins the Day

Instead of fighting Orochi with brute strength, Susanoo used his brain to come up with a smart plan. This reminds us that being clever can help us solve problems.

Bravery Comes in Many Forms

Susanoo wasn't afraid to face a dangerous dragon to help others. True bravery means standing up for what's right, even when things seem scary.

Kindness Changes Everything

Although Susanoo started as a troublemaker, he showed that even someone wild can change and do good.

From that day forward, the sword Kusanagi became one of the most treasured items in Japanese mythology, passed down through generations as a symbol of courage and wisdom. And as for Susanoo? He continued to have adventures—but that's a story for another day!

Are you ready for the next legend? There are even more gods, heroes, and magical creatures waiting to meet you! Let's keep going on this exciting journey through the world of Japanese legends!

CHAPTER 3:
URASHIMA TARO - THE FISHERMAN'S ADVENTURE UNDER THE SEA

A long time ago, in a small fishing village by the sparkling sea, there lived a kind and gentle fisherman named Urashima Taro (pronounced er-AH-sheema TAH-roh). Taro loved nothing more than sailing his boat and casting his nets into the ocean. He always treated the sea creatures with care, never taking more fish than he needed. Everyone in the village admired Taro for his kindness and honesty. But little did Taro know that one day, he would embark on a magical adventure that would change his life forever.

Saving the Turtle

One bright morning, as Taro walked along the beach with the waves gently lapping at the shore, he noticed a group of rowdy children gathered around something in the sand. The children were shouting and laughing, and as Taro got closer, he saw what they were doing—they were bullying a small turtle!

"Leave the turtle alone!" Taro called out. But the children just laughed and continued to poke at the poor creature, who flailed its tiny legs helplessly.

Taro wasn't about to stand by and do nothing. He rushed over and gently scooped up the turtle, shielding it from the children. "This turtle hasn't done anything to you," Taro said firmly. "Let's be kind to animals!"

The children, feeling a bit guilty, apologized and ran off. Taro looked down at the little turtle in his hands. "You're safe now, little one," he said, smiling warmly. Then, he carefully placed the turtle back into the ocean.

The turtle floated for a moment, looking up at Taro with what almost seemed like a grateful smile. Then, with a splash, it disappeared beneath the waves.

Taro dusted off his hands and turned to leave, thinking his day was over. But suddenly, the water began to shimmer and bubble! Out of the waves popped the same turtle—only now it was much larger, with glittering scales that sparkled like jewels.

"Thank you, kind Taro!" the turtle said. "You saved me, and now I wish to repay your kindness. Climb on my back, and I will take you to a place you've never seen before—the palace of the Dragon King, deep beneath the sea!"

Journey to the Dragon King's Palace

Taro blinked in amazement. A talking turtle? A magical palace under the sea? It sounded like a dream! But Taro had always been curious, so he decided to trust the turtle. He climbed onto its back, and with a mighty splash, the turtle dove deep into the ocean.

Down they went, past colorful coral reefs and schools of shimmering fish. Taro's eyes grew wide as they swam deeper than any fisherman had ever gone. The light from the surface faded, but glowing sea creatures lit their way, making the ocean feel like a magical, starry sky.

At last, they reached the Dragon King's palace. It was the most beautiful place Taro had ever seen! The palace walls shimmered like pearls, and the gates were made of shining gold. Fish in every color of the rainbow swam gracefully through the halls, and gentle music echoed softly through the water.

Waiting at the entrance was Otohime, the Dragon King's daughter. She wore a dress made of seaweed and pearls, and her smile was as warm as sunlight on the ocean.

"Welcome, Urashima Taro," Otohime said. "Thank you for saving the turtle. Please, stay in our palace and enjoy the wonders of the sea!"

A Magical Life Beneath the Sea

Taro couldn't believe his luck. Everywhere he looked, there was something new and amazing to see. The fish danced and twirled to music, and the sea creatures treated Taro like an honored guest.

Each day, Otohime (pronounced OH-to-him-eh) showed Taro the ocean's wonders. They rode on dolphins, explored coral gardens, and even danced with jellyfish that sparkled like fireworks. It was like living in a dream—Taro never wanted it to end.

But time under the sea seemed different. Days felt short, and nights passed like the blink of an eye. Before Taro knew it, many days, maybe even years, had gone by. Though he was happy in the Dragon King's palace, Taro began to think about his home.

"I've had such a wonderful time here," Taro told Otohime one day. "But I miss my village and my family. I think it's time for me to go back."

Otohime smiled sadly. "I understand," she said. "But before you leave, I want to give you a gift—a special box called the Tamatebako."

She handed Taro a beautiful lacquered box tied with a silk ribbon. "Whatever you do, Taro, don't open the box. Keep it safe, and it will protect you."

Taro thanked Otohime, climbed onto the turtle's back once more, and began the journey back to the surface.

Returning Home

When Taro reached the shore of his village, he smiled with relief. The waves sparkled, and the beach felt just as warm and inviting as he remembered. Yet as he walked into the village, something felt... strange.

The houses were different, the people looked unfamiliar, and everything seemed older. "Where is everyone I know?" Taro wondered. He asked the villagers about his family and friends, but no one recognized their names.

Taro's heart sank. "How long was I really gone?" he whispered. He realized that while he felt like he had spent only a few days under the sea, many, many years had passed on land. Everyone he knew was gone, and the world had changed.

Feeling lost and alone, Taro sat on the beach, holding the mysterious Tamatebako in his hands. He remembered Otohime's warning not to open the box, but curiosity gnawed at him.

"What's the harm?" he thought. "Maybe the box holds something that can help me."

The Mystery of the Tamatebako

With trembling hands, Taro untied the silk ribbon and opened the box. A soft white mist swirled out, wrapping around him like a cloud.

Suddenly, Taro felt strange—his body became heavy, and his hair turned white as snow. In moments, Taro had aged into an old man, his strength fading away. The magic of the palace had kept him young under the sea, but now that the box was open, time had caught up with him.

Taro looked at his wrinkled hands and sighed. Though he had lost his youth, he smiled softly. He knew that life was full of both happy moments and sad ones, and the time he had spent under the sea was a gift he would always cherish.

The Lesson of Urashima Taro's Adventure

Urashima Taro's story teaches us many important lessons.

Kindness Always Comes Back to You

Taro's adventure began because he showed kindness to a small turtle. When we help others, good things often happen in return.

Time Is Precious

Taro's time under the sea felt magical, but life on land kept moving forward. This reminds us to cherish every moment and spend time with the people we love.

Curiosity Comes with Consequences

Taro opened the Tamatebako out of curiosity, even though he was warned not to. This teaches us to think carefully about our actions and their consequences.

Though Urashima Taro's life changed in ways he never expected, his story reminds us that every adventure is valuable, even if it doesn't turn out the way we planned. Life is full of surprises, and every moment—whether it's joyful or sad—helps us grow wiser.

As Taro gazed at the waves, he knew he would always carry the memories of the Dragon King's palace in his heart, like a secret treasure from a distant dream.

Are you ready for the next adventure? There are more magical stories waiting just beyond the horizon. Let's dive into the next chapter and see what wonders await!

CHAPTER 4: MOMOTARO - THE PEACH BOY'S BRAVE QUEST

A long time ago, in a peaceful village surrounded by green hills and blooming flowers, there lived an old man and an old woman. They were kind and hardworking, spending their days collecting firewood and washing clothes in the nearby river. Though they were happy, the couple felt lonely. They had always wished for a child, but no child had come to them.

One day, everything changed when the old woman went to the river to wash clothes. As she hummed a cheerful tune, she saw something floating down the river. It wasn't a fish or a log—it was a giant peach glowing in the sunlight!

"Look at that peach!" the old woman exclaimed. "It's the biggest peach I've ever seen!"

She reached into the water and pulled the giant peach onto the riverbank. It was heavy but so beautiful that she decided to take it home to share with her husband.

The Magical Birth of Momotaro

The old woman carried the peach back to their little house. "Husband, look what I found!" she called. The old man's eyes widened when he saw the enormous peach.

"This will make a wonderful feast!" he said, picking up a knife to slice the peach open.

Just as the knife touched the peach's soft skin, something amazing happened! The peach split open with a gentle pop, and inside, they found a baby boy!

The baby yawned and smiled at the old couple. "Hello!" he said cheerfully.

The old man and woman couldn't believe their eyes. "A baby—inside a peach!" the old woman gasped.

The old man clapped his hands with joy. "It's a miracle! We've always wanted a child, and now we have one!"

They decided to name the boy Momotaro, which means "Peach Boy," since he had come to them in a peach. Momotaro (pronounced MO-mo-tah-roh) grew quickly;by the time he was a young boy, he was already stronger and braver than anyone in the village.

The Oni Threat

One day, the old man and woman told Momotaro about the terrible Oni—evil ogres who lived on a distant island. These Oni were huge and scary, with sharp horns and teeth. They came to the village frequently, stealing food and treasures and making life miserable for the villagers.

"They're too strong for us to fight," the old man said sadly.

But Momotaro stood tall and declared, "Don't worry, Father and Mother. I will go to Oni's island and defeat them! I'll bring back the treasures they stole and make sure they never bother anyone again."

The old couple was proud of their son's bravery, though they also worried for his safety. To help him on his journey, they made special rice cakes called kibi-dango. "Take these with you," the old woman said, "and they will give you strength."

With a bundle of kibi-dango tied to his belt, Momotaro set off on his adventure, his heart filled with courage.

Momotaro's Animal Companions

As Momotaro traveled toward Oni's island, he met a hungry dog. The dog growled at him, but Momotaro wasn't afraid.

"Where are you going, boy?" the dog asked.

"I'm going to Oni's island to defeat the ogres!" Momotaro replied.

The dog's ears perked up. "That's a dangerous mission. What's in that bag?"

"These are kibi-dango," Momotaro said. "If you help me fight the Oni, I'll share them with you."

The dog wagged his tail happily. "Deal! I'll fight by your side."

The two of them continued their journey until they met a mischievous monkey swinging from a tree.

"Where are you two going?" the monkey asked.

"We're off to defeat the Oni on their island!" Momotaro replied.

The monkey scratched his head. "That sounds like fun. What's in the bag?"

"These are kibi-dango," said Momotaro. "If you help us, you can have some too."

The monkey grinned. "Count me in!"

As they traveled further, they met a colorful pheasant flying above them.

"Where are you all going?" the pheasant asked, fluttering down to land on a branch.

"We're going to fight the Oni!" Momotaro explained.

The pheasant ruffled its feathers. "Sounds exciting! If I help, can I have a kibi-dango too?"

"Of course!" Momotaro said, handing the pheasant a rice cake.

Now, Momotaro had three loyal companions—a dog, a monkey, and a pheasant. Together, they continued toward Oni's island, ready for adventure.

The Battle with the Oni

At last, the group reached Oni's island. The sky was cloudy, and the waves crashed against the rocky shore. Momotaro and his animal friends could see the Oni's castle in the distance, its gates guarded by huge, snarling ogres.

The dog growled, the monkey scratched his head, and the pheasant flapped its wings. "Let's show these Oni what we're made of!" Momotaro said, tightening his grip on his sword.

The pheasant flew ahead, swooping down to distract the Oni guards. "Hey, ugly ogres! Over here!" the pheasant squawked, pecking at their heads.

While the Oni were busy swatting at the pheasant, the monkey climbed over the castle walls and opened the gates from the inside. "Come on, everyone!" the monkey shouted.

Momotaro and the dog charged into the castle, ready for battle. The dog bit the Oni's legs, the monkey pelted them with rocks, and Momotaro slashed at them with his sword. The Oni were no match for the brave team. One by one, the ogres were defeated; finally, they gave up.

"We surrender!" the Oni cried. "Please don't hurt us anymore! Take all the treasures we stole and leave us in peace!"

The Return Home with Treasures

With the Oni defeated, Momotaro and his companions gathered all the treasures the ogres had stolen from the villagers. They packed up gold, silk, and other valuables and returned to the village, proud of their victory.

When they returned, the villagers cheered and celebrated. "Momotaro has saved us!" they cried. "The Oni will never trouble us again!"

The old man and woman hugged Momotaro tightly. "We knew you could do it," they said with joyful tears.

Thanks to Momotaro's courage—and the help of his loyal animal friends—the village was safe and happy once more.

What We Can Learn from Momotaro's Adventure

Momotaro's story teaches us some important lessons.

Bravery and Teamwork

Momotaro couldn't defeat the Oni alone—he needed his friends' help. This reminds us that working together makes us stronger.

Kindness Goes a Long Way

Momotaro shared his kibi-dango with the dog, the monkey, and the pheasant; in return, they helped him on his quest. Helping others brings help back to us.

Never Give Up

Even though the Oni were big and scary, Momotaro didn't let fear stop him. His determination shows us that we can overcome any challenge if we keep trying.

Momotaro became a hero, remembered not just for his bravery but also for his kindness and teamwork. His adventure reminds us that even the biggest challenges can be conquered with a little courage and the right friends by our side.

Are you ready for the next exciting story? There are even more adventures waiting in the world of Japanese legends!

CHAPTER 5:
KAGUYA-HIME - THE BAMBOO PRINCESS FROM THE MOON

A long time ago, in a quiet forest filled with rustling leaves, there lived an old bamboo cutter and his wife. Every day, the old man would walk deep into the forest to cut bamboo, which he sold to make a living. He was happy with his simple life, but one thing was missing: he and his wife had no children.

Sometimes, the old man would pause while cutting bamboo and wish quietly, "If only we had a child to fill our hearts with joy."

One evening, something extraordinary happened. As the sun began to set and the forest grew dark, the old man noticed a glowing bamboo stalk among the trees. It shimmered like moonlight, lighting up the forest around it. Curious, the old man carefully cut the bamboo stalk open; inside was the most beautiful, tiny baby girl he had ever seen! She was no bigger than his hand, with skin as fair as moonlight and eyes that sparkled like stars.

The Bamboo Cutter's Wish Comes True

The old man gently picked up the tiny girl, cradling her in his hands. "What a miracle!" he whispered. He carried her home and showed her to his wife, who was just as amazed. "She is a gift from the heavens," the wife said. "We will raise her as our own daughter."

The old couple named the baby Kaguya-hime, which means "Radiant Princess." To their surprise, the tiny baby grew quickly. In just a few days, she became a lovely young girl. Her beauty was beyond anything the old couple—or anyone in the village—had ever seen. Her long, black hair shimmered like silk, and her smile could light up the darkest night.

Kaguya-hime (pronounced kah-GU-yah HEE-meh) brought great joy to her new parents, who loved her more than anything in the world.

Suitors from across the Land

As word spread about Kaguya-hime's beauty, young men from near and far began to visit the bamboo cutter's home, hoping to marry the beautiful princess. They came dressed in fine clothes, riding horses, and bringing expensive gifts. They told Kaguya-hime how much they admired her and promised to make her happy if she would marry them.

Kaguya-hime was not interested in marrying any of the suitors. "I'm grateful for your kindness," she said politely, "but I cannot marry anyone."

Some of the suitors persisted. They begged Kaguya-hime to change her mind. Finally, to discourage them, she gave each one of them an impossible task. "If you can complete the task I give you," she said, "then I will marry you."

The Impossible Tasks

The first suitor was told to bring back a jeweled branch from the legendary island of Horai. The second suitor was told to retrieve a robe made of Fire Rat fur that could not be burned. The third suitor was sent to fetch a crystal bowl from the bottom of the dragon's lair. The fourth suitor was asked to bring a shell that sings like a bird, and the fifth suitor was asked to find a magical stone that glows in the dark.

The suitors tried their best to complete these tasks, but each of them failed. One suitor claimed he had found the jeweled branch, but Kaguya-hime knew it was fake. Another brought back a robe, but when Kaguya-hime threw it into the fire, it burned to ashes. None of the suitors could complete their tasks, and one by one, they gave up and left, realizing that they were not worthy to marry the extraordinary Kaguya-hime.

Kaguya-hime's Secret

Though Kaguya-hime lived happily with her parents, she often seemed sad and thoughtful, especially when she looked up at the moon. "Is everything all right, my dear?" her father would ask.

Kaguya-hime smiled gently but said nothing. As much as she loved the old bamboo cutter and his wife, she knew a secret she hadn't shared with anyone. Kaguya-hime was not from the Earth—she was from the moon, and her time on Earth was coming to an end.

One evening, as she gazed at the full moon, tears filled her eyes. She knew that soon, she would have to leave her parents and return to her true home in the sky.

The Bittersweet Farewell

One night, as the bamboo cutter and his wife sat with Kaguya-hime, the princess finally told them the truth. "I am not an ordinary girl," she said softly. "I come from the moon, and the time has come for me to return."

The old man and woman were heartbroken. "Please don't leave us," they begged. "We love you as our daughter. We don't care where you're from—we just want you to stay with us."

Kaguya-hime's heart ached, but she knew she had no choice. "I love you too," she whispered, "but the moon is calling me back. I will always carry you in my heart."

The night of Kaguya-hime's departure finally arrived. The sky was clear, and the full moon shone brightly. As her parents held her hand, a glowing chariot descended from the sky, carrying celestial beings dressed in white robes.

"Kaguya-hime, it is time to return," they said gently.

The old man and woman hugged Kaguya-hime tightly, their tears falling like rain. "We will never forget you," they whispered.

"And I will never forget you," Kaguya-hime replied, her voice filled with love.

With one last look at her earthly parents, Kaguya-hime stepped into the glowing chariot. As it rose into the sky, a soft, shimmering light surrounded her. The bamboo cutter and his wife watched as the chariot carried their beloved daughter higher and higher until she disappeared into the light of the moon.

Though their hearts ached with sadness, the old couple knew that Kaguya-hime was happy, and they felt grateful for the time they had shared with her.

The Lesson of Kaguya-hime's Story

Kaguya-hime's story teaches us that some things in life are beautiful but fleeting.

Cherish Every Moment

Just like the bamboo cutter and his wife treasured their time with Kaguya-hime, we should enjoy every moment with the people we love.

True Love Is Letting Go

The old couple loved Kaguya-hime so much that they let her return to her true home, even though it saddened them. This teaches us that love sometimes means letting go.

Not Everything Can Be Possessed

Kaguya-hime's beauty was admired by many suitors, but they couldn't win her heart with treasures. Some things—like love and happiness—can't be earned with wealth.

Though Kaguya-hime returned to the moon, the memory of her time on Earth lived on in the hearts of those she left behind. And even now, when you look up at the full moon, you might just see the soft glow of Kaguya-hime's smile, reminding us that love shines brighter than anything in the sky.

CHAPTER 6:
THE TANUKI - THE SHAPE-SHIFTING RACCOON DOG

Deep in the forests of Japan, where the trees grow thick and the rivers run clear, lives a magical creature called the Tanuki. Tanuki are not like ordinary animals—they are shape-shifters, able to turn into anything they want! Sometimes, they become teapots or statues. Other times, they disguise themselves as people, creating all sorts of mischief and fun. With their round tummies, big eyes, and friendly smiles, Tanuki are always up to something exciting.

But be careful! Though Tanuki love to play pranks and jokes, their tricks don't always go as planned. Some of their pranks are so silly that even they end up learning important lessons about kindness and responsibility. Are you ready to hear the playful and heartwarming adventures of these tricky creatures? Let's dive into the world of Tanuki magic!

The Playful Tanuki and His Many Tricks

Tanuki (pronounced tah-NU-kee) are known throughout Japan as tricksters. They love to change form and play pranks on humans, animals, and even other spirits. Here are some of the most famous tricks Tanuki has pulled off.

The Tanuki Teapot

One Tanuki once transformed himself into a teapot and sat quietly in a shop. A customer bought the teapot and took it home, but when he placed it over the fire, the Tanuki couldn't handle the heat! The teapot suddenly grew arms and legs and ran away, leaving the poor customer staring in shock.

The Tanuki's Disappearing Rice Cakes

One day, a farmer prepared a stack of delicious rice cakes for a festival. As soon as he turned his back, Tanuki sneaked in and snatched every last one! When the farmer chased after the Tanuki, the mischievous creature turned himself into a tree stump, standing perfectly still. The farmer scratched his head, wondering where the thief had gone. Meanwhile, the Tanuki giggled quietly from his hiding spot.

The Tanuki as a Human Traveler

Sometimes, Tanuki love to pretend to be humans. One Tanuki turned himself into a wandering traveler and stopped at a village, claiming he had magical treasures to sell. The villagers gave him food and gifts, hoping to see the treasures. But when they returned the next morning, the traveler had vanished—along with all the food! All that was left was a pile of leaves where the Tanuki had slept.

When Tanuki's Tricks Go Too Far

While most of Tanuki's tricks are harmless, sometimes their pranks cause trouble. One day, a mischievous Tanuki named Shiro decided to pull a prank on a kind farmer named Jiro. The farmer was known for his gentle heart, always sharing food with animals and helping those in need. But Shiro, being a bit selfish, wanted to see if he could steal all of Jiro's food without getting caught.

Shiro turned himself into an old, hungry man and knocked on the farmer's door. "Please, kind sir, may I have some rice?" the disguised Tanuki begged, acting weak and tired.

Jiro welcomed the visitor warmly. "Of course! No one should go hungry," he said, offering the Tanuki a big bowl of rice.

But the greedy Tanuki kept coming back every day, disguised as different travelers—sometimes an old woman, sometimes a young boy. Each time, Jiro smiled and gave him food.

One evening, Jiro caught Tanuki in the act. "I see what you're doing!" Jiro laughed, surprising Shiro. "You've been playing tricks on me all along, haven't you?"

The Tanuki felt embarrassed and ashamed. "I'm sorry," he admitted. "I didn't mean to cause any harm—I just wanted to have some fun."

Jiro smiled kindly. "It's not wrong to have fun, but it's important to be honest and think about others. Tricks should make people laugh, not cause them trouble."

Shiro the Tanuki nodded thoughtfully. From that day on, he decided to use his shape-shifting abilities for good.

How Tanuki Learned to Be Helpful

After his encounter with Jiro, Shiro the Tanuki wanted to make up for his past pranks. He began thinking of ways to use his magic to help people instead of tricking them.

One day, Shiro came across a group of villagers trying to build a bridge over a river. The work was hard, and the people were tired. "If only we had more hands to help," one villager sighed.

That's when Shiro had an idea. He transformed into a strong young man and joined the workers, carrying heavy stones and planks. "Wow! Where did this helpful stranger come from?" the villagers wondered. Thanks to Shiro's help, the bridge was finished in no time!

When the villagers turned to thank him, Shiro transformed back into his Tanuki form and gave a playful bow. "Surprise! It was me all along!" he said with a grin.

The villagers laughed and clapped. "Thank you, Tanuki! You're not just a trickster—you're a true friend."

More Helpful Adventures of the Tanuki

As Shiro continued to explore the world, he found many ways to spread joy and kindness.

Helping the Lost Traveler

One night, Shiro found a traveler who had lost his way in the forest. Instead of playing a trick, Shiro transformed into a glowing lantern and guided the traveler safely back to the village.

Cheering Up the Lonely Child

When Shiro noticed a little girl sitting sadly by herself, he decided to cheer her up. He transformed into a beautiful butterfly and fluttered around her, making her giggle with delight.

A Feast for the Animals

During a cold winter, Shiro saw the forest animals struggling to find food. He transformed into a big tree full of juicy fruits, giving the animals a place to eat and take shelter from the snow.

Through these adventures, Shiro realized that kindness was even more magical than any prank. He still loved to play tricks, but now they were the kind that made others grateful and joyful.

What We Can Learn from the Tanuki's Story

The story of the Tanuki teaches us that fun and kindness go hand in hand. Here are some important lessons we can learn from Shiro's adventures.

Think about Others

It's okay to have fun, but we should always think about how our actions affect the people around us.

Kindness Brings Joy

Just like Shiro found happiness by helping others, being kind makes the world a better place for everyone.

Use Your Talents for Good

The Tanuki had the power to shape-shift, and once he used that power to help others, he became a true friend to everyone he met.

Though Tanuki love to play pranks, their stories remind us that life is better when we share joy and kindness. Whether you're playing a game, telling a joke, or helping a friend, remember that the best kind of magic is the kind that makes people smile.

And who knows? The next time you see something strange—a teapot with feet, a tree stump that wasn't there before, or a glowing lantern in the forest—it might just be a playful Tanuki on another adventure!

CHAPTER 7:
THE RABBIT ON THE MOON
-A STORY OF SELFLESSNESS

A long, long time ago, when the world was young and the skies sparkled with stars, animals lived together in peace. Among these animals was a kind rabbit who always tried to help others. The rabbit had soft white fur, big ears, and bright eyes. All the animals admired him because he was always willing to share what little he had, even when times were tough.

One cool autumn night, the rabbit sat under the glowing full moon with his friends—a monkey and a fox. As the breeze rustled the leaves, the three friends talked about how they could do good in the world.

"It's important to help those in need," the rabbit said thoughtfully. "Even if it means we have to give up something for ourselves."

A Visitor in Disguise

As they were talking, a strange old man appeared from the forest. His clothes were tattered, and he looked very tired and hungry. "Oh, kind animals," the old man said, leaning on a stick. "I have been traveling for days, and I am terribly hungry. Could you spare me something to eat?"

The rabbit, the monkey, and the fox looked at each other. They all felt sorry for the poor old man. But they didn't know that this wasn't just any ordinary traveler—he was actually a god in disguise, testing the animals to see how kind and generous they were.

"I will find some food for you," the monkey said. He scampered up the nearest tree and gathered a bunch of juicy fruits. He proudly offered them to the old man.

"I'll help too," said the fox, darting into the bushes. He returned with a fish he had caught from the river and laid it at the old man's feet.

Now, it was the rabbit's turn. But the rabbit was troubled—unlike the monkey and the fox, he couldn't climb trees or catch fish. All he could do was gather grass, which didn't seem like much of a gift.

The rabbit thought hard. "How can I help this poor traveler if I have nothing to give?" he wondered. With a heavy heart, he made a brave decision.

The Rabbit's Selfless Act

The rabbit hopped over to the old man and said, "I'm sorry I don't have any food to offer you. But if you are very hungry, you can take me. I will offer myself so you won't go hungry."

The monkey and the fox gasped. "No, rabbit, you can't!" they cried. "There must be another way!"

But the rabbit smiled gently. "It's okay," he said. "I'd rather help someone in need, even if it means giving up everything."

With that, the rabbit gathered sticks and made a small fire. He looked at the old man one last time and said, "Please eat and feel better." Then, the rabbit jumped into the flames without hesitation.

The God Reveals Himself

The moment the rabbit jumped into the fire, the old man's disguise vanished in a flash of light. He was no longer a frail traveler—he was a god, shining brilliant light and showing mighty power! With a wave of his hand, the flames disappeared. The rabbit stood safely on the ground, completely unharmed.

"You are truly kind and selfless," the god said, his voice full of admiration. "You were willing to give up everything for someone you thought was in need. Such generosity deserves to be remembered forever."

The rabbit looked at the god in surprise. "But I didn't do anything special," he said.

"Oh, but you did," the god replied with a warm smile. "Your kindness is more powerful than any treasure."

To reward the rabbit's selflessness, the god gave him a very special place in the sky. "From now on," the god said, "you will live on the moon as a shining reminder of kindness and generosity. Anyone who looks up at the moon will see your shape and remember your story."

With a flick of his hand, the god lifted the rabbit high into the sky. The stars twinkled as the rabbit floated higher and higher until he landed softly on the glowing surface of the moon.

And so, the rabbit became the Rabbit on the Moon. If you look up at the full moon on a clear night, you can still see the silhouette of the rabbit. His ears, nose, and paws are visible in the moon's soft light, reminding everyone of his kindness and selflessness.

The rabbit didn't mind living on the moon. From there, he could watch over all the animals and people on Earth. And every time he saw someone helping others or showing kindness, he smiled, knowing that his story had inspired them.

A Story to Remember

The story of the Rabbit on the Moon teaches us that true kindness comes from the heart. Here are some important lessons we can learn from the rabbit's adventure.

Kindness is Powerful

The rabbit had nothing to give but himself, yet his selflessness touched the heart of a god. This reminds us that even small acts of kindness can make a big difference.

Generosity Means Giving without Expecting Anything in Return

The rabbit didn't expect a reward—he just wanted to help someone in need. True generosity is about giving simply because it's the right thing to do.

Our Actions Live On

The rabbit's story is remembered every time someone looks at the moon. This shows us that good deeds have a way of lasting forever, even after we're gone.

Look Up at the Moon

The next time you see the full moon shining in the night sky, take a moment to search for the rabbit's shape. Imagine him sitting quietly on the moon, watching over the world with a kind heart. And remember, just like the rabbit, you have the power to make the world a better place with kindness and generosity.

And who knows? Maybe the rabbit is smiling at you right now, proud of all the good things you do.

Let's continue on our journey through Japanese legends! There are still many more stories filled with magic, adventure, and wisdom waiting to be told. Are you ready for the next one? Let's go!

CHAPTER 8: HACHIKO - THE LOYAL DOG

A long time ago, in the bustling streets of Tokyo, Japan, there lived a special dog named Hachiko. Hachiko wasn't just any dog—he was an Akita, a breed known for its loyalty and bravery. What made Hachiko truly famous wasn't just his fluffy fur or friendly bark—it was his heart full of love and loyalty. This is the story of how Hachiko became a symbol of faithfulness that is still remembered and celebrated to this day.

Hachiko and His Beloved Owner

When Hachiko was just a little puppy, he was adopted by a kind man named Professor Ueno, who lived in the heart of Tokyo. From the very first day they met, Hachiko and Professor Ueno became the best of friends. Hachiko loved following the professor around the house, wagging his tail happily. And the professor treated Hachiko with great care, always making sure his furry friend was well-fed and loved.

Every morning, the professor took a train from Shibuya Station to his job at the university. And every morning, Hachiko would happily trot beside his owner to the station. When the professor got on the train, Hachiko would sit quietly at the station entrance, watching the train pull away.

But here's what made Hachiko so special—every afternoon, when the professor's train returned, Hachiko would be waiting right there at the station entrance, wagging his tail with excitement. As soon as the professor stepped off the train, Hachiko would greet him with a joyful bark, and together they would walk home.

Day after day, Hachiko waited faithfully at the station for his beloved owner. Rain or shine, no matter how cold or hot the weather, Hachiko was always there, patiently waiting for the professor to come back. The station workers and neighborhood people grew fond of Hachiko, calling him the "loyal dog of Shibuya."

A Sad Day at the Train Station

One afternoon, something tragic happened. Professor Ueno went to work as usual but he didn't come back. That day, the professor fell ill while at the university and passed away. Hachiko waited at the station entrance, just like always, his eyes watching every train that arrived. But the professor didn't step off any of them.

The people at the station tried to explain to Hachiko that the professor wasn't coming back but Hachiko didn't understand. He continued to wait, his tail still wagging in hope every time a train arrived. Day after day, Hachiko returned to the station, waiting for the professor to come home.

Even though the professor's family moved away and no one came to pick up Hachiko, the loyal dog never stopped waiting. The station workers and neighbors were so touched by Hachiko's loyalty that they began to care for him. They fed him, petted him, and made sure he was safe and warm during the cold winter months. No matter how much time passed, Hachiko never gave up hope.

The Years Go By

For ten long years, Hachiko came to Shibuya Station every single day, waiting patiently for the professor. The people of Tokyo admired his loyalty, and many of them would stop to say hello or leave treats for him. Even the train conductors and station staff knew Hachiko well and looked forward to seeing him each day.

Over time, Hachiko became a symbol of loyalty and love. His story began to spread throughout Japan, and people from all over the country visited Shibuya Station just to meet the faithful dog. Children would point excitedly and say, "Look! That's Hachiko, the dog who waits!"

Though Hachiko grew older and slower, he never missed a day at the station. He sat in his usual spot, his soft brown eyes watching every train, hoping to see his beloved owner again.

Hachiko's Legacy

One peaceful day, Hachiko lay down in his favorite spot at the station and quietly passed away, still waiting for the professor. When the people of Tokyo learned that Hachiko had passed, they felt a deep sadness, but they also felt grateful for the beautiful lesson he had left behind: true loyalty never fades, even when times are hard.

To honor Hachiko's memory, the people of Tokyo decided to build a statue of him at Shibuya Station, right where he used to wait. The statue shows Hachiko sitting proudly, just as he did every day while waiting for his friend. The Hachiko statue quickly became a beloved landmark, and people from all over the world visit it to remember the faithful dog who never gave up hope.

Even today, you can visit the Hachiko statue in Tokyo, where people gather to take pictures, leave flowers, and tell stories about his loyalty. Some visitors bring their own dogs to see Hachiko's statue, and others stop for a moment of silence, remembering the love and dedication of a very special dog.

What We Can Learn from Hachiko's Story

Hachiko's story teaches us some important lessons about love, loyalty, and friendship.

True Loyalty Never Fades

Hachiko kept waiting for his owner, even though he didn't understand what had happened. His story reminds us to stay loyal to the people we care about, no matter how hard things get.

Kindness Inspires Kindness

The people of Tokyo took care of Hachiko because they admired his loyalty. When we are kind and faithful, we inspire others to be kind in return.

Memories Keep Love Alive

Even though the professor was gone, Hachiko's love for him lived on. This reminds us that the people we love stay in our hearts, even if they are no longer with us.

Hachiko's Statue Today

Today, the statue of Hachiko stands proudly outside Shibuya Station, welcoming visitors from all over the world. This memorial is a symbol of love and loyalty. People still gather there to take pictures, meet friends, and tell Hachiko's story.

If you ever visit Tokyo, be sure to stop by the Hachiko statue. You might even spot a few dogs sitting beside the statue as if keeping Hachiko company. And as you stand there, think about the story of a dog who waited every day, rain or shine, just to see the person he loved.

The next time you see a dog wagging its tail or sitting patiently by the door, remember Hachiko— the loyal dog who taught the world the true meaning of friendship and devotion.

CHAPTER 9:
TENGU - THE MYSTERIOUS MOUNTAIN GOBLINS

High in the misty mountains of Japan, hidden among ancient trees and rocky paths, live the Tengu—mysterious creatures that are part bird and part human. The Tengu are known for their bright red faces, long noses, and feathered wings that allow them to fly silently through the forest. Some Tengu look more like humans, while others have beaks and feathers like birds of prey.

The Tengu are magical beings whose moods can change as fast as the wind. Sometimes, they like to play tricks on travelers; other times, they teach wisdom and valuable lessons to those who are lost. Whether you meet a helpful Tengu or a mischievous one depends on your behavior. If you are respectful and kind, the Tengu might teach you something important. But if you're greedy or rude, you'd better watch out—because the Tengu are not afraid to teach you a lesson you won't forget!

Tengu's Mischief in the Mountains

The forests and mountains of Japan are home to many mysteries, and the Tengu love to use their magic to cause a little chaos.

Disguising Themselves as Monks

One of the Tengu's favorite tricks is to disguise themselves as traveling monks or wandering priests. They stop travelers on the road and ask tricky questions. If the traveler gives a clever answer, the Tengu will leave them alone. But if the traveler stumbles or acts rudely, the Tengu will lead them in circles through the forest until they become hopelessly lost!

Switching Paths and Moving Stones

Tengu are known to change the shape of paths in the mountains, making travelers think they are on the right track, only to find themselves back where they started. They also like to move stones and leave strange signs to confuse people. If a traveler panics, the Tengu will laugh, their voices echoing through the trees like the sound of birds.

Borrowing Hats and Umbrellas

Tengu loves collecting unusual items from humans—especially hats and umbrellas! If you leave your things unattended in the forest, don't be surprised if they disappear! The Tengu might borrow them for a while, just to see if you can make it home without them.

But don't worry—most of the time, the Tengu's tricks are meant to test your patience and cleverness. If you keep your cool, you might even earn the Tengu's respect!

Learning Wisdom from the Tengu

While the Tengu enjoy playing tricks, they also have a lot of wisdom to share. Many legends tell of Tengu teaching special skills to monks and warriors who come to the mountains to learn. The Tengu respect those who seek knowledge and are willing to work hard to improve themselves.

One famous story is about a young monk named Yamato, who climbed the mountains to meditate and improve his martial arts. Yamato had heard rumors that the Tengu knew secret techniques that could make him stronger, so he decided to search for them.

After days of climbing steep paths and sleeping under the stars, Yamato finally reached a mysterious forest at the top of the mountain. There, he found a Tengu waiting for him, standing silently beneath a tall pine tree with wings folded neatly behind its back.

The Tengu's Challenge

"You seek wisdom?" the Tengu asked, its voice deep and echoing like the wind in the trees.

"Yes," Yamato replied, bowing respectfully. "Please teach me how to be strong."

The Tengu tilted its head and gave Yamato a sharp look. "Strength is not just about muscles," the Tengu said. "It comes from the mind and the heart as well. If you truly wish to learn, you must prove yourself."

The Tengu gave Yamato three challenges:

> Climb to the top of the tallest tree without fear.
> Meditate under a freezing waterfall without moving.
> Solve a riddle that only the wise can answer.

Yamato nodded. "I will do my best."

The Three Challenges

The first challenge was difficult, but Yamato climbed the tallest tree in the forest. Though the branches swayed in the wind, he stayed calm and reached the top. The Tengu watched from below, its sharp eyes gleaming with approval.

Next, Yamato found the freezing waterfall. The icy water roared over the rocks, but he sat beneath it, still and silent, as the cold water poured over him. Though the cold stung his skin, Yamato did not move. The Tengu watched quietly, impressed by the young monk's determination.

Finally, Yamato was ready to hear the riddle. The Tengu stood before Yamato, folded its wings, and asked: "What is something that grows when you give it away but shrinks when you keep it?"

Yamato thought hard. He sat beneath a tree, watching the wind rustle the leaves. Then, smiling, he said, "The answer is kindness. When you give kindness to others, it grows. But if you keep it to yourself, it fades away."

The Tengu nodded, satisfied. "You have learned well," it said. "You are ready."

A Gift from the Tengu

Because Yamato had passed the three challenges, the Tengu shared with him a secret martial arts technique, one that would make him not only strong in body but also wise in spirit. "Remember," the Tengu said, "true strength comes from the balance of mind, body, and heart. Use your skills to help others, not just yourself."

With that, the Tengu spread its wings and soared into the sky, disappearing into the mist. Yamato bowed deeply, grateful for the wisdom he had received. He returned to his temple and became a great teacher, passing down the Tengu's lessons to future generations.

The Lesson of the Tengu's Stories

The Tengu may be tricky and mischievous, but their stories teach us some important lessons.

Stay Calm and Think Clearly

The Tengu's tricks test your patience. If you stay calm, you can figure out even the trickiest situations.

Respect Others, Even When They Seem Strange

The Tengu might look frightening, but they can be wise teachers if treated with respect.

True Strength Comes from Within

As Yamato learned, being strong isn't just about muscles—it's about having a sharp mind and a kind heart.

Even today, people in Japan tell stories about the Tengu, and they remain mysterious figures in folklore. Some say the Tengu live in ancient forests, watching over travelers and testing those who climb too high into the mountains. Others believe the Tengu appear only to those with pure intentions, ready to teach important lessons to those who seek wisdom.

You might even see statues of the Tengu at certain temples in Japan. These statues show Tengu with long noses and wings, standing proudly as protectors of the mountains. Some people leave offerings, like rice or flowers, at the statues—just in case the Tengu are watching!

What Can We Learn from the Tengu?

The stories of the Tengu remind us that life is full of tests and challenges, but each one is a chance to grow wiser and stronger.

- When faced with challenges, stay calm and use your mind to solve problems.
- Treat others with respect, no matter how different they seem.
- Remember that true strength comes from having a kind heart and a clear mind.

The next time you walk through a forest or hike up a mountain, keep an eye out—you never know when a Tengu might be watching! And if you do meet one, remember to stay respectful. Who knows? You might just learn something magical.

CHAPTER 10: THE CRANE WIFE - A TALE OF LOVE AND SACRIFICE

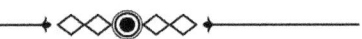

A long time ago, in a quiet village surrounded by snowy mountains, there lived a kind and humble man named Taro. He had no family of his own, but he lived a simple, happy life, chopping firewood and taking care of the forest animals. One cold winter day, Taro went out into the forest to gather wood when he spotted something unusual—a beautiful white crane tangled in a hunter's trap.

The poor crane struggled to free herself, her wings flapping desperately, but the trap only tightened around her slender leg. Taro's heart ached for the poor creature. "Don't worry, little one," he said gently. "I'll set you free."

Taro carefully untangled the crane's leg and patted her softly on the head. "Fly away now," he whispered, "before the hunters return." The crane flapped her wings and soared into the sky, her white feathers gleaming like fresh snow. Taro smiled, happy that he could help. Little did he know that this kind act would change his life forever.

A Mysterious Visitor

That night, just as Taro was settling in by the fire, he heard a knock at his door. "Who could that be on such a cold night?" he wondered. When he opened the door, he found a young woman standing outside. She wore a simple white robe, her long black hair flowing over her shoulders, and her smile was warm despite the cold air.

"I've lost my way," the woman said softly. "May I stay here for the night?"

Taro welcomed the woman into his small home, offering her a warm blanket and a bowl of rice. As they sat by the fire, the two talked and laughed, and Taro found that her voice was as gentle as the winter breeze.

One night turned into many, and soon, the two became close friends. It wasn't long before Taro and the woman decided to get married, and Taro's lonely home became a place filled with love and happiness.

The Magical Cloth

One evening, Taro's new wife had a surprise for him. "I wish to help support our home income," she said. "I will weave a special cloth that will bring us fortune."

She led Taro to a small room in the back of the house. "I must weave in private," she told him. "Promise me you will never look inside while I work."

Taro agreed, curious but respectful. Day after day, his wife stayed in the room, weaving from morning until night. When she finally emerged, she held a cloth so beautiful that it looked like moonlight woven into silk. The cloth shimmered with patterns of feathers that seemed to move in the light.

Taro took the cloth to the village market, where merchants were amazed by its beauty. "I've never seen anything like this!" they cried, offering bags of gold for the magical fabric.

Taro was overjoyed. With the money, he and his wife were able to buy everything they needed—food, firewood, and warm clothes for the winter. Despite their new wealth, Taro's wife continued to weave. Each time she brought out another piece of cloth, it was even more beautiful than the last.

Curiosity and a Broken Promise

At first, Taro was content with their happy life, but over time, curiosity began to gnaw at him. "How does she create such magical cloth?" he wondered. "And why must she weave in secret?"

One snowy evening, while his wife was busy weaving in the back room, Taro couldn't resist any longer. He tiptoed to the door and peeked inside. What he saw made him gasp in surprise.

Instead of a woman sitting at the loom, there was the white crane he had rescued! Her wings moved gracefully as she pulled feathers from her own body and wove them into the shimmering cloth. Every feather was a part of her, and the cloth she made was woven with her love and sacrifice.

At that moment, the crane turned her head and saw Taro at the door. Her eyes were filled with sadness. "You have seen my true form," she whispered. "Now I can no longer stay with you."

A Bittersweet Farewell

Taro's heart broke. "Please don't leave," he begged. "I love you, whether you are a woman or a crane. Stay with me!"

The crane smiled sadly. "I wanted to stay with you forever," she said. "But I can no longer weave the magical cloth, and I must return to the sky, where I belong."

Taro tried to hold her hand, but before he could, the crane transformed back into her bird form. With a final, loving glance, the crane spread her wings and flew out the window, soaring high into the night sky.

Taro stood at the window, watching the crane disappear into the clouds, his heart heavy with sorrow. Though he knew he could never see her again, he whispered a quiet "thank you" toward the sky, grateful for the love she had shared with him.

The Lesson of the Crane Wife's Story

The story of the Crane Wife teaches us about love, sacrifice, and trust. Here are some important lessons we can learn from Taro's adventure.

Respect the Promises You Make

Taro broke his promise by looking into the weaving room, costing him the person he loved. This reminds us that keeping our promises is important, especially to those we care about.

True Love Requires Sacrifice

The crane gave up parts of herself to create the magical cloth, showing us that love often means giving without expecting anything in return.

Appreciate What You Have

Taro had a wonderful life with his wife, but his curiosity caused him to lose her. This story teaches us to cherish the moments and people in our lives instead of always seeking more.

A Love that Lives in the Wind

Though the crane was gone, Taro never forgot her. On quiet nights, when the wind whispered through the trees, he liked to imagine it was the sound of the crane's wings brushing against the sky, carrying her love across the mountains.

Even today, people tell the story of the Crane Wife as a reminder that love is about trust and kindness and that sometimes, the greatest gifts come from the heart.

The story of the Crane Wife reminds us that even the smallest acts of kindness can create magic in our lives. Just as Taro saved the crane from the hunter's trap, we can all make a difference by helping those in need. And just like the crane's love, the kindness we give to others will stay with them, even if we must part ways.

Next time you hear the wind rustling through the trees, think of the Crane Wife and her sacrifice. And remember, love is strongest when it's built on trust, kindness, and the joy of giving.

Are you ready for the next adventure? There are still many more magical stories waiting to be discovered. Let's continue exploring the enchanting world of Japanese legends!

CHAPTER 11: KITSUNE - THE FOX SPIRITS OF JAPAN

Deep in the forests and fields of Japan, where the moonlight dances on streams and winds whisper through the trees, live the Kitsune—magical fox spirits. Kitsune are no ordinary foxes. They are shape-shifters with the ability to transform into anything they desire—sometimes even people!

The word *Kitsune* (pronounced kit-SOO-nay) means fox, but these creatures are much more than just animals. Some Kitsune are known for their playful tricks, while others perform acts of great kindness and wisdom. Whether a Kitsune chooses to help or cause mischief depends on how they feel—and how they are treated by humans.

Let's dive into the mysterious world of Kitsune and discover their clever tricks and magical adventures!

Kitsune: The Clever Shape-Shifters

In Japanese legends, Kitsune grow smarter and more powerful as they get older. Young Kitsune start with just one tail, but the oldest and wisest Kitsune have nine tails, each tail glowing with magic. As Kitsune grows, they become so wise and powerful that they can change shape with ease—transforming into anything from a teapot to a beautiful princess!

One of the Kitsune's favorite forms is that of a human woman. They love to disguise themselves and visit villages, sometimes for fun, sometimes to help someone in need, and other times just to see what it's like to be human. But no matter how well they hide, Kitsune often give themselves away with a tiny mistake—like forgetting to hide their fox tails or twitching their noses when excited!

A Story of a Kitsune in Disguise

One of the most famous stories about the Kitsune is the tale of Yuki, a beautiful woman who lived in a quiet village. Yuki was kind and gentle, and everyone loved her, especially a young farmer named Taro. The two fell in love and were soon married.

For years, Yuki and Taro lived happily together. Yuki was a wonderful wife, always caring for their home and helping Taro with his farm. But there was one thing strange about her—no matter how warm the weather got, Yuki always wore a thick scarf wrapped around her neck.

One summer afternoon, while Yuki was working in the garden, a playful breeze blew her scarf off—and to Taro's surprise, he saw a soft fox tail poking out from under her robe!

Yuki gasped and tried to hide her tail, but it was too late. "I didn't want you to know," she whispered sadly. "I am a Kitsune. I used my magic to become human so I could live with you."

Taro was shocked, but he still loved Yuki. "You've been kind and loving," he said. "It doesn't matter to me that you are a Kitsune. Please stay with me."

Yuki's eyes filled with joyful tears. And so, the Kitsune and the farmer continued to live happily together, their love as strong as ever—proving that kindness and love can overcome any difference.

Kitsune's Playful Tricks

Not all Kitsune are as gentle as Yuki! Many Kitsune love to play tricks on humans. They enjoy confusing travelers, borrowing people's belongings, and stirring up a little harmless trouble. Here are some of their favorite tricks.

Swapping Roads

A Kitsune might change the shape of a path in the forest, leading a traveler in circles. Just when the traveler feels lost, the Kitsune appears with a grin and points them in the right direction.

Borrowing Faces

Kitsune sometimes disguise themselves as someone familiar to play a friendly prank. Imagine seeing your best friend, only to realize it's a fox in disguise!

Stealing Lanterns

Kitsune love light and often borrow lanterns or candles from homes, leaving the owners scratching their heads about where they've gone. But don't worry—Kitsune always return what they take.

While their tricks can be frustrating, Kitsune don't mean any harm. They play pranks to make people laugh and remind them not to take life too seriously. But Kitsune are also fair—if someone treats them kindly, they will repay that kindness in unexpected ways.

A Kitsune's Act of Kindness

One cold winter's night, a traveler named Sora was walking through the forest. Snow covered the ground, and the wind howled through the trees. Sora shivered, wrapping his coat tightly around him. He had lost his way and feared he wouldn't reach the village before dark.

Just when Sora thought all hope was lost, a small fox appeared on the path. The fox's golden eyes sparkled as it nudged Sora's hand gently as if saying, "Follow me."

Sora, with no other choice, followed the fox through the forest. After a short walk, they reached a warm little cabin with a fire glowing inside. The fox trotted inside and, before Sora's eyes, transformed into a beautiful woman with soft red hair and a kind smile.

"Come inside," the Kitsune said warmly. "You can rest here until the storm passes."

Sora was amazed but grateful. He spent the night by the fire, and when morning came, the Kitsune gave him food for his journey. "Go safely, traveler," she said.

When Sora finally reached the village, he looked back toward the forest. Though the cabin was nowhere to be seen, he smiled, knowing he had been helped by a kind-hearted Kitsune.

Kitsune and the Balance of Mischief and Kindness

Kitsune remind us that life is full of surprises and lessons. Sometimes, they play pranks to teach people not to take things too seriously, while other times they show great kindness to those in need.

The stories of Kitsune teach us lessons like these.

Don't Judge by Appearances

Just like the farmer who loved Yuki, we learn that what's on the inside matters most.

Kindness Goes a Long Way

Treating others well—even mischievous fox spirits—can bring unexpected rewards.

Life Should Be Enjoyed with a Little Fun

The Kitsune's playful tricks remind us to laugh and enjoy life's surprises.

The Kitsune's Legacy Today

Even today, Kitsune are celebrated in Japan. Statues of foxes can be found at many shrines, especially those dedicated to Inari, the god of rice and prosperity. People leave offerings of rice, candles, and fox-shaped charms at these shrines, hoping to receive the Kitsune's blessings.

Some believe that the Kitsune still wander the forests and fields, watching over travelers and playing tricks on those who forget to laugh. If you ever feel a breeze tickling your neck or hear a strange sound in the forest, it just might be a Kitsune nearby, having a little fun!

The next time you hear a strange rustle in the bushes or see a fox dart across a path, think about the Kitsune. Is it a fox simply running by? Or could it be a tricky spirit in disguise, watching to see if you can keep up with its clever tricks?

If you ever find yourself lost in a forest, don't worry—maybe, just maybe, a Kitsune will guide you home. But be prepared! You never know if the fox will leave you with a laugh or a lesson.

CHAPTER 12: THE BATTLE OF THE KAPPA -THE MISCHIEVOUS RIVER SPIRITS

Down by the rivers of Japan, hidden beneath the cool waters, live strange and playful creatures called Kappa. These water-dwelling spirits have bodies like frogs or turtles, webbed hands and feet for swimming, and beaked faces that make them look both curious and mischievous. But their most unusual feature is the dish on the top of their heads, which holds water from their home rivers. As long as their dish stays full, the Kappa are strong and powerful—but if the water spills out, the Kappa becomes weak and helpless.

Kappa are known to be both mischievous and tricky. They love playing pranks on people, especially those who wander too close to the water's edge. Some Kappa tricks are harmless and silly, but others can cause real trouble. Yet, just as these river spirits can be sneaky, they can also be outsmarted—sometimes with a bit of kindness, and other times by making them bow in respect!

Kappa's Tricks and Trouble

Kappa love to spend their days causing mischief. If you've ever lost a shoe by a river or fallen into the water unexpectedly, it just might have been the work of a Kappa!

Here are some of their favorite tricks.

Stealing Vegetables

Kappa are especially fond of cucumbers. They sneak into gardens to steal these refreshing vegetables, leaving behind muddy footprints and a trail of wet leaves. Some families write their names on cucumbers and toss them into the river, hoping to keep the Kappa satisfied and away from their crops.

Tugging People into the Water

Kappa like to hide just below the river's surface and grab the legs of people who wade too close. With a splash and a giggle, the Kappa pulls the person into the water, laughing as the captive struggles to return to shore.

Switching Fish Baskets

Fishermen who leave their baskets on the riverbank often return to that their fish have been replaced with slimy river weeds! The Kappa loves to confuse people and play pranks like these.

While most of these tricks are playful, some Kappa enjoy challenges—and they dare people to wrestle with them by the river. But if a person isn't careful, the Kappa might try to drag them underwater! Fortunately, there are clever ways to defeat a Kappa without needing to wrestle at all.

How to Outsmart a Kappa

Even though Kappa are tricky, they have one major weakness: they are obsessed with politeness and respect. If you ever meet a Kappa, here are a few ways to outsmart them.

Make the Kappa Bow

Kappa are known for their love of manners. If you bow to a Kappa, it will feel obligated to bow back. But when the Kappa bows, its dishwater will spill—and without the water, the Kappa loses all its strength! The Kappa will be too weak to cause any more trouble, giving you time to escape.

Defeat Them with Kindness

Kappa are not all bad. If someone treats them kindly, the Kappa may become a friend instead of a foe. One story tells of a boy named Hiroshi who met a Kappa by the river. Instead of running away or playing tricks, Hiroshi offered the Kappa a cucumber.

The Kappa was so touched by the boy's kindness that it decided to help him. From that day on, whenever Hiroshi needed water for his fields, the Kappa would fill buckets from the river and bring them to his farm. The two became good friends, showing that even mischievous spirits can become kind when treated with respect.

The Battle of the Kappa

One of the most famous stories about Kappa is called The Battle of the Kappa. In a small village by the river, the Kappa had become too mischievous, playing pranks day and night. They stole cucumbers from gardens, frightened children, and splashed anyone who tried to cross the bridge. The villagers were tired of the tricks and decided that something had to be done.

The strongest man in the village, named Jiro, stepped forward. "I will go down to the river and challenge the Kappa to a wrestling match," he declared. "If I win, the Kappa must leave the village in peace!"

The villagers cheered, but many were worried. "Be careful, Jiro," they warned. "The Kappa are very strong."

Jiro nodded and marched to the riverbank, where the Kappa were playing in the water. "I challenge you to a wrestling match!" Jiro shouted. The Kappa, excited by the challenge, agreed at once.

The Clever Plan

Jiro knew he would need more than strength to defeat the Kappa—he needed a clever plan. Before the match began, he bowed politely to the Kappa.

Being a creature of manners, the Kappa felt that it had to bow back. As soon as it did, the water from the dish on its head spilled out, and the Kappa wobbled and fell to the ground, too weak to stand!

The other Kappa watched in amazement. "You have defeated us fairly," they said. "From now on, we promise to leave the village in peace."

The villagers cheered as the Kappa, now respectful and humbled, returned to the river. Jiro had saved the village—not with brute strength, but with cleverness and respect.

The Kindness Pact

After the wrestling match, the villagers made a pact with the Kappa. Every year during the summer festival, they would throw cucumbers into the river as a gift to the Kappa. In return, the Kappa promised to stay friendly and helpful, using their magic to keep the river clean and protect the fish from harm.

From that day forward, the Kappa became protectors of the river, and the villagers lived in peace, knowing that they could rely on the Kappa's help whenever they needed it.

What We Can Learn from the Kappa

The stories of the Kappa teach us that even mischievous creatures can become friends when treated with kindness and respect. Here are some lessons we can learn from the Kappa's adventures.

Politeness Is Powerful

Just like Jiro outsmarted the Kappa by making it bow, politeness can sometimes solve problems better than force.

Kindness Can Change Hearts

The boy Hiroshi showed kindness to the Kappa, and in return, the Kappa became his friend. A little kindness can go a long way.

Trickiness Isn't Always Bad

While the Kappa love to play pranks, they also remind us that life can be fun when we don't take things too seriously.

Meeting the Kappa Today

Even today, people in Japan tell stories about the Kappa. Statues of Kappa can be found near rivers and ponds, and some people still offer cucumbers to keep the Kappa happy. Children are warned not to play too close to the water, just in case a playful Kappa is lurking nearby, waiting to tug at their toes!

If you ever meet a Kappa, remember this: treat it with respect, and you might make a magical friend. And if a Kappa challenges you to a match, don't forget to bow first—you just might win the battle with a little cleverness and a lot of politeness.

Next time you're near a river, keep an eye out for ripples and bubbles—who knows? A playful Kappa might be watching from the water, ready to offer you a splash and a smile.

CHAPTER 13: RAIJIN AND FUJIN -THE GODS OF THUNDER AND WIND

In the skies high above Japan, where clouds swirl, and the winds howl, live two powerful gods who control the weather. Their names are Raijin and Fujin.

Raijin (pronounced (rye-GEEN), is the God of Thunder, with a wild mane of hair and a fierce face. He carries drums wherever he goes, and each time he strikes them, thunder rumbles across the sky. His eyes flash like lightning, and his laughter sounds like the crack of a storm.

Fujin, the God of Wind, is Raijin's friend—and sometimes his rival. Fujin (pronounced foo-GEEN) is a giant with a sack full of wind slung over his shoulder. When he opens the sack, the wind roars out, scattering leaves and rattling windows. Together, Raijin and Fujin bring storms to the world, but they are also guardians of the heavens, protecting the earth from harm.

JAPANESE LEGENDS FOR KIDS

Raijin and Fujin: A Stormy Friendship

Though Raijin and Fujin are brothers, they have very different personalities. Raijin is loud and energetic, always ready for a thunderous adventure. Fujin, on the other hand, is a bit more laid-back, preferring to watch the clouds drift by as the wind whispers through the trees. When these two gods come together, the skies explode with storms!

The brothers are known to argue from time to time. Raijin loves to make big, noisy thunderstorms, but Fujin sometimes thinks his brother is too wild. "Calm down, Raijin," Fujin says as the wind blows gently. "Not every day needs to be a thunderstorm!"

Raijin just laughs. "Where's the fun in that?" he booms, beating his drum and sending thunder rumbling across the sky.

Despite their differences, Raijin and Fujin are also a great team. When they work together, they can move storms across the world, sending rain to dry fields and clearing the skies for sunshine. Let's dive into some of their most exciting adventures!

The Storm over the Village

One summer day, the people of a small village were desperate for rain. The fields were dry, the rivers were low, and the crops were wilting in the sun. The villagers prayed to Raijin and Fujin for help, hoping the storm gods would send rain to save their crops.

Raijin heard the prayers first. "A storm? I can do that!" he said with a grin. He climbed into the sky, beat his thunder drums, and filled the clouds with lightning and thunder. Soon, dark clouds gathered over the village, and the air buzzed with electricity.

But Fujin, sitting on a mountaintop nearby, shook his head. "This is too much, brother," he called. "If you keep this up, the storm will scare the people!"

Raijin rolled his eyes. "A storm isn't fun without a little thunder!" he said. But Fujin opened his sack of wind just enough to calm the skies. The wind blew gently, spreading the storm clouds evenly across the sky.

Together, Raijin and Fujin brought just the right amount of rain. The fields were saved, and the villagers danced with joy. "Thank you, Raijin and Fujin!" they cheered.

Raijin and Fujin Battle a Sea Monster

Though Raijin and Fujin sometimes cause trouble, they are also heroes. One of their most famous adventures is the battle against a sea monster that threatened the land.

One day, a massive sea monster rose from the ocean. Its body was covered in scales; it was so big that it blocked out the sun. The monster sent waves crashing onto the shore, destroying villages and terrifying the people.

The storm gods knew they had to stop the beast. Raijin leaped into the sky, pounding his drums to summon a mighty storm. Thunder roared, and lightning flashed across the ocean.

Meanwhile, Fujin opened his sack and sent powerful winds to push the monster back into the sea. The storm and wind worked together, creating mountainous waves that surrounded the monster.

The battle raged for hours. The sea monster fought back, but the storm gods were too strong. Finally, with a great roar, the monster sank beneath the waves, defeated by the thunder and wind.

The people cheered as the skies cleared. Raijin and Fujin had saved the land, and the sea monster was never seen again.

A Lesson in Teamwork

Though Raijin and Fujin sometimes argue and play tricks on each other, their adventures show us that working together makes them stronger. When they team up, they can bring rain to dry fields, defeat monsters, and protect the heavens from danger.

The story of Raijin and Fujin teaches us important lessons.

Teamwork Is Powerful

Raijin and Fujin are strongest when they work together, just like we are stronger when we help one another.

Balance Is Important

Raijin loves wild storms, but Fujin reminds him that too much chaos can cause trouble. Finding the right balance between fun and responsibility is important in life.

Every Talent Has Value

Raijin's thunder and Fujin's wind are different, but both are needed to make a storm. This reminds us that everyone has something unique to offer.

Raijin and Fujin Today

Even today, Raijin and Fujin are remembered in Japan. You might see their statues at temples, with Raijin holding his thunder drums and Fujin carrying his sack of wind. Some people leave small offerings at the statues, asking the gods to bring gentle rain or protect them from storms.

During thunderstorms, children sometimes imagine that Raijin is playing his drums in the clouds, and when the wind blows through the trees, they say that Fujin is racing through the sky. Though the storm gods may be mischievous, they are also beloved protectors of the world.

The next time you hear thunder rumbling or feel the wind tugging at your clothes, think of Raijin and Fujin. Are they having a friendly argument, or are they working together to bring rain to the fields?

If the storm feels too wild, remember that just like Raijin and Fujin, we all need a little balance in life. Even the wildest storms can bring good things, like fresh rain and cool breezes.

The adventures of Raijin and Fujin remind us that storms, like life, can be full of surprises. With a little teamwork and balance, we can face any challenge—whether it's a thunderstorm or a tricky problem.

Next time the sky rumbles with thunder, don't be afraid. Just imagine Raijin playing his drums and Fujin racing through the sky with his sack of wind. Who knows? Maybe they're working together to send a little magic your way!

CHAPTER 14: JIZO - THE PROTECTOR OF CHILDREN AND TRAVELERS

In the peaceful forests, quiet streets, and temple grounds of Japan, you might spot a small stone statue of a gentle figure wearing a red hat and a bib. This is Jizo, one of the most beloved figures in Japanese folklore and religion. Jizo (pronounced JEE-zoh) is known as the protector of children, travelers, and those in need. His face is kind and calm, and he is always ready to help anyone who is lost or afraid. Whether you are a child, a traveler on a journey, or just someone looking for comfort, Jizo will always be there to guide you.

Who Is Jizo?

Jizo, also called Ojizo-sama, is a *Bodhisattva*, which means he is someone who has chosen to stay in the world to help others, even though he could have gone to a peaceful place. His mission is to protect those in need—especially children and travelers.

When children feel scared, Jizo comforts them. When someone gets lost on a long journey, Jizo helps them find their way. Because of his kindness, people all over Japan love Jizo and often leave small offerings at his statues to thank him for his protection. Jizo is easy to recognize by his peaceful face and his bright red hats and bibs, which are gifts from families grateful for his care.

The Story of Jizo Helping Lost Children

One of the most famous stories about Jizo tells of how he helps children who find themselves far from home.

Long ago, in a small village, there was a little boy named Taro. One day, Taro wandered into the forest to pick flowers, but soon, he realized he had lost his way. The trees looked the same in every direction, and the sun began setting. Taro sat on a rock, hugging his knees, as tears began to fall down his cheeks.

Just then, Taro saw a small stone figure standing beneath a tree—a Jizo statue!

Even though it was made of stone, the statue seemed warm and friendly, as if it was smiling just for Taro.

"Don't be afraid," Taro whispered to himself, imagining that the Jizo was watching over him. Feeling a little braver, Taro curled up next to the statue and fell asleep under the stars.

When morning came, Taro woke up to find an old traveler standing nearby, smiling kindly. "You must be lost," the traveler said. "I saw the Jizo statue and knew someone might need help."

With the traveler's help, Taro found his way home. "Thank you, Jizo!" Taro whispered, \grateful to the stone figure who had kept him safe through the night. From that day on, whenever Taro passed by a Jizo statue, he would leave a small offering of flowers to thank him.

The Red Hats and Bibs of Jizo

If you ever visit Japan, you'll notice that many Jizo statues are dressed in red hats, bibs, and scarves. But why do people leave these special gifts? There's a beautiful reason behind it.

Long ago, a family lost their young daughter to an illness. They were heartbroken, but they found comfort in believing that Jizo would protect her spirit and guide her safely to a peaceful place. As a way of thanking the Jizo, the family made a tiny red hat and a bib and placed them on a Jizo statue.

Soon, other families started doing the same. They dressed the statues in red to honor Jizo's kindness and to keep his spirit warm, believing that Jizo helps both living children and the spirits of those who have passed away. Today, you can still see these red hats and bibs on Jizo statues across Japan. It's a way of showing love, gratitude, and trust in Jizo's protection.

The Story of Jizo Helping a Traveler

Jizo's kindness isn't just for children—he also watches over travelers who are far from home. Here is one such story about a farmer named Sora who set out on a long journey through the mountains.

Sora needed to reach the next village to sell his rice, but the weather took a turn for the worse. Rain poured down, and the wind howled through the trees. Soon, the path became muddy and slippery, and Sora wasn't sure if he could find his way through the storm.

Just when he thought all hope was lost, Sora saw a Jizo statue standing along the path. The statue's face looked calm and kind, even in the pouring rain. "I will rest here for a moment," Sora thought, sitting beside the statue.

As he rested, the rain eased, and the wind calmed. Sora felt a warm sense of comfort, as if Jizo's presence was giving him strength. With renewed energy, Sora stood up and continued along the path, eventually reaching the village safely.

When the storm had passed, Sora returned to the Jizo statue with a gift—a red scarf to keep Jizo warm during future storms. "Thank you, Jizo," Sora whispered. "I couldn't have made it without your guidance."

Why People Leave Offerings for Jizo

In Japan, it's common to see small offerings of flowers, rice, or stones placed by Jizo statues. These gifts are a way of saying thank you to Jizo for his protection and kindness. Here are a few reasons people leave these offerings.

- To thank Jizo for protecting their children.
- To honor loved ones who have passed away, believing that Jizo will guide their spirits to peace.
- To ask for protection on a journey, leaving an offering before traveling, and returning with another gift after safely coming home.

Some children also leave pebbles near Jizo statues, believing that Jizo will use them to build a bridge to help lost spirits find their way to a peaceful place. Whether leaving flowers, food, or a small stone, every offering left for Jizo is given with love and gratitude.

The Lesson of Jizo's Kindness

Jizo's stories teach us important lessons about kindness, compassion, and helping others.

Here are some things we can learn from Jizo.

Kindness Makes a Difference

Even small acts of kindness—like leaving a flower for Jizo—can brighten someone's day.

We Are Never Truly Alone

Just like Taro and Sora found comfort in Jizo's presence, we can find strength in believing that someone is always watching over us.

Helping Others Is Powerful

Jizo teaches us that we should try to help those in need, just as he helps lost children and travelers.

Jizo's Legacy Today

Today, you can find Jizo statues all across Japan, from busy cities to quiet forests. People of all ages still visit these statues, leaving gifts and saying prayers. Some families bring their children to place a small pebble or flower by Jizo's feet, teaching them about kindness and gratitude.

Even though Jizo is a stone statue, his message of love and protection is something everyone can carry in their hearts. Next time you see a Jizo statue—whether in Japan or in a picture—remember that Jizo is always watching over those in need, ready to lend a helping hand.

A Guardian for All

Whether you are a child on a walk, a traveler on a long journey, or someone just trying to find their way, Jizo will always be there. His calm face reminds us that even when life feels uncertain, we are never truly alone. With kindness and care, Jizo teaches us that helping others is the greatest gift of all.

Next time you see a statue of Jizo, consider leaving a small offering—a pebble, a flower, or even just a kind thought. And remember: Jizo's kindness lives in all of us, and we can share it with the world every day.

CHAPTER 15: THE SPIDER'S THREAD – A LESSON IN KINDNESS

Once upon a time, in a peaceful garden full of blooming flowers and gentle breezes, the Buddha was quietly strolling beside a pond. As he admired the beauty of the lotus flowers floating on the water, something caught his eye—a small spider weaving a delicate, silvery thread between two leaves. The spider worked carefully, its thin silk glistening in the sunlight.

The Buddha smiled. Even the smallest creatures, like the spider, had a place in the world. And sometimes, even a thread as thin as a spider's silk could hold great meaning. As he watched, the Buddha had an idea.

The Man Trapped in Hell

Far below the peaceful garden was a dark and frightening place known as Hell, where those who had lived selfishly were trapped. In this grim world, souls wandered in endless darkness, weighed down by their past mistakes.

Among these souls was a man named Kandata. In life, Kandata had been a thief, taking things that didn't belong to him and caring only about himself. Because of his selfish ways, Kandata found himself in Hell, wandering through the shadows, lost and hopeless.

But there was one good deed Kandata had done. Once, as he walked through a forest, he saw a small spider crawling across the ground. Instead of stepping on it, Kandata decided to let the little creature live. "It's only a spider," he thought. "There's no need to crush it." Though it was a small act, it was enough to catch the attention of the Buddha.

A Thread from the Heavens

As the Buddha thought of Kandata's one small act of kindness, he decided to give the man a chance. From the spider in his garden, the Buddha took a single, shimmering thread and gently lowered it down from the heavens, through the clouds, all the way into Hell.

Kandata was sitting by a dark, murky river when he noticed something bright glimmering above him. It was a silver thread, dangling just within reach!

"This is my chance!" Kandata exclaimed. He leaped to his feet and grabbed the thread with both hands. To his surprise, the thread felt strong, even though it was as thin as silk. Slowly, hand over hand, Kandata began to climb upward, leaving the dark world of Hell behind.

A Climb Full of Hope

As Kandata climbed, light from the heavens began to shine down on him. He could feel the warmth of the sun, and his heart filled with hope. "I'll escape this terrible place," he thought. "I'll be free!"

But just as he was climbing higher and higher, Kandata heard whispers and shuffling below him. He looked down and saw that other souls in Hell had noticed the thread too. They were grabbing onto the silk and climbing after him, hoping to escape just as he was.

Kandata's heart raced. "What if the thread isn't strong enough for all of us?" he thought. Fear and selfishness filled his mind. "If they all climb, the thread will break, and I'll fall back into Hell!"

Without thinking, Kandata shouted down at the other souls. "Let go! This thread is mine! I found it first!"

The Thread Breaks

The moment Kandata yelled in anger, the thread gave a sudden snap! It broke with a sharp twang, and Kandata and all the other souls tumbled back down into the darkness of Hell.

As Kandata fell, he realized his mistake. If only he had shared the thread, they might have all climbed to safety together. But his selfishness had cost him his one chance at freedom.

Far above, the Buddha sighed. He gently gathered the broken thread and returned it to the spider, who continued weaving without complaint.

The Lesson of the Spider's Thread

The story of Kandata and the spider's thread teaches us some important lessons.

Selfishness Hurts Us and Others

Kindness and sharing make us stronger. Kandata could have escaped if he had let the others climb with him. Instead, his selfishness caused the thread to break.

Invite Others into Opportunities

Opportunities are better when shared. Like Kandata's thread, life's blessings are more meaningful when we share them with others.

Little Kindness Makes Much Difference

A small act of kindness can make a big difference. Even though Kandata was a thief, his one small act of sparing the spider gave him a chance at redemption.

Kindness Is a Thread that Connects Us

Even though Kandata's story has a sad ending, it teaches us that every moment is an opportunity to be kind. Whether sharing a toy, helping a friend, or simply being patient with others, small acts of kindness are like threads that connect us and make life better for everyone.

When you feel tempted to keep something all to yourself, remember Kandata's story. Imagine how different things might have been if he had reached down and helped the other souls climb instead of pushing them away. Kindness grows stronger the more we share it, just like a spider's web becomes stronger with every thread.

This story also shows that even small actions can have big effects. Kandata probably didn't think much about sparing the spider's life, but that tiny moment of kindness gave him a chance to escape from Hell. In the same way, the kind things we do—even if they seem small—can mean a lot to someone else.

Next time you help a friend, say a kind word, or share what you have, know that you're weaving your own threads of kindness that make the world a better place.

What Will You Do with Your Thread?

Every day, we are given chances to choose kindness—just like Kandata had his chance. Will you share your thread with others? Or will you try to hold onto it all by yourself?

Remember, life is better when we help each other climb, whether we are reaching for a dream or just trying to get through a tough day. If we lift each other up, there's no limit to how high we can go.

Look for those little moments—like holding the door for someone or sharing a toy—and know that you are spinning threads of kindness that connect us all.

CHAPTER 16: YUKI-ONNA - THE MYSTERIOUS SNOW WOMAN

On cold winter nights, when the snow falls silently and the wind whispers through the trees, people say you can catch a glimpse of a beautiful yet mysterious figure: Yuki-onna, the Snow Woman. Yuki-onna (pronounced YOU-kee AH-nah) is a spirit of the snow, said to appear during fierce winter storms. Some say her beauty is like freshly fallen snow, with skin as pale as ice and long black hair that flows like the wind. But beware—Yuki-onna is as mysterious as the winter weather itself.

Sometimes, she shows kindness to lost travelers and guides them to safety. Other times, she is said to bring danger to those who are unkind or disrespectful. No one knows which Yuki-onna they will meet—the gentle protector or the fierce spirit of the storm.

A Cold Night and a Mysterious Woman

Once upon a time, two woodcutters, Minokichi and his older friend Mosaku, were returning home after a long day in the forest. The path was covered with thick snow, and the wind blew fiercely, stinging their faces. The two men knew they wouldn't reach home before nightfall, so they decided to stay in a small cabin they had found along the path.

The wind howled outside the cabin as the snow piled high. Tired from their journey, Minokichi and Mosaku lay down to sleep. But just after midnight, Minokichi (pronounced min-AH-ki-chee) woke up to a strange coldness in the air. He blinked and gasped—in the doorway stood a tall, pale woman, her dark hair flowing like shadows and her kimono as white as snow.

She glided silently toward them, her breath turning into icy mist. Minokichi was too frightened to move. The Snow Woman leaned over Mosaku, her icy breath covering him in a cold so deep that he never woke again. Then, she turned to Minokichi.

"Young one," she whispered, her voice soft but cold as a winter breeze. "I will spare your life, but only if you never tell anyone what you have seen tonight."

Minokichi nodded, trembling with fear. With a swirl of snow, the woman disappeared into the storm, leaving the cabin as silent as before.

A Chance Encounter Years Later

Minokichi never told anyone about that strange, cold night. Time passed, and he went on with his life. One day, while walking along a snowy path, he met a beautiful young woman named Yuki. She had skin as pale as snow and long black hair. Yuki and Minokichi became friends, and soon they fell in love. The two married and lived happily together, raising a family in their cozy little home.

Yuki was always kind and gentle, and she seemed to bring warmth to even the coldest winter days. She helped Minokichi with his work, cared for their children, and filled their home with joy. Yet, there was always a mysterious air about her, as if she carried a part of the winter in her heart.

The Secret Revealed

One cold winter night, as the snow fell softly outside, Minokichi and Yuki sat by the fire, talking about old times. Without thinking, Minokichi began to tell Yuki the story of the Snow Woman who had visited him and Mosaku years ago in the cabin.

"I still remember her," Minokichi said, staring into the flames. "She was beautiful, like a spirit of the snow. She spared my life and told me never to tell anyone—but I guess it's safe to tell you now."

As soon as Minokichi finished speaking, he noticed that Yuki's expression had changed. Her eyes, which had always been warm, now looked as cold as ice. A chill filled the room.

"I am the Snow Woman," Yuki whispered, her voice soft but sorrowful. "I spared you that night, but you have broken your promise."

Minokichi's heart raced. "But… you are my wife! I love you! Please don't leave!"

Yuki's eyes softened, and tears sparkled like snowflakes on her cheeks. "I love you too," she whispered. "But I can't stay. The snow is where I belong."

With those words, Yuki kissed Minokichi one last time. Then, with a swirl of snow, she disappeared into the night, leaving only the sound of the wind behind.

The Mystery of Yuki-onna

The story of Yuki-onna is filled with mystery. No one knows whether she is a kind spirit or a dangerous one—perhaps she is both. Some say she comforts lost travelers, guiding them safely through snowstorms. Others believe she is a warning to those who are selfish or unkind.

People tell stories of Yuki-onna visiting children and tucking them in with blankets of snow to keep them safe from harm. But they also say she can appear suddenly in a storm, testing travelers to see if they are worthy of her help.

If you meet Yuki-onna on a snowy night, how she treats you will depend on how you treat others. If you show kindness and respect, she may guide you to safety. But if you act selfishly or break a promise, she may vanish into the snow, leaving you to find your way alone.

The Lesson of Yuki-onna

The story of Yuki-onna teaches us several important lessons.

Kindness Matters

How we treat others—whether friends, family, or strangers—shapes the world around us. Kindness is like a warm fire on a cold night.

Promises Are Important

Just as Minokichi learned, a promise is something that must be kept, even when it's difficult. Trust is built on keeping our word.

Some Things Remain a Mystery

Like Yuki-onna, life is sometimes filled with questions that don't have easy answers. That's okay—there is beauty in mystery, too.

Even today, people in Japan tell stories of Yuki-onna. When the snow falls, and the wind howls through the trees, some say she is near, watching over travelers. Others say you can feel her presence when the world falls silent under a blanket of snow.

Parents sometimes tell their children, "If you get lost in the snow, stay calm and be kind—Yuki-onna might guide you home." And when the first winter snow arrives, people whisper her name, wondering if she'll visit again.

When you find yourself outside on a snowy night, take a moment to listen to the wind. Imagine the swirling snowflakes as Yuki-onna's gentle touch drifts through the air. Remember: life, like snow, can be cold and mysterious—but kindness and promises will always keep you warm.

Are you ready for the next adventure? More magical creatures, wise spirits, and thrilling stories await just beyond the next page. Let's keep going!

CHAPTER 17: HOICHI THE EARLESS -THE TALE OF A GHOSTLY ENCOUNTER

A long time ago, in a quiet village by the sea, lived a young man named Hoichi. Hoichi (pronounced ho-EE-chee) was blind, but he was gifted with an incredible talent—he could play the *biwa*, a kind of lute. He played it so beautifully that anyone who heard him would feel as if they were drifting through a dream. His music told stories of heroes, battles, and love, and people came from all around to listen to him play.

One day, Hoichi's music caught the attention of unusual listeners—listeners from the spirit world. That was how Hoichi became known as Hoichi the Earless.

A Visit from a Mysterious Stranger

One warm summer night, Hoichi sat outside the temple where he lived, strumming his biwa softly under the stars. The other monks were inside, fast asleep, but Hoichi enjoyed the quiet night.

As he played, a cold wind swept through the temple grounds, and suddenly, he heard footsteps approaching. Before he could react, a deep voice called out from the darkness.

"You there—are you Hoichi, the famous musician?"

Hoichi turned his head toward the sound. "Yes, I am Hoichi," he replied politely.

"I have come to take you to perform for my master," the voice said. "He has heard of your skill and wishes to hear you play tonight."

Though Hoichi was curious, he could tell from the voice that the stranger was important and powerful. So, without hesitation, Hoichi picked up his biwa and followed the sound of the stranger's footsteps into the night.

A Performance for Ghostly Guests

The stranger led Hoichi through the village and down a winding path toward the sea. Hoichi couldn't see where they were going, but soon, he heard the distant sound of waves crashing against rocks. After what felt like hours, the stranger stopped and said, "We are here. Play your biwa for my master and his guests."

Hoichi sat down, cradled his biwa in his arms, and began to play. His music told the story of the Battle of Dan-no-Ura, a famous battle between two powerful clans, the Heike and the Genji. As Hoichi played, he heard whispers and soft footsteps moving around him as if many people were gathering to listen.

The sound of rustling robes and faint murmurs filled the air, but Hoichi focused on his music. He played with all his heart, imagining scenes of warriors fighting bravely and ships sinking into the sea. When he finished, the mysterious audience clapped softly, and Hoichi felt the chill of cold hands brush against his arms in approval.

"Excellent," the stranger said. "My master is very pleased. You will return tomorrow night to play again."

Hoichi bowed politely, and the stranger led him back to the temple just before dawn.

The Monks Discover the Truth

Night after night, the mysterious visitor came to take Hoichi to play his biwa. Each time, Hoichi poured his heart into the music, unaware of the strange presence surrounding him. Soon, the monks who lived at the temple grew worried.

"Hoichi has been sneaking out every night," one monk whispered. "He looks pale and tired. Something strange is happening."

One night, a few monks secretly followed Hoichi. They watched as he left the temple and made his way to an old graveyard by the sea, where he sat among the ancient tombstones and began to play his biwa. To their horror, they realized that Hoichi was playing for ghosts! The spirits of the Heike clan, who had perished in the Battle of Dan-no-Ura, were still haunting the place, and they believed Hoichi's music was meant for them.

The monks rushed back to the temple to tell the head priest what they had seen.

A Plan to Protect Hoichi

The head priest knew that Hoichi was in danger. "If the spirits continue to believe Hoichi belongs to them, they may take him away forever," the priest warned. "We must protect him."

That night, the priest and the other monks brought Hoichi inside the temple and sat him down. "We will write sacred words on your body to protect you from the spirits," the priest explained. "These words will make you invisible to them, and they will no longer be able to find you."

The monks dipped their brushes in ink and carefully wrote sacred prayers all over Hoichi's body—on his arms, legs, back, and even his face. When they were done, Hoichi's skin was covered with protective writing.

"There," the priest said. "Now the spirits will not see you."

In their rush to finish the task, the monks had forgotten one important detail—they hadn't written any words on Hoichi's ears.

The Ghost Returns

Just before midnight, the mysterious visitor came again, calling Hoichi's name. But this time, Hoichi sat perfectly still, silent and hidden by the protective writing on his body.

The spirit roamed the temple grounds, searching for the musician. "Where is Hoichi?" the voice growled. "I know he is here!"

As the spirit moved closer, it scanned the darkness—but all it could see were two floating ears! Because the monks had forgotten to write prayers on Hoichi's ears, the spirit thought the ears were all that remained of him.

The next morning, the monks rushed to check on Hoichi. They were shocked to find him sitting quietly. His ears were gone, but he was otherwise unharmed. Though he had lost his ears, the protective writing had saved his life, and the spirits never returned for him again.

From that day forward, Hoichi became known as "Hoichi the Earless." Despite his injury, Hoichi continued to play his biwa, and his music became even more beautiful. People from far and wide came to hear his songs, and they admired not just his talent but also his courage and kindness.

The Lesson of Hoichi the Earless

Hoichi's story teaches us many important lessons.

Kindness Can Reach Beyond Worlds

Hoichi's music brought peace to the spirits, even though he didn't realize it at the time.

Courage Comes In Many Forms

Hoichi's bravery in the face of fear helped him survive a ghostly encounter.

Small Mistakes Can Have Big Consequences

The monks' mistake of forgetting Hoichi's ears reminds us to pay attention to the details, especially when helping others.

A Musician Remembered Forever

Even today, people in Japan tell the story of Hoichi the Earless. His tale is about bravery, kindness, and resilience. Though Hoichi lost his ears, he never lost his spirit, and his music continued to inspire those around him.

Next time you hear a beautiful song, think of Hoichi and his biwa. Remember that courage and kindness can help us overcome even the most difficult challenges, whether they come from the living or the spirit world.

CHAPTER 18:
THE TALE OF THE FIREFLIES
-A STORY OF LOVE AND LOSS

On warm summer nights in Japan, if you wander near the rivers and forests, you might see tiny lights twinkling in the dark. These glowing lights belong to fireflies, known as *hotaru* in Japanese. Did you know that there's a beautiful legend behind these magical creatures? The fireflies are said to be the spirits of two lovers who were separated long ago, their love shining forever in the night. This is the Tale of the Fireflies—a story of love, loss, and the beauty of never giving up.

The Young Lovers: Hikari and Akihiro

Long ago, in a small village nestled between lush forests and a clear river, there lived a kind and gentle girl named Hikari. Her name meant "light," and she was known for her bright smile and warm heart. Hikari (pronounced hee-KAH-ree) would spend her days helping her family and picking flowers by the riverbank, where she often met a young boy named Akihiro ah-kih-HEE-roh).

Akihiro was the son of a farmer, and he was just as kind-hearted as Hikari. He loved visiting the river to fish, and whenever he saw Hikari there, he would sit and talk with her. Over the years, their friendship blossomed into love.

Hikari and Akihiro dreamed of being together forever. But their families did not approve. Akihiro's family needed him to work on the farm, and Hikari's parents wanted her to marry someone from a wealthier family. No matter how much they tried, the two young lovers were told they could not be together.

A Secret Promise by the River

One summer evening, as fireflies danced around them, Hikari and Akihiro sat together by the river, tears glimmering in their eyes. They knew they could not stay in the village much longer—Hikari's family was sending her away to live with relatives in another town.

"Even if we are separated, I will always find a way to be with you," Hikari whispered.

"And I will wait for you," Akihiro promised. "Every summer night, I will think of you when the fireflies glow."

They held hands under the soft light of the fireflies, vowing that no matter what happened, their love would never fade. As the moon rose above the river, they made a promise:

"Even if we must leave this life," Hikari whispered, "we will find each other again—as fireflies, glowing in the night."

A Tragic Farewell

The next morning, Hikari was taken away by her family, leaving Akihiro heartbroken by the river. Every evening, he would sit where they had made their promise, hoping to see her one last time. But the seasons changed, and years passed without a sign of Hikari.

Akihiro's heart ached with sadness, and he spent many nights by the river, hoping that fate would somehow bring them together again. He grew weaker and weaker until one summer night, under the soft glow of fireflies, Akihiro quietly passed away by the riverbank, still holding on to the memory of his beloved Hikari.

Far away, in the town where Hikari lived, the news of Akihiro's death reached her. Heartbroken, Hikari ran to the river where they had made their promise. There, under the same glowing fireflies that had witnessed their love, Hikari passed away, longing to be reunited with Akihiro.

The Fireflies' Eternal Dance

The gods, touched by the pure love of Hikari and Akihiro, decided to grant the young lovers a second chance—but not as humans. Instead, the gods transformed Hikari and Akihiro into fireflies, their spirits glowing softly in the summer night.

Now, every summer, you can see two glowing fireflies dancing together by rivers and in the forests. These tiny lights are believed to be Hikari and Akihiro, reunited at last. They float through the night, side by side, their lights shimmering as a reminder of their eternal love.

It is said that on the nights when fireflies shine the brightest, Hikari and Akihiro are happiest, celebrating their love under the stars. Their lights flicker and glow, telling the world that true love never fades, even when life becomes difficult.

A Lesson in Love and Patience

The tale of Hikari and Akihiro teaches us many valuable lessons.

Love Is Eternal

Like Hikari and Akihiro's love, true love can survive even the hardest challenges.

Patience Is Powerful

Even though they couldn't be together in life, they patiently waited for each other in the future.

Little Moments Matter

The fireflies' tiny lights show us that small acts of love—like a kind word or a kept promise—can shine brightly, even in the darkest times.

Even today, when people see fireflies glowing in the night, they remember the story of Hikari and

Akihiro. Couples often visit riverbanks and forests during the summer firefly season, hoping to catch a glimpse of the two fireflies dancing together. Some believe that making a wish on a glowing firefly will bring good luck in love.

There is also a Japanese saying: "The firefly's light is the light of love." It reminds us that love is not about how big or grand something is—it's about the little things, like the quiet glow of a firefly on a summer night.

Next time you see fireflies dancing in the dark, pause for a moment. Watch their tiny lights flicker and glow, and think of Hikari and Akihiro. Their story reminds us that love, no matter how far apart we are, can always find a way to shine.

And maybe, just maybe, one of those fireflies will be Hikari and Akihiro, dancing side by side, glowing with the light of their eternal love.

CONCLUSION: THE LESSONS HIDDEN IN THESE LEGENDS

As we reach the end of our journey through the magical world of Japanese legends, we can look back at the stories we've discovered and see that they are more than just tales about gods, spirits, and magical creatures. These legends carry important lessons about life—teaching us about courage, kindness, respect, and friendship. These stories are like treasures from the past, shared through generations, reminding us to live with good hearts and brave spirits.

The Power of Courage

In many of the legends we explored, characters showed great courage. Whether learning about Momotaro bravely facing the Oni on a distant island or Hoichi the Earless standing up to ghosts, these stories teach us that courage is about facing fear and doing the right thing, even when it's hard.

- Momotaro teaches us that being brave doesn't mean you have to act alone—you can gather friends to help you on your journey.
- Susanoo, the storm god, shows us that even when things seem overwhelming, courage and clever thinking can help us overcome any obstacle, just as he defeated the eight-headed dragon Orochi.

These stories remind us that everyone can be brave—even in small ways. Being brave can mean speaking up when something is unfair, trying something new, or helping a friend in need. Courage doesn't always mean fighting battles; sometimes, it just means believing in yourself.

Kindness Always Shines Bright

From Jizo's gentle protection of children to the fireflies' glowing love, kindness flows through every story. Acts of kindness, even small ones, can change the world—whether sharing food with a friend, sparing a tiny spider, or helping someone who is lost.

- The tale of the Crane Wife shows us that love means giving without expecting anything in return.

- Urashima Taro's adventure under the sea reminds us to be kind to animals and to cherish our time with others.

These stories show that kindness spreads like ripples in a pond. One kind action leads to another, making the world a better place. You don't need magic powers to make a difference—every smile, kind word, and good deed helps.

The Importance of Respect

Respect is a lesson that appears often in these legends. Many characters learned that treating others with respect—whether they are human, spirit, or animal—can lead to unexpected rewards.

- The Tanuki, a mischievous raccoon-dog spirit, learns to be kind and respectful through his adventures, teaching us that even playful hearts can grow.

- Taro, in the story of the Kappa, discovers that politeness can outsmart even the trickiest of creatures. A simple bow helps him escape from danger.

These stories remind us that respect isn't just about using polite words—it's about treating others kindly, listening, and being fair. Respect makes it easier to solve problems and builds strong friendships.

Friendship and Selflessness

Some of the most touching stories we explored were about friendship and sacrifice. True friendship is about caring for others, even if it means making difficult choices.

- The Red Oni and the Blue Oni show us that true friends sometimes make sacrifices for one another, even if it's hard to say goodbye.
- The Tale of the Fireflies teaches us that love and friendship can shine on, even after life changes or things feel difficult.

These stories teach us that friendship means sharing, helping, and being there for one another through good times and bad.

Celebrate the Legends Today

Even though these stories are ancient, they are still celebrated in Japan today. You can see reminders of these legends everywhere!

- Shrines and statues of Jizo can be found in temples and along roads, where people leave offerings to thank him for protecting children and travelers.
- Kappa statues sit near rivers, reminding people to be careful around water and to show respect for the spirits.
- During the Tanabata Festival, people celebrate the love of two star-crossed lovers by writing

wishes on colorful paper strips and hanging them from bamboo trees—just like the glowing fireflies in our story about Hikari and Akihiro.

- Every summer, firefly festivals take place all over Japan. At these festivals, families gather to watch the fireflies dance and share stories of love and magic.

These legends aren't just stories from long ago—they live on in festivals, art, and traditions. Each time people share these tales or leave an offering by a statue, they keep the magic of the legends alive.

Explore More and Share the Stories

There are so many more legends and stories waiting to be discovered. Whether you read them from a book, hear them from a friend, or visit places in Japan where these stories began, each legend is a chance to learn and grow.

Maybe one day, you'll even share these stories with your family and friends. The lessons hidden in these tales—about courage, kindness, and respect—are treasures that never fade. And the best part? Each time you share them, you keep their magic alive for the next generation.

What's Your Favorite Legend?

As you've read through these stories, which one did you like the most? Was it the tale of Momotaro's brave quest? Or perhaps the gentleness of the Crane Wife? Did the playful Tanuki make you smile, or did Yuki-onna's story send a little shiver down your spine?

Each story has its own special magic, just like every person has their own unique qualities. The legends remind us to embrace who we are, to find joy in learning, and to always treat others with kindness and respect.

A Final Thought to Carry with You

As we say goodbye to these wonderful legends, remember this: the lessons we learn from stories can help guide us through life. Courage helps us overcome challenges, kindness brings joy to the people around us, and respect builds strong friendships.

Just like the fireflies that glow each summer night, these legends shine brightly, reminding us that love, bravery, and kindness are the most magical things of all.

Thank you for reading! Though our book has come to an end, the stories will stay with you forever.

Who knows? Maybe one day, you'll create a story of your own—one filled with courage, kindness, and a little bit of magic!

BONUS: AND FUN FACTS - EXPLORE THE WORLD OF JAPANESE LEGENDS!

Now that you've finished reading these amazing stories, it's time to have some fun! In this chapter, you'll find activities that let you dive deeper into the world of Japanese legends. You'll also discover fun facts about the stories, characters, and traditions that make these tales so special. Are you ready to explore, create, and learn? Let's go!

Activities Inspired by Japanese Legends

1. Create Your Own Oni Mask!

Materials: Paper plates, markers or paints, scissors, and string.

- *Instructions:*

    Draw the face of an Oni (you can make it red, blue, or even green!). Add big horns, sharp teeth, and fun designs. Use scissors to carefully cut holes for the eyes.

> Paint or color the mask and punch two small holes on the sides to tie string for wearing it.
> Put on your Oni mask and act out a scene from the Momotaro story!

- *Challenge:* Can you make one mask for Red Oni and one for Blue Oni?

2. Make Firefly Glow Jars 🌸

- *Materials:* A jar with a lid, glow-in-the-dark paint, paintbrush, and glitter (optional).
- *Instructions:*
  > Use the paintbrush to make tiny dots inside the jar—these will look like glowing fireflies when the lights are off!
  > Sprinkle glitter inside for extra sparkle if you like.
  > Let the paint dry, then take your jar to a dark room and watch it glow!
- *Idea:* While your glow jar shines, retell The Tale of the Fireflies to your friends and family.

3. Write a New Legend ✍️

- What if you created your own magical story? Use your imagination to write a short legend about a new spirit or hero. Will it be about a kind dragon? A brave fox? Or maybe a magical creature that protects forests?

- Share your story with your friends and family, or act it out like a play!

4. Make an Offering to Jizo ✳

- Find a small stone or flower to leave as an offering to someone special. You could make an offering to a plant, tree, or garden in your neighborhood, just as people leave flowers and pebbles for Jizo statues in Japan.

- Say a kind thought when you leave your offering—like wishing for someone's happiness or hoping for a safe journey.

5. Play the Tanuki Trickster Game 🐼

In this game, one person is the Tanuki and tries to trick the others! The Tanuki hides a small object (like a coin or a key) somewhere in the room. The others have to ask yes-or-no questions to figure out where it's hidden. But the Tanuki can only tell the truth half the time—the other half, they must trick the players with playful answers!

FUN FACTS ABOUT JAPANESE LEGENDS

1. Oni Are Celebrated in Festivals!

- Every year during the Setsubun Festival, people in Japan throw roasted soybeans to chase away Oni and bring good luck to their homes. Families shout, "Oni wa soto! Fuku wa uchi!" which means, "Out with the Oni! With good fortune!"

2. Fireflies Are a Symbol of Love

- In Japan, fireflies (hotaru) are believed to represent love and the souls of people who have passed away. Many couples visit firefly festivals during the summer to watch these glowing creatures and enjoy the romantic atmosphere.

3. Yuki-onna Is Part of Winter Folklore

- The Snow Woman, Yuki-onna, is still a popular figure during winter in Japan. Some parents tell their children bedtime stories about her to encourage kindness during the cold season.

4. Jizo Statues Have Special Red Hats and Bibs

- The red hats and bibs on Jizo statues aren't just for decoration! Families dress these statues to thank Jizo for protecting their children or to honor loved ones who have passed away.

5. The Kappa Loves Cucumbers

- One of the Kappa's favorite foods is the cucumber. Some families write their names on cucumbers and throw them into rivers to make peace with the mischievous water spirits.

6. Tanuki Are Real Animals!

- The Tanuki is based on a real animal called the Japanese raccoon dog, which can still be found in forests across Japan. These animals are known for their curious behavior, making them perfect for the playful legends.

7. Hoichi's Story Is Told through Theater

- The story of Hoichi the Earless has been adapted into Noh theater, a traditional Japanese performance with masks and music. The haunting tale of Hoichi continues to captivate audiences today.

8. Raijin and Fujin Guard Japanese Temples

- Statues of Raijin (the thunder god) and Fujin (the wind god) are often found at the entrance of temples in Japan. They are there to protect the temple grounds from harm.

9. Amaterasu's Story Explains the Sun

- The tale of Amaterasu, the Sun Goddess, is used to explain the cycle of day and night. When she hides in her cave, the world becomes dark—but when she returns, the sun shines brightly again.

10. Japanese Festivals Celebrate Legends

- Many of Japan's festivals are tied to the stories and legends you've read. For example, during Tanabata (the Star Festival), people celebrate the reunion of two star-crossed lovers with colorful decorations and parades.

Now that you've read the stories and explored the activities, keep the magic alive—go out, explore, and share what you've learned with others!

The End… or Just the Beginning? 🎉

REFERENCES

The stories and information in this book are inspired by traditional Japanese folklore, mythology, and cultural traditions passed down for generations. Below is a list of references and sources that helped bring these legends to life.

Books and Publications

- Aston, W.G. – Shinto: The Ancient Religion of Japan
    - A foundational text on Shinto myths and deities, including stories of gods like Amaterasu and Susanoo.
- Yei Theodora Ozaki – *Japanese Fairy Tales*
    - A collection of retold Japanese folk stories, including Urashima Taro and Momotaro.
- Lafcadio Hearn – Kwaidan: Stories and Studies of Strange Things
    - This book offers insights into ghost stories such as Hoichi the Earless and other supernatural encounters.

- Foster, Michael Dylan – The Book of Yokai: Mysterious Creatures of Japanese Folklore
  - A deep dive into the world of yokai, including Kappa, Tanuki, and Yuki-onna.
- Sei Shonagon – *The Pillow Book*
  - This classical text gives glimpses into ancient Japanese culture and seasonal events, including early references to fireflies and nature spirits.

Online Resources

- The Japanese Folklore Database – https://www.japanese-folklore.com
  - A detailed digital archive of traditional Japanese legends and stories.
- National Geographic Kids – Japanese Culture
  - A kid-friendly guide to Japanese festivals and traditions, including the Tanabata Festival and Setsubun.
- Encyclopedia of Shinto – http://k-amc.kokugakuin.ac.jp/
  - A comprehensive resource on Shinto gods, festivals, and practices, including Raijin and Fujin.

Cultural and Museum Resources

- Kyoto National Museum – Exhibitions on Japanese mythological art and Noh theater performances, including tales like Hoichi the Earless.
    - Website: https://www.kyohaku.go.jp/eng/
- Ghibli Museum – Exploration of Japan's influence on modern storytelling through folklore-inspired films.
    - Website: https://www.ghibli-museum.jp/en/

Folklore and Oral Traditions

1. Many of these stories, such as The Tale of the Fireflies, The Red Oni and the Blue Oni, and Jizo the Protector, come from oral traditions that have been shared by families and communities for centuries.
2. Interviews with storytellers and historians in Japan were used to capture the cultural meaning behind some of these tales.

Acknowledgments

We also thank the many teachers, parents, and cultural experts who keep these legends alive by sharing them with young readers across the world. These stories not only entertain but also teach important values that continue to inspire people today.

This list of references ensures the legends were accurately retold and adapted in a way that remains true to their spirit, while also making them fun and accessible for children. Thank you for embarking on this magical journey!

THAI LEGENDS FOR KIDS:

KINGS, QUEENS, DEMONS, HEROES, MYTHS, SACRED TALES & MORE FROM THAILAND

TABLE OF CONTENTS

INTRODUCTION 1

CHAPTER 1: THE LEGEND OF PHRA RAHU – THE ECLIPSE GOD 8

CHAPTER 2: THE TALE OF MAE NAK – THE LOVING GHOST .. 15

CHAPTER 3: NANG PHAYA – THE QUEEN OF AMULETS 22

CHAPTER 4: HANUMAN – THE MONKEY WARRIOR 29

CHAPTER 5: THE LEGEND OF THE NAGA – THE SACRED SERPENT 36

CHAPTER 6: THE TALE OF THE GOLDEN SWAN – HONGSA .. 42

CHAPTER 7: THE STORY OF BUDDHA AND THE MANGO TREE 49

CHAPTER 8: THE WHITE ELEPHANT – A SYMBOL OF GOOD FORTUNE 56

CHAPTER 9: THE ORIGIN OF SONGKRAN – THE WATER FESTIVAL 63

CHAPTER 10: THE GIANT OF WAT ARUN – YAKSHA THE PROTECTOR 72

CHAPTER 11: THE MAGIC OF KRATHONGS – FLOATING LIGHTS ON THE WATER 81

CHAPTER 12: THE LEGEND OF THE TIGER SPIRIT – PROTECTOR OF THE FORESTS 90

CHAPTER 13: THE TALE OF SANG THONG – THE GOLDEN PRINCE 100

CHAPTER 14: THE FESTIVAL OF THE FULL MOON – YI PENG 109

CHAPTER 15: THE STORY OF KHUN PHAEN – THE WARRIOR AND HIS CHARMS 117

CHAPTER 16: THE LEGEND OF THE PHI TA KHON – THE GHOST FESTIVAL 127

CHAPTER 17: THE PRINCESS AND THE KRAHASA – A TALE OF SACRIFICE 136

CHAPTER 18: THE STORY OF THE KHMER RUINS – A GLIMPSE INTO THE PAST 146

CHAPTER 19: THE LEGEND OF THE LOTUS BLOSSOM – A SYMBOL OF PURITY 154

CHAPTER 20: THE TALE OF THE MYSTERIOUS KINNAREE – HALF-BIRD, HALF-WOMAN 162

CHAPTER 21: THE KING AND THE MONK – A LESSON IN WISDOM 169

CHAPTER 22: THE LEGEND OF PHI AM – THE SPIRIT OF DREAMS 178

CHAPTER 23: THE STORY OF THE PHAYA NAGA – GUARDIAN OF THE MEKONG RIVER 186

CONCLUSION – THE ENDURING MAGIC OF THAI LEGENDS 194

ACTIVITIES 201

FUN FACTS 208

REFERENCES 211

INTRODUCTION

Welcome, young adventurer! It's time to step into a world filled with magic, bravery, and wonder—the land of Thai legends. In this book, you will explore stories that have been told for centuries across the lush jungles, peaceful villages, and bustling cities of Thailand. These legends are more than just tales—they are windows into the heart of Thai culture, teaching lessons about kindness, courage, and wisdom. Get ready to meet mythical creatures, brave heroes, and powerful spirits that will guide you through the enchanting world of Thailand's folklore.

Some of the most fascinating legends in the world come from Thailand, which is a country filled with rich history and beautiful landscapes. The purpose of these stories is not just simple entertainment—they were created to pass down important lessons from one generation to the next. Whether you are reading about the legend of *Hanuman*, the Monkey King, or the story of *Nang Phisuea Samut*, the Mermaid Princess, each tale holds a little bit of magic and a lot of wisdom.

Who Are the Thai People?

Thailand, known as the "Land of Smiles," is located in Southeast Asia. It is a country full of beautiful beaches, misty mountains, and ancient temples. The Thai people are known for their warm hospitality, strong family ties, and deep-rooted traditions. Unsurprisingly, many of these traditions are tied to Thai stories and legends. Thai culture also has a unique blend of religious influences—from Buddhism to ancient "animist" beliefs (a religion where people honored spirits in nature).

The Thai people love storytelling. As such, legends are often shared during important festivals or around the family table. Even more interestingly, these stories aren't just found in books, but also in everyday life. If you walk through a bustling market in Thailand or visit a temple, you'll find murals, statues, and art that depict scenes from these tales. Even the names of rivers, mountains, and towns are linked to ancient legends that remind people of their cultural heritage.

In these stories, you'll learn about the values that are important to the Thai people—like compassion, humility, loyalty, and perseverance. You'll also see how the stories reflect Thailand's love for nature and the importance of living in harmony with the surrounding world.

The Importance of Storytelling in Thai Culture

Storytelling is like a treasure chest in Thai culture—it keeps wisdom, lessons, and traditions safe and passes them on to future generations. Just like bedtime stories teach children valuable lessons around the world, Thai legends are meant to guide people on how to live a good life. These tales often feature challenges and obstacles, which teach that bravery, patience, and kindness are more important than strength alone.

Many Thai stories come from ancient epics, such as the *Ramakien*—Thailand's version of the Indian *Ramayana ( )*. The Ramakien tells the story of Prince

Rama and his journey to rescue his beloved, *Sita,* from the demon king *Ravana.* It's an epic full of battles, friendships, and heroic acts. In this epic, the trickster monkey god, *Hanuman, also* steals the show due to his cleverness and loyalty.

Other stories come from local legends that have been told for generations in Thai villages—like the story of *Mae Nak,* the ghost wife who shows the power of love even after death, or the *Naga* serpents that protect rivers and bring rain to farmers. These legends are more than just fairy tales—they shape how people behave, treat one another, and respect nature and their ancestors.

What You'll Discover in These Tales

In this book, you will explore the wonders of Thai folklore through exciting stories filled with adventure and magic. Some stories will take you to enchanted forests where magical creatures dwell. Others will guide you across the sparkling waters of Thailand's rivers, where the ancient *Naga* sea serpents slither far below the surface. You will also journey to mountain top temples, meet powerful spirits, and discover the secrets hidden within ancient cities.

The tales you'll find inside this book include:

> Mythical creatures like the *Naga* serpents, who are the guardian spirits of Thai rivers.
>
> Brave heroes and heroines who fight for what's right, like Prince *Rama* and *Hanuman* (the mischievous Monkey King).
>
> Ghostly spirits and friendly phantoms who teach lessons about love, loss, and forgiveness.
>
> Festivals and traditions that keep these legends alive, like the colorful *Loy Krathong* Festival, where people release floating lanterns on water to honor spirits and make wishes.

Throughout the book, you'll also discover how these legends reflect Thai values—like the importance of family, respect for elders, and living in harmony with nature. You'll also see how Thai people celebrate life through music, dance, and festivals, and how these traditions are still alive today in Thailand's modern world.

A Journey Through Heroes, Faeries, and Magical Lands

Get ready to dive into some incredible adventures! Imagine exploring the jungles where magical creatures live, meeting heroes who fight for justice, and learning from spirits who protect their homes. You'll meet characters like:

Mae Nak (the ghost wife), whose love was so powerful it crossed the boundaries of life and death.

The *Garuda*, a mighty bird who symbolizes courage and strength, and also serves as Thailand's national emblem.

As you read these stories, you'll feel like you're right there with the heroes and spirits—facing challenges, learning valuable lessons, and discovering the magic of Thailand's legendary world. These tales are perfect for sparking your imagination, and each story holds a lesson you can carry with you.

A World of Adventure Awaits

Use this book and your imagination to help you explore a magical world that has shaped the culture and values of Thailand. Whether you dream of flying through the sky on the back of a *Garuda* or solving riddles like the clever *Hanuman*, these stories will inspire you to think, imagine, and dream big.

THAI LEGENDS FOR KIDS

So, are you ready to begin your journey into the world of Thai legends? There's so much to discover—heroes to meet, adventures to go on, and lessons to learn. As you read, try to imagine yourself in the heart of each story. What would you do if you were in Hanuman's place? How would you feel meeting a Naga serpent guarding a river? These tales are not just ancient—they are alive in the hearts of everyone who reads them, including you!

Turn the page, and let the adventure begin.

CHAPTER 1: THE LEGEND OF PHRA RAHU - THE ECLIPSE GOD

In the magical world of Thai legends, few stories are as exciting as the tale of *Phra Rahu*, the mysterious god of eclipses. This story will take you to a time when the sky was filled with gods and powerful beings, and every sunrise and sunset held a little bit of magic. But what happens when something or someone tries to swallow the light? Buckle up, because the story of Phra Rahu is about to take you on an unforgettable adventure through darkness and light.

How Phra Rahu Swallowed the Sun and Moon

Long ago, in the days when gods ruled the heavens, there lived a powerful deity named Phra Rahu. He wasn't like the other gods who were bright and cheerful—Rahu was dark and mysterious. With a body as black as the deepest night, Rahu often hid in the shadows. But don't be fooled—he was a trickster at heart and always looked for ways to cause mischief.

One day, the gods prepared a special potion called the "nectar of immortality." Anyone who drank it would live forever! But the gods, wanting to keep the potion for themselves, guarded it carefully. Rahu, however, was clever. He disguised himself as another god and slipped into the feast, quietly drinking the potion when no one was looking. Just as the nectar touched his lips, the Sun God and the Moon God spotted him! They shouted, "Rahu is not one of us—stop him!"

Before the nectar could spread through Rahu's entire body, the mighty god Vishnu swung his sword and cut Rahu in half! But, because Rahu had already swallowed some of the nectar, he didn't die. Instead, his two halves became two different celestial beings. His upper half, still alive, drifted into the heavens, while the lower half vanished into the darkness. From that day on, Rahu swore revenge against the Sun and the Moon for exposing him.

Whenever Rahu manages to see the Sun or the Moon traveling through the sky, he leaps up and swallows them whole. This automatically causes an eclipse. But because Rahu is only a shadowy head, he is not powerful enough to swallow the Sun or the Moon whole. So, the Sun and Moon always manage to escape from his mouth, bringing back the light to the world. This is why eclipses don't last forever—Rahu's power can only hold back the light of these two gods for a little while before they slip free again.

The Origin of Eclipses in Thai Beliefs

For centuries, Thai people have explained solar (of the sun) and lunar (of the moon) eclipses through the legend of Phra Rahu. Imagine looking up at the sky and suddenly seeing the Sun or Moon slowly disappear. In ancient times, this was a mysterious and even frightening event. People believed that Rahu was swallowing the celestial lights, and they needed to do something to help the Sun and Moon escape from his jaws!

During an eclipse, villagers would gather outside, banging drums, pots, and pans, and making as much noise as possible. They believed that if Rahu heard their noise, he would get scared and spit out the Sun or Moon. Families would also light firecrackers or play loud music to chase Rahu away. And sure enough, after a little while, the Sun or Moon would return, causing everyone to cheer in celebration!

Even today, in some parts of Thailand, people continue these old traditions during an eclipse to honor the legend of Rahu. The story reminds them that, just like the Sun and Moon, light always returns, no matter how dark it seems.

Lessons About Darkness and Light

The legend of Phra Rahu teaches us important lessons about life. One of the biggest lessons is that darkness is not something to fear. Just like the Sun and Moon return after every eclipse, hard times in life will also pass, and better days will come. Darkness and light are both natural parts of the world, and we need both to grow. Without night, we wouldn't appreciate the day. Similarly, without challenges, we wouldn't understand the value of happiness.

Another lesson the legend of Rahu teaches us is about forgiveness. Even though Rahu causes trouble for the Sun and Moon, they never fight him—they simply escape and continue their journey through the sky. This teaches us that sometimes it's better to let things go rather than hold onto anger. Just like the Sun and Moon move on, we can learn to move past problems and focus on the good things that lie ahead.

Finally, the story of Phra Rahu also shows that everyone has a role to play, even in the grand scheme of the universe. Rahu may seem like a villain, but without him, the magic of eclipses wouldn't exist. This reminds us that even things that seem scary or bad can have a purpose. Every part of life, whether bright or dark, helps shape the world in some way.

The Magic of Eclipses

So, have you ever seen a solar or lunar eclipse? Each is an amazing sight! During a solar eclipse, the moon passes between the Earth and the sun, covering the sun's light for a short time. During a lunar eclipse, the Earth casts a shadow over the moon, making it appear red or dark. Unlike the ancient Thai people, we now know that eclipses are part of the natural movements of the planets—making them even more special!

Eclipses remind us that just like in famous legends, there's always more to discover about the world around us. Next time you look up at the sky, think about Rahu and his mischievous quest to swallow the Sun and Moon. And remember, even when the sky goes dark, the light will always return—just as it does in the legend.

Bringing the Story to Life

The next time you see an eclipse, you can tell the story of Phra Rahu to your friends and family. Imagine Rahu lurking in the shadows, waiting for his chance to grab the Sun or Moon. You could even act out the story—have someone pretend to be Rahu, another person be the Sun or Moon, and the rest of the group make noise to help free the light! Storytelling is a fun way to keep legends like this alive and share the magic of Thai culture with others.

And who knows? Maybe one day, you'll visit Thailand and see a festival where people celebrate these ancient beliefs. You might hear drums, fireworks, and laughter filling the air as the community comes together to honor their legends.

Through stories like Phra Rahu's, we see that every culture has its own way of explaining the mysteries of life—and each story brings a little more magic to the world.

CHAPTER 2: THE TALE OF MAE NAK - THE LOVING GHOST

Beyond the battle between darkness and light, another story about a ghost whose love for her husband was so strong that it reached beyond the grave lies in the heart of Thailand's many legends. This is the story of *Mae Nak*, the ghost wife. This tale, filled with both warmth and chills, has been told for generations. It's a story about love, loss, forgiveness, and learning how to let go. While Mae Nak's tale has moments of fright, at its heart, it's a story that shows us the power of love and the importance of moving on.

The Story of a Woman's Love Beyond the Grave

A long time ago, in a small village by the *Chao Phraya* River, there lived a beautiful young woman named *Nak*. Nak was known not only for her beauty but also for her kind heart. She lived happily with her husband, *Mak*, in a small wooden house surrounded by fields and lush greenery. The couple loved each other deeply and soon found out they were going to have a child.

But before their baby could be born, Mak was called to serve as a soldier in a faraway battle. With a heavy heart, he kissed Nak goodbye and promised to return soon. As Mak marched off with the other soldiers, Nak watched him disappear into the distance. Her heart was still full of hope and love, as she wasn't aware of how her life would soon take a heartbreaking turn.

While Mak was away, Nak began to give birth to their baby. But, something terrible happened. During childbirth, Nak grew weak, and despite the efforts of the local healer, both she and the baby passed away. The villagers were heartbroken. However, they knew of an ancient belief: spirits could sometimes cling to the world if their love or sadness was too strong.

And that's exactly what happened to Mae Nak.

Determined to wait for her husband, Nak's spirit refused to leave. She stayed in her home by the river, rocking her baby in her arms, waiting for Mak to return. When the villagers tried to tell Mak what had happened, Mae Nak's ghost became angry. She didn't want her husband to know the truth—she just wanted to be with him again, no matter what.

How Mae Nak's Spirit Both Helped and Frightened the Villagers

After many months, Mak finally returned from the battlefield. He was eager to reunite with his wife and meet his child. And, to his surprise, everything seemed perfectly normal when he arrived home. Mae Nak greeted him warmly as their baby slept peacefully in a cradle. Mak was overjoyed to be back with his family, unaware that they were now ghosts.

For a while, Mak lived happily with his wife and child, thinking nothing was wrong. Mae Nak's love for Mak was so strong that she did everything she could to make their home feel just like it had before. But something strange began to happen in the village. The villagers, who knew the truth, started to avoid Mak and his house. They were afraid of Mae Nak's spirit and didn't dare speak to Mak, fearing the ghost's wrath.

One day, however, the truth began to reveal itself. As Mae Nak was cooking in the kitchen, she accidentally dropped a lime through the floorboards. Without thinking, she stretched her arm through the wooden planks to grab it—a movement no living person could make. Mak saw this from the corner of his eye, and in that moment, he realized the truth: his wife was no longer alive.

Filled with fear, Mak fled the house, running to the temple, where the monks could protect him from Mae Nak's spirit. Heartbroken and angry, Mae Nak chased after him, her cries of sorrow echoing through the night. The villagers, terrified of her ghostly presence, hid in their homes, praying that the monks could help.

The End of the Tale and Letting Go

At the temple, the monks performed ancient rituals to calm Mae Nak's spirit. They understood that she was not evil—she was just a soul trapped between two worlds, unable to let go of the love she had for Mak. With great care, the monks gathered her spirit into a clay pot and sealed it, placing it beneath the river to let her rest peacefully at last.

In some versions of the story, a wise monk helps Mae Nak understand that it's time to move on. The monk tells her that love is not about holding on forever, but about accepting how it changes. Mae Nak, with tears in her eyes, forgives Mak and promises to let him live his life. With that, her spirit finds peace, and the river gently carries her memory away.

No matter which version of the story people believe, the villagers never forgot Mae Nak. To this day, many people believe that her spirit is still watching over the *Chao Phraya* River, protecting families and bringing good fortune to those who remember her story with kindness.

Lessons About Love, Forgiveness, and Letting Go

The tale of Mae Nak teaches us many valuable lessons. One of the most important is that sometimes true love means letting go, no matter how strong that love is. Mae Nak's love for Mak was so strong that even death couldn't separate them. But in the end, she learned that to prove her true love for Mak she had to let him go. Sometimes, the hardest thing we can do is let someone we love move forward, even when it feels impossible.

This legend also teaches us about the importance of being understanding and compassionate. Mae Nak wasn't a scary ghost because she wanted to harm anyone—she was simply lost and sad, just like many people can feel when they lose someone they care about. This story reminds us to show kindness to others, even when they seem different or frightening.

Finally, the legend of Mae Nak teaches us that it's okay to let go of the past. Life is always changing, and holding on to something for too long can keep us from moving forward. Just as Mae Nak found peace by letting Mak go, we can also find happiness by accepting change and embracing new beginnings.

Keeping Mae Nak's Memory Alive Today

The story of Mae Nak is still told in Thailand today. There is even a shrine dedicated to her near the Chao Phraya River, where people leave offerings and pray for good luck and protection. Some visitors leave flowers or toys for Mae Nak's child, believing that her spirit still watches over families and children. The shrine is a reminder that, even though Mae Nak's story is sad, it's also filled with love and hope.

People who visit the shrine often reflect on the story of Mae Nak and the lessons it teaches. They are reminded that Mae Nak's power lies in her ability to remind us that love can become a beautiful and powerful memory if we find the strength to let it go.

A Story to Tell and Retell

So, whether you're sitting by the river, watching the moonlight dance on the water, or listening to the sound of the wind through the trees, you can imagine that Mae Nak's spirit is nearby, waiting for someone to remember her story. And, if you ever feel sad, just think about Mae Nak's journey and remember: love always finds a way to bring peace, even when it seems impossible.

So the next time you tell someone about Mae Nak, remember that you're not just sharing another ghost story—you're sharing a tale about the power of love, the importance of forgiveness, and the courage to let go. And who knows? Maybe, just maybe, Mae Nak will be listening, and is grateful that her story continues to be told.

CHAPTER 3: NANG PHAYA - THE QUEEN OF AMULETS

Let's continue further down the road of supernatural Thai beliefs by moving on from honoring a powerful ghost to admiring an impressive object. In the heart of Thailand's traditions and legends lies a special story about an amulet so powerful that it became known as the "Queen of Amulets." This amulet is known as *Nang Phaya*. It is cherished in Thai mythology not only for its beauty but also for the protection and strength it offers to those who carry it. The legend of Nang Phaya is about faith, courage, and the power of belief. And, we will soon find out small objects can hold great meaning.

How a Queen's Amulet Became a Symbol of Protection

Long ago, in a kingdom nestled in the northern forests of Thailand, there lived a wise and kind-hearted queen named *Phaya*. Queen Phaya was deeply loved by her people. Not only was she known for her beauty and intelligence, but also for her ability to lead with compassion. During her reign, the kingdom faced many challenges—enemies threatened the land and people worried for their safety. But Queen Phaya did not give up.

To protect her people and give them hope, Queen Phaya had special amulets created by trusted craftsmen. Each amulet was made with blessed clay and shaped carefully with sacred symbols. These amulets were small enough to carry, yet they were believed to be incredibly powerful. Queen Phaya gave them to her soldiers, farmers, and villagers, telling them that the amulet would guard them from harm and fill their hearts with courage.

The people believed in the power of the queen's amulet. Whenever they felt afraid, they would touch the small clay token, remembering that their queen had faith in their strength. The soldiers who wore the amulets fought bravely, and the villagers and farmers worked hard, as they believed that the queen's spirit was with them. Over time, the amulets became a symbol of protection for anyone who carried one.

The Power of Amulets in Thai Traditions

In Thailand, amulets play an important role in people's everyday lives. An amulet is more than just a lucky charm—it is believed to carry spiritual power and protect its wearer from danger. Some amulets are blessed by monks, while others are tied to ancient legends, like the story of Nang Phaya. People believe that wearing an amulet can bring good luck, safety, and inner strength.

Amulets are often made from special materials, such as clay, stone, or metal. Some are decorated with images of the Buddha, while others show animals or mythical figures. The Nang Phaya amulet, in particular, is known for its elegant shape. This amulet resembles the image of a queen sitting gracefully, and represents protection, wisdom, and power.

Thai people wear amulets not only to guarantee their own strength and prosperity (money, luck, etc.), but they also give these powerful objects to ensure said benefits for others. As such, these amulets are often given as gifts to friends and family. Amulets are an especially popular gift for those facing challenges, such as students preparing for exams or travelers heading on long journeys. These gifts are a way to show love, care, and belief in the person's success and safety.

Stories of Strength Through Nang Phaya Amulets

The story of the Nang Phaya amulet is more than just a legend—it has become part of Thai culture. There are even real-life stories that show the power of faith and belief in its power! One famous story tells of a group of soldiers who wore Nang Phaya amulets during a battle long ago. Despite being outnumbered, the soldiers fought with incredible bravery, believing that their queen's spirit was protecting them. The amulets gave them the courage to keep going, and they returned home as heroes.

In another tale, a merchant traveling through the dense forests of Thailand carried a Nang Phaya amulet given to him by his mother. The journey was filled with dangers—such as wild animals and bandits that lurked in the woods. Despite these challenges, the merchant kept moving forward in his journey, holding onto his amulet and believing that, no matter what, the amulet would keep him safe. The merchant did indeed complete his journey safely, never once doubting the power of the small clay token.

These stories remind people that though strength comes from within, faith in something as simple as an amulet can make all the difference. The Nang Phaya amulet itself has thus become a symbol of hope and courage, helping people through difficult times because of the many stories that prove its power..

Lessons About Strength and Faith

The legend of Nang Phaya teaches us that strength isn't always about physical power—sometimes, it's about the courage to keep going even when things are tough. Queen Phaya's amulets gave people the confidence to face challenges, but it was their own belief in themselves that truly helped them succeed. The amulet served as a simple reminder that they were not alone, and that they had the power to overcome any obstacle.

This story also shows us the importance of faith. Whether it's faith in ourselves, in others, or in something greater, believing in something gives us strength. The people of Queen Phaya's kingdom trusted in her amulets, and that belief made them braver. Even today, people wear amulets not just as a symbol of protection, but as a reminder to stay hopeful and courageous, no matter what life throws their way.

Finally, the story of Nang Phaya teaches us about the power of kindness and giving. Just as Queen Phaya gave her people amulets to protect them, we can also offer kindness and encouragement to those around us. A small act of kindness—like giving someone a good-luck charm or a word of encouragement—can have a big impact, just like the Nang Phaya amulet did for the people of her kingdom.

Keeping the Spirit of Nang Phaya Alive Today

Today, the Nang Phaya amulet is still cherished by many people in Thailand. It is often worn by those seeking protection and strength, and some families even pass down Nang Phaya amulets from one generation to the next so the strength of ancestors is also carried along with each charm...

There are even festivals and ceremonies where people bring their amulets to be blessed by monks, adding another layer of meaning and power to these special objects. Whether worn by students taking exams, travelers exploring new places, or parents watching over their children, the Nang Phaya amulet is still a symbol of faith, strength, and protection today.

A Story to Carry With You

So, just like the soldiers, farmers, and travelers who carried the queen's amulets, we too can face life's challenges with courage and hope. The story of Nang Phaya reminds us that, no matter how small something may seem—whether it's a kind word, a lucky charm, or a simple belief—it can have a powerful impact on both ours and the lives of others.

So, the next time you feel unsure or scared, imagine that you're carrying a Nang Phaya amulet with you. Though you should remember the story of Queen Phaya and how she believed in her people, it is more important that you believe in yourself. Just as the amulet brought strength and protection to those who carried it, your own faith in yourself can guide you through any challenge.

CHAPTER 4: HANUMAN - THE MONKEY WARRIOR

In the world of ancient Thai legends, where amulets like the Nang Phaya and ghosts like Mae Nak demonstrate the power of faith and love, few characters are as beloved and admired as Hanuman, the brave and loyal monkey warrior. Known for his strength, cleverness, and devotion, Hanuman plays an important role in Thai culture, especially through the epic story of *Ramakien*. Ramakien is Thailand's version of the Indian *Ramayana*. This story not only tells of Hanuman's amazing adventures, but also teaches us valuable lessons about courage, friendship, and perseverance (which means "never giving up").

How Hanuman Helped Rama Rescue Sita

This legend begins with a terrible event: *Sita*, who was the wife of a noble prince named *Rama*, was kidnapped by the demon king, *Ravana*. Ravana took Sita away to his distant island kingdom, *Lanka*, and locked her in a palace. Rama was devastated as he knew he couldn't rescue Sita on his own. Rama would need the help of strong allies to rescue his beloved—and that's when Hanuman, the monkey warrior, appeared.

Hanuman wasn't an ordinary monkey—he was blessed with magical powers which allowed him to grow as large as a mountain or shrink as small as a fly. His strength, bravery, and unshakable loyalty to Rama made him the perfect ally for this mission. When Hanuman heard of Rama's troubles, he immediately vowed (an unbreakable promise) to bring Sita back safely.

But, finding Sita wasn't easy. She was hidden far away on Ravana's island, surrounded by oceans and guarded by fierce demons. Hanuman's first task was to search for her and deliver a message from Rama that would let her know help was on the way.

Hanuman's Adventures Across Mountains and Oceans

Hanuman's journey to find Sita was filled with incredible challenges. He had to journey over vast mountains and even cross the ocean to reach the distant island of Lanka. This ocean crossing was one of the most exciting parts of the story, as Hanuman used his magical powers to grow as tall as the sky and leaped from the shore of India all the way to Lanka in a single bound. Imagine the sight— a giant and mighty monkey soaring through the air as his shadow stretched across the sea!

When Hanuman finally reached Lanka, he had to sneak into Ravana's palace without being seen. Using his cleverness, he shrank himself down to the size of a mouse and quietly slipped past the guards. As he searched the palace, he finally found Sita, sitting sadly in a garden. He gave her Rama's message, and Sita's heart filled with hope. She knew that Rama was coming to save her, and she just needed to be brave for a bit longer.

But Hanuman's adventures weren't over yet! Before leaving, he wanted to cause some trouble for Ravana and his demons. So, he returned to his full size and wreaked havoc (or, caused lots of destruction) in the palace. Hanuman set parts of the palace on fire with his magical tail, causing chaos to break out. Although the demons tried to capture him, Hanuman was too quick and clever. He escaped back across the ocean, ready to help Rama plan the rescue mission.

The Battle to Save Sita

With Hanuman's help, Rama gathered a great army of monkeys and animals to fight Ravana and rescue Sita. Unsurprisingly, Hanuman played a key role in this battle. The great monkey warrior fought bravely on the front lines, lifting boulders, smashing demons, and protecting his friends. At one point, when Rama's brother, *Lakshmana (who had come to help with the fight),* was wounded, Hanuman performed one of his most famous feats—he flew all the way to a distant mountain! And just so he could find a magical healing herb to help Lakshmana. But when he couldn't find the herb, Hanuman lifted the entire mountain and carried it back to save Lakshmana!

Thanks to Hanuman's courage, cleverness, and loyalty, Rama's army was able to defeat Ravana in the end. Sita was rescued and reunited with Rama, and the two returned home, grateful for the help of their loyal friend Hanuman.

Lessons About Courage, Loyalty, and Friendship

The story of Hanuman teaches us many important lessons, but one that is particularly important is that of courage. Hanuman faced countless dangers—crossing the ocean (in one giant leap!), sneaking into a demon's palace, and battling powerful enemies—but he never gave up. Even when things seemed impossible, Hanuman trusted in his abilities and kept going. His story reminds us that courage isn't about being fearless—it's about doing the right thing, even when you're afraid.

Another lesson from Hanuman's story is about loyalty and friendship. Hanuman's devotion to Rama and Sita shows us the importance of standing by the people we care about, no matter how difficult the situation. True friends don't give up on each other. Friends should offer each other help, support, and encouragement, just as Hanuman did for Rama and Sita.

Hanuman's tale also teaches us about the power of cleverness and resourcefulness. The brave monkey warrior didn't just rely on strength to solve problems—he used his brain as well as his brawn (strength). When Hanuman needed to sneak into the palace, he shrank himself to the size of a mouse. When he couldn't find the healing herb, Hanuman lifted the entire mountain instead. As such, his story shows us that sometimes, the key to success is thinking creatively and finding new solutions.

Hanuman in Thai Culture Today

Hanuman's story is still celebrated in Thailand today, especially in traditional dance dramas called *Khon*. In these performances, actors dressed in colorful costumes tell the story of Rama, Sita, Ravana, and Hanuman through music, dance, and gestures. The character of Hanuman, with his lively movements and playful spirit, is always a favorite among audiences.

People also look up to Hanuman as a symbol of strength and protection. Some wear amulets with Hanuman's image, believing that it will give them courage and keep them safe from harm. In Thai culture, Hanuman represents bravery, cleverness, and loyalty—qualities that everyone can admire and strive for.

A Story That Lives On

The legend of Hanuman, the monkey warrior, is more than just an adventure—it's a story filled with important lessons about how to live our lives. Whether we are facing challenges at school, helping our friends, or trying to solve a tricky problem, we can all learn something from Hanuman's example.

The next time you feel scared or unsure, think of Hanuman leaping over the ocean to find Sita. When you feel tired or want to give up, remember how he carried an entire mountain to save his friend. And when you wonder how to help a friend in need, think of the way Hanuman stood by Rama and Sita, no matter how hard things got.

Hanuman's story teaches us that everyone has the power to be a hero, no matter how big or small. With a little courage, cleverness, and kindness, we can face any challenge that comes our way if we channel the spirit of Hanuman, the mighty monkey warrior.

CHAPTER 5: THE LEGEND OF THE NAGA - THE SACRED SERPENT

Let's move onto another one of Thailand's most famous creatures from ancient tales. Where Hanuman stood out for his bravery and connection to his friends, this creature is known for its mysterious power and deep connection to water and nature. This creature is the *Naga*, or a great serpent that lives in rivers, lakes, and temples. This serpent serves to protect and symbolize wisdom, as it is believed that it brings blessings, guards sacred places, and helps humans live in harmony with nature. In this chapter, let's take a literal deep dive into the waters of the fascinating world of the Naga, explore its role in Thai traditions, and discover what lessons this legendary serpent can teach us.

How the Naga Protects the Rivers and Temples of Thailand

The Naga is said to live deep beneath the surface of the water, hidden in rivers and lakes, but its presence can be felt all around Thailand. Some say the Naga controls the flow of water, keeping rivers peaceful and providing rain to help farmers grow crops. In temples across Thailand, you might see beautiful sculptures of the Naga wrapped around staircases or gates. Though impressive, these statues aren't just decorations—they are meant to protect the temple and those who visit it.

One famous legend tells of a Naga named *Muchalinda*, who saved the Buddha from a storm. When the Buddha was meditating beneath a tree, a heavy rainstorm began. Muchalinda rose from the water and coiled his great body around the Buddha, spreading his hood to shield Buddha from the rain. This legend is part of the reason that the Naga is seen as a guardian of peace and enlightenment.

Another tale tells of the Naga protecting entire villages when treated with respect. Villagers who revere (or, respect) the Naga are offered protection from droughts and floods, whereas those who pollute rivers or act with disrespect may be punished. In such cases, the Naga might stir the water, causing floods or storms to remind people to care for the environment.

The Naga's Role in the Festival of Lights (Loy Krathong)

One of the most beautiful celebrations in Thailand is the *Loy Krathong* festival, also known as the Festival of Lights. On this night, people release small floating baskets, or *krathongs*, into rivers and lakes as a way of asking for forgiveness from the water spirits and offering gratitude. Many believe that the Naga watches over these rivers and ensures that the krathongs safely float away, carrying these wishes and prayers to the heavens.

During Loy Krathong, families gather along the water's edge, carefully decorating their krathongs with flowers, candles, and incense. Some add coins or personal wishes to the baskets, believing that the

Naga will help bring them good fortune and blessings. As the flickering lights of the krathongs float down the river, it feels like the Naga is swimming beneath the surface, silently watching over the people and their prayers.

In some parts of Thailand, especially along the Mekong River, people tell stories of Naga fireballs rising from the water during the festival. These glowing orbs are believed to be a sign of the Naga's presence, a reminder that the sacred serpent is always near.

Lessons About Respect for Nature and Water

The Naga teaches us many important lessons, especially about respecting nature. In Thai beliefs, rivers, lakes, and oceans are sacred places that need care and protection. The Naga reminds us that when we take care of the water, the water will take care of us in return, bringing rain for crops and keeping floods away. But if we treat rivers poorly by polluting them or wasting water, we not only harm the environment—we also disrespect the Naga.

This lesson is especially important today, as we learn more about how important water is for the world. Just like the Naga protects rivers and reminds people to respect them, we can also play a part by keeping rivers clean, saving water, and appreciating nature. Every drop of water matters, and every small action—like not littering near rivers or using less water—makes a difference.

The Naga also teaches us about balance. Like the peaceful rivers the sacred serpent guards, life can flow smoothly when we act with kindness, respect, and patience. But when we make unwise choices, like harming nature or acting carelessly, it's as if we were disturbing the river. And, when we disturb the river, we also disrespect it, which can make things get stormy and difficult.

The Naga's Presence in Everyday Life

Even today, the image of the Naga is a part of daily life in Thailand. As mentioned, temples often feature the image of this serpent, but homes and even bridges also display statues of the Naga. These statues remind people of the serpent's protection. It is also believed that if you dream about a Naga, it is a sign that good things are coming your way. Others wear amulets featuring images of the Naga in hopes of receiving its strength and protection, especially in times of hardship.

The Naga also appears in art, dance, and storytelling. In traditional Thai performances, dancers sometimes move gracefully like serpents, paying tribute to the Naga's presence in their culture. In these stories and dances, the Naga is not just a symbol—it represents the spirit of Thailand itself, showing strength, wisdom, and a deep connection to nature.

A Legend That Lives On

As all legends, people's belief in the Naga mean this sacred serpent is more than just a story—it's a reminder to live with respect, patience, and kindness. The Naga shows us that when we honor nature and take care of water, good things will flow into our lives. Whether we are watching the krathongs float away during Loy Krathong or simply drinking a glass of water, we can remember the lessons of the Naga.

So, the next time you drop a krathong into a river or look up at the stars, imagine the Naga swimming below the surface. And remember—like the peaceful flow of a river, life is smoother when we act with care and respect. The Naga is always watching, ready to guide us toward a better, more thoughtful way of living.

CHAPTER 6: THE TALE OF THE GOLDEN SWAN - HONGSA

In the heart of Thailand's mythical stories, one animal shines brighter than the Naga, Hanuman, and all the rest—the golden swan, known as the *Hongsa*. This elegant creature has long been admired for its beauty, grace, and wisdom. It flies across Thai folklore, teaching people about kindness, nobility, and the importance of inner peace. In this chapter, we will follow the golden swan on its journey to the sacred mountain, explore its role as a symbol of Thai culture, and discover what we can learn from this graceful bird.

The Journey of the Swan to the Sacred Mountain

The legend of the Hongsa begins with a magical journey. Long ago, the Hongsa, a golden swan, lived in a peaceful forest filled with flowers, rivers, and sunlight. This was no ordinary bird—the Hongsa's feathers gleamed like gold, and its flight was so graceful that anyone who saw it felt calmer and more peaceful. However, the swan was not content. The Hongsa had heard stories about a sacred mountain far away, where the wise spirits lived. This mountain was said to hold the secret to true wisdom, and the Hongsa wanted to learn it.

The journey to the sacred mountain was not easy. The golden swan had to fly over vast forests, deep rivers, and stormy skies. But the Hongsa never gave up, knowing that the wisdom waiting on the mountain was worth every challenge. Along the way, the Hongsa helped other animals in need. It shared food with a starving squirrel, sheltered a bird from the rain under its wings, and guided lost travelers toward safety.

After a long journey, the Hongsa finally reached the top of the sacred mountain. There, it met the ancient spirits, who welcomed the swan warmly. They told the Hongsa that the secret of true wisdom was not hidden on the mountain—it had been inside the swan all along, and had been revealed through its acts of kindness and patience during the journey. The spirits blessed the swan, and from that moment, the Hongsa became a symbol of grace and inner wisdom for all who heard its story.

How the Hongsa Became a Symbol of Grace and Nobility

In Thai tradition, the Hongsa is a powerful symbol of nobility, beauty, and kindness. Its golden feathers represent not just outer beauty but the goodness of the heart. Just like the swan in the story, people are encouraged to be graceful in their actions, to fly above difficulties with patience, and to help others along the way.

The Hongsa also teaches us about humility. Although this golden swan is obviously a majestic bird, it flies close to the earth, never forgetting the people or animals below. This humility has made the Hongsa a beloved figure in Thai culture. In some Thai temples and royal ceremonies, you can see statues or carvings of the Hongsa, symbolizing the importance of wisdom, respect, and inner peace. The swan reminds both rulers and everyday people to act with honor and kindness, no matter how high they fly in life.

In the ancient city of *Sukhothai*, the Hongsa appears in art and architecture, representing the beauty and serenity of the land. Some festivals in Thailand even include dances inspired by the swan's elegant movements, reminding people of the bird's lesson: true nobility lies in how we treat others.

Lessons About Wisdom and Kindness

The tale of the golden swan teaches us many things, but at its heart, it's a story about kindness and patience. Just as the Hongsa helped others during its journey, we too can find joy in helping those around us. When we show kindness, even in small ways—like sharing with a friend or helping someone in need—we grow stronger and wiser, just like this swan.

The Hongsa also teaches us about the importance of staying calm during life's challenges. Despite flying through many storms and difficult skies, the Hongsa kept moving forward with grace and patience. This elegant swan reminds us that even when things get tough, we can find peace within ourselves if we remain patient and kind.

Another important lesson from the Hongsa is that wisdom comes from experience. The swan believed it had to reach the sacred mountain to find wisdom, but instead of finding said wisdom at the peak, the Hongsa learned that the journey itself was its real teacher. In the same way, we grow wiser by learning from our experiences—whether they are easy or difficult—and by paying attention to the lessons life offers.

The Hongsa's Presence in Everyday Life

Even today, the Hongsa is a part of Thai culture. You can find images of the golden swan in artwork and decorations. And, during some important celebrations, people release paper lanterns shaped like swans into the sky or float them on rivers, symbolizing the spirit of the Hongsa taking flight.

In Thai literature and music, the Hongsa appears in poems and songs about love, peace, and kindness. Parents tell their children stories of the golden swan to remind them that kindness is a treasure more valuable than gold. Just like the Hongsa, children are encouraged to be gentle, patient, and helpful, knowing that even small acts of kindness can make a big difference.

As mentioned before, the Hongsa also appears in traditional Thai dance. These dances feature performers that imitate a swan's graceful movements. These dances are often performed during festivals, reminding people to move through life with grace and purpose. When people watch these dances or see statues of the Hongsa in temples, they are reminded of the swan's message: true beauty comes from a kind heart and a peaceful spirit.

A Legend to Carry in Your Heart

The story of the Hongsa reminds us that whether we are soaring high or facing storms, we should remember the lessons of this golden swan. When we help others, even in small ways, we are like the Hongsa, spreading light and kindness wherever we go.

So, the next time you see a bird flying across the sky or a swan gliding peacefully on the water, think of the Hongsa and its journey to the sacred mountain. You, too, are on a journey, and, just like the golden swan, you carry the power to make the world a better place through your kindness, patience, and inner wisdom.

The Hongsa's story reminds us that the real treasures in life are not found in distant places but in how we treat others and ourselves. Every kind word, every act of patience, and every small effort to help someone else brings us closer to the wisdom and beauty of the golden swan. Fly gracefully, like the Hongsa, and let your kindness be your wings.

CHAPTER 7: THE STORY OF BUDDHA AND THE MANGO TREE

Another figure in Thai mythology who was just as graceful and patient as the Hongsa is the Buddha. This next legend, which features him, begins long ago, in a peaceful village surrounded by lush forests and sparkling rivers. In this village there was a mango tree that grew in the heart of a garden. And, this particular mango tree was said to have the juiciest, sweetest fruit anyone had ever tasted. The villagers loved this tree and its delicious fruit, and every year, they eagerly waited for the mangoes to ripen.

But one day, when the Buddha himself visited the village, his encounter with the mango tree would leave behind a lesson that people would remember for generations.

How a Mango Tree Taught a Lesson in Generosity

It was a sunny morning when the Buddha and his disciples arrived in the village. They had been traveling for days, spreading messages of kindness, wisdom, and peace. As they entered the village, the Buddha noticed the mango tree, heavy with bright yellow fruit. A gentle smile appeared on his face. He knew that the mango tree held an opportunity to teach a valuable lesson.

The villagers gathered around the Buddha, eager to hear his words. One man in the crowd stepped forward and said, "Oh wise teacher, would you like to taste one of our mangoes? They are the best in the land!"

The Buddha nodded kindly. "Yes," he replied, "but let me ask you a question: What will happen if all the mangoes are picked, and the tree is left bare?"

The villagers looked at one another, confused. They hadn't thought much about what would happen after the harvest. One boy raised his hand and said, "If we take all the mangoes now, the tree will have no more fruit until next year."

The Buddha smiled at the boy's answer. "That is true," he said. "Now, let me ask: What if we picked only some of the mangoes, leaving the rest for others to enjoy? What if we gave a few away to travelers, and people passing by who are hungry?"

The villagers thought about the Buddha's words. They realized that if they shared the fruit and left some on the tree, they could help others and still enjoy the mangoes themselves. The Buddha continued, "A mango tree gives its fruit freely, expecting nothing in return. It does not keep all of its sweetness for itself. It teaches us that true joy comes from giving, not just from having."

The villagers nodded, understanding that the mango tree was more than just a source of food—it was a symbol of generosity and sharing.

The Buddha's Message about Sharing and Compassion

As the villagers listened closely, the Buddha shared a story with them—a parable (or, a story that is specifically created to teach a lesson) about giving without expecting anything in return.

"Once," the Buddha began, "a wise king planted many mango trees along the roads of his kingdom. He told his people, 'These mango trees are not for me but for the travelers and the poor. Let them enjoy the fruit.' And so, the mango trees grew, and everyone—rich or poor—was welcome to take what they needed.

"But one day, a selfish man said, 'Why should these trees belong to everyone? I will gather all the mangoes and sell them at the market!' He filled his basket with fruit, leaving nothing behind. However, a storm came that night and uprooted many trees. When the selfish man returned the next day, hoping to collect more fruit, he found the trees bare and broken. He had taken too much, and now there was nothing left for anyone—including himself."

The villagers listened in silence, taking in the meaning of the story. "Generosity," the Buddha explained, "creates abundance, while greed leads to loss." He reminded them that sharing makes life richer, not just for those who receive but also for those who give.

Four Lessons About Giving and Gratitude

The story of the mango tree and the Buddha's message teaches us some very important lessons—lessons that children and adults alike can carry in their hearts.

1. **Giving Brings Joy:** Just like the mango tree gives its fruit freely, we can find happiness by sharing what we have with others. Whether it's sharing toys with friends, helping a sibling, or giving food to someone in need, small acts of kindness make the world a better place.

2. **Leave Some for Others:** Just like the Buddha taught the villagers, it's important to remember that the world's resources are meant to be shared. If we take only what we need and leave some for others, there will always be enough for everyone.

3. **Gratitude for What We Have:** The villagers learned that being thankful for what we have is as important as sharing it. When we appreciate the things in our lives—whether it's a delicious meal, a favorite book, or a kind friend—we feel more content.

4. The Power of Compassion: The Buddha's story shows us that kindness and compassion create harmony. When we care for others, we grow stronger as a community. The mango tree did not keep its sweetness for itself, and neither should we. Helping others makes our hearts grow bigger.

How the Mango Tree Became Part of Thai Traditions

Even today, the lessons of the mango tree and generosity are remembered in Thai culture. The idea of sharing food and helping others is an important part of festivals, family life, and traditions. During the Loy Krathong festival, the very same festival where people release floating lanterns on the rivers to express gratitude and offer blessings to others, the message of giving to others flows through the celebration.

In many Thai households, people offer food to monks as a way of sharing what they have. This tradition, called *almsgiving*, is a way to practise generosity and gratitude every day. Just like the mango tree, these small acts of giving help create a more caring and connected world.

A Story That Lives On in Every Act of Kindness

The legend of the mango tree and the Buddha's explanation of generosity are a lesson that we can learn from today. Whenever we share something, no matter how small, we are planting the seeds of kindness. Whether it's sharing a smile, a meal, or a helping hand, each act of kindness makes the world a little brighter.

So, the next time you eat a mango or see a fruit tree, think of the Buddha's lesson. Just as the mango tree gives its fruit freely, we can share what we have and make life sweeter for others. Generosity is a gift that never runs out—it only grows the more we give.

So, as you go about your day, remember the golden mango tree and the Buddha's words: "True joy comes not from what we keep but from what we give."

Will you blossom like the mango tree, and share your sweetness with the world?

CHAPTER 8: THE WHITE ELEPHANT - A SYMBOL OF GOOD FORTUNE

Though the Buddha has taught us a very important lesson in generosity, there's still more to learn from Thai mythology! Let's talk about a rare and majestic creature who lived long ago in the tropical forests of Thailand. This creature was the white elephant. In Thai culture, the white elephant has always been considered sacred, and is known for bringing blessings and prosperity to the land. In the past, its appearance was a sign that good fortune was coming for the king and his entire kingdom. This is the story of how the white elephant became one of Thailand's most beloved symbols.

The Legend of the Sacred White Elephant in Thai History

According to legend, there was once a wise and gentle king who ruled over a vast and beautiful kingdom. His people loved him because he cared for the land and ensured that everyone was treated fairly. One evening, the king had a dream that a sacred white elephant would soon appear, bringing peace and blessings to his kingdom.

The king's dream came true soon after when his scouts rushed back from the forest one morning with exciting news. "Your Majesty!" they cried, "We have found a rare white elephant deep in the jungle!" The king was overjoyed. It was believed that finding a white elephant was a gift from the gods, a sign that the kingdom would prosper, and the people would live in happiness.

The king immediately sent his best caretakers to bring the white elephant to the palace. Unlike other elephants, the white elephant was not put to work or used in battles. Instead, it was treated like royalty, given the finest food, and housed in a golden pavilion. The people of the kingdom were delighted, and they celebrated the arrival of the sacred animal with parades, music, and dance. They believed that the presence of the white elephant would bring rain for their crops, peace to their villages, and good fortune to all. And, all of their wishes came true! Sure enough, the arrival of the white elephant brought great prosperity to the kingdom.

How the White Elephant Brings Blessings to the Land

In Thai culture, the white elephant is a symbol of peace, power, and prosperity. It has always been closely associated with the monarchy. So naturally throughout history, whenever a white elephant was discovered, it was presented to the king. The more white elephants a king had, the more powerful and blessed his reign was believed to be. A king with many white elephants was considered to be a ruler favored by the gods.

White elephants were believed to bring many kinds of blessings to the land. They were said to have the power to call forth rain, ensuring that the farmers' crops would grow strong. They also symbolized peace meaning that as long as the white elephant remained in the kingdom, the people believed that no harm would come to them. And just as the white elephant was treated with kindness and respect, the people of the kingdom were inspired to treat each other with care and compassion.

In times of trouble, the people would pray to the white elephant for help, believing that its gentle spirit would guide them through difficult times. Even today, the white elephant remains a symbol of Thailand's rich culture and traditions, reminding people of the importance of kindness, respect, and good fortune.

Lessons About Respect for Animals and Luck

In Thailand, animals—especially elephants—are cherished and treated with care. But, as the white elephant holds such symbolic value, here are some of the key lessons we can learn from this legend:

Respect for Animals

The white elephant was treated with great honor because the people believed it carried the blessings of the gods. But, just like the white elephant, every creature has a role to play in the world, meaning we should learn to care for all animals and treat them with compassion.

Good Luck Comes to Those Who Do Good

The people believed that the presence of the white elephant would bring fortune to the kingdom. But luck isn't just something that happens by chance. Kindness, hard work, and generosity can attract good fortune into our lives. When we treat others with care and do good deeds, good things often come our way.

Prosperity in Unity

The arrival of the white elephant brought the kingdom together in celebration. The people shared food, danced, and enjoyed one another's company. This reminds us that communities thrive when people work together and support one another.

Taking Care of What Is Precious

The story of the white elephant teaches us to treasure the things that are special—whether it's an animal, a friend, or a gift from nature. Just as the people cared for the white elephant, we should care for the special things in our lives and treat them with love.

The White Elephant in Thai Traditions Today

Even today, the white elephant holds a special place in Thai culture. The image of the white elephant appears on flags, statues, and even coins, reminding people of the importance of respect and good fortune. In some parts of Thailand, stories are still told about how white elephants bring blessings and protect the land. There are even festivals and parades where people dress up as elephants, honoring the role these magnificent creatures have played in Thai history.

Though white elephants are nearly impossible to see, elephants are cared for and protected in Thailand's national parks, reminding visitors of the importance of preserving wildlife. The Elephant Conservation Center, for example, is a place where children can learn about elephants, help care for them, and understand the need to protect these gentle giants. The story of the white elephant inspires people to value all animals and to work toward a future where humans and nature can live in harmony.

A Legend That Teaches Kindness and Hope

The story of the white elephant is more than just a tale of good fortune. It teaches us about the power of kindness, respect, and unity. Just like the people of the ancient kingdom, we can find joy and happiness by being kind to others and caring for the world around us. When we treat animals, nature, and people with respect, we create a world filled with good fortune and happiness.

The next time you see an elephant—whether it's in a storybook, at a zoo, or on a postcard—remember the white elephant. Just as the white elephant is cherished, we can cherish the people and animals in our lives. Good fortune follows those who care for others.

So, as you remember the white elephant, think about the fact that the greatest blessings come from the heart. You should ask yourself what treasures can you share with the people around you that come from your heart? Remember, every act of kindness, no matter how small, makes the world a better place.

CHAPTER 9: THE ORIGIN OF SONGKRAN - THE WATER FESTIVAL

While some treasures come from the heart and the unity of people due to their belief in a very rare animal (like the white elephant), others come from the outward display of joy. The Thai people are aware of these treasured moments, as every year the whole country bursts into celebration in honor of their traditional New Year. They welcome this day with splashes, sprays, and laughter. This joyful holiday is known as *Songkran*, and is also sometimes called the Water Festival. Such a joyous festival has, unsurprisingly, become one of Thailand's most beloved celebrations.

During Songkran, people take to the streets armed with buckets, water guns, and hoses, ready to soak each other with water. But there's more to Songkran than just fun and games; this festival is rooted in ancient legends, traditions, and meanings that stretch back hundreds of years. Let's dive into the story of Songkran and discover how this Thai

New Year became a celebration of water, renewal, and togetherness.

How the Thai New Year Became a Festival of Water

Songkran, celebrated in mid-April, marks the start of the traditional Thai New Year. Long ago, before the festival became a water-soaked celebration, it was a time for cleaning homes, visiting temples, and spending time with family. The idea was to start the New Year with a fresh outlook and a clean slate. People would clean their houses, offer food to monks, and pay respects to their elders in hopes these actions would bring good luck and blessings for the year to come.

The tradition of splashing water began as a gentle and respectful custom. People would pour water over the hands of their elders as a way of showing respect and asking for blessings. This water was often scented with flowers, making it feel special and sacred. Gradually, this act of respect turned into a joyous activity where everyone in the community joined in, sharing the coolness of water in the heat of April.

As time went on, the small splashes grew into big splashes, and soon, Songkran transformed into a nationwide water fight! Today, people of all ages gather in the streets to celebrate with water in every form, from buckets to water balloons. But, while the celebration has grown, the spirit of Songkran remains the same: it's a time to come together, start fresh, and celebrate the blessings of life.

The Legend of the Water Spirits Bringing Rain

One of the most enchanting tales surrounding Songkran is the legend of the Water Spirits. In ancient Thai beliefs, water was seen as a gift from the spirits, and it played a very important role in the lives of the Thai people. In these ancient times, water symbolises life, growth, and renewal. According to legend, there are special spirits who control the rain and ensure that water flows freely to nourish the fields and crops.

One of the most popular stories tells of a time when a terrible drought hit the land. The rivers and lakes dried up, the crops withered, and people feared they would starve. The villagers prayed to the Water Spirits, asking them to bring rain to quench the thirsty earth. In answer to their prayers, the Water Spirits appeared and performed a beautiful dance, pouring water from magical urns to create rain clouds. Soon, rain began to fall, reviving the plants and filling the rivers once more. The people were saved, and from that day forward, they celebrated the gift of water with gratitude.

Songkran honors this legend by celebrating water's power to bring life and growth. People believe that splashing water on one another is a way to honor the Water Spirits and share in the joy of life-giving water. It is a way to call forth good fortune and thank the spirits for the rain that helps the land thrive.

Lessons About Renewal and Community

Songkran is also a time for reflection on the year that has passed and looking forward to the future. This festival teaches us valuable lessons about renewal, gratitude, and community. Here are some of the important lessons we can learn from Songkran:

The Power of Fresh Starts

Songkran marks the beginning of a new year, reminding everyone that every ending brings a new beginning. Just as water washes away dirt and refreshes the land, we too can wash away our worries, mistakes, and challenges from the past year. It's a time to forgive, let go of grudges, and start with a clean heart.

Gratitude for Nature's Gifts

Songkran celebrates water as a precious gift from nature. The festival is a reminder of how important water is for life. It teaches us to respect natural resources and to appreciate the blessings we have. By honoring water, we show our gratitude to the earth for all it provides.

Strengthening Bonds in the Community

During Songkran, families come together to visit temples, pay respects to their elders, and enjoy the festivities. This strengthens the bonds between family members and within the community. Songkran teaches us that when people come together in joy and kindness, it creates a powerful sense of unity. This festival is a time where the Thai people can connect with family, friends, and neighbors, making everyone feel like they belong in their communities.

Finding Joy in Simple Things

While Songkran has evolved into a big celebration, its roots are still firmly planted in the simple joys that being together brings. Whether it's splashing water with friends or pouring a gentle stream of water over someone's hands in respect, Songkran reminds us that happiness doesn't always come from grand gestures. Sometimes, it's the small, meaningful acts that bring the most joy.

How Songkran Is Celebrated Today

Today, Songkran is celebrated with three main traditions: water splashing, paying respects to elders, and temple visits.

Water Splashing

Water fights are the highlight of Songkran, especially in big cities like Bangkok and Chiang Mai. Travelers from all over the world come to Thailand to join in the water festival. From children to grandparents, everyone joins in the fun, bringing people together in a playful celebration of life.

Paying Respects to Elders

On the first day of Songkran, families gather to pour scented water over the hands of their elders, usually their grandparents and parents. This gesture is known as *Rod Nam Dum Hua,* and is a way to ask for blessings for the year ahead. It also shows respect, gratitude, and love toward the older generation. By honoring their elders, families strengthen their connections and show that they value the wisdom and guidance of their loved ones.

Visiting Temples and Offering Food to Monks

Many people visit temples during Songkran to offer food to monks and receive blessings. Some also participate in the Buddha bathing ritual, where they pour water over Buddha statues as a symbol of cleansing and renewal. These rituals are done by people who hope to start the New Year with good karma and positive energy.

The Spirit of Songkran Around the World

The joyful spirit of Songkran has spread far beyond Thailand. Thai communities in other countries, like the United States, Canada, and Australia, celebrate Songkran to keep their traditions alive. Even in places where water fights might not be possible, people still gather to honor their elders, visit temples, and enjoy Thai food. These celebrations help Thai families feel connected to their culture, no matter where they live.

For those who are not Thai, Songkran has become an opportunity to learn about Thai culture and values. Many people who have experienced Songkran say it's one of the happiest and most memorable celebrations they've ever seen. The festival serves as a reminder that the joy of renewal, unity, and gratitude is universal and can be shared by people of all backgrounds.

The Meaning of Songkran in Our Lives

The Songkran festival teaches us that each year, we have a chance to wash away the past and welcome a fresh start. Whether it's in a big water fight or a simple moment of reflection, Songkran encourages us to be grateful for our families and communities and to look forward to what's to come.

Just like the Water Spirits in the old legends, Songkran reminds us that life is full of cycles—of growth, renewal, and celebration. The next time you turn on the faucet or take a drink of water, remember the story of Songkran and the blessings that water brings to our lives. And perhaps you'll feel inspired to celebrate renewal in your own way, showing kindness to others and honoring the precious resources that help our world grow.

Songkran is a time to reflect, renew, and rejoice. So whether you're splashing in a puddle, watering plants, or just enjoying the sound of rain, remember the spirit of Songkran, and let it remind you of the simple joys that make life beautiful.

CHAPTER 10: THE GIANT OF WAT ARUN - YAKSHA THE PROTECTOR

As you well know from the first chapters, the Thai people revere their legends as much as they do their festivals and other traditions. One of the most important said traditions is their religion, Buddhism. Due to this faith, there are many magnificent buildings around the country that have been built to honor it. One such building exists on the banks of the *Chao Phraya* River in Bangkok. Here you will see a magnificent temple rise to the sky. Known as *Wat Arun*, or the Temple of Dawn, it's one of Thailand's most beautiful and famous landmarks. Its tall, spire-like towers gleam as the sun rises, creating a scene so magical that it has captivated visitors for centuries. However, Wat Arun is not only known for its beauty. It is also protected by a legendary giant known as the *Yaksha*. This powerful guardian stands watch at the temple gates, towering over visitors with a fierce and mighty appearance.

In Thai folklore, giants, like Yaksha, play important roles as protectors and guardians. The tale of Yaksha, the protector of Wat Arun, is a story of strength, responsibility, and dedication. It teaches us about the role of protectors in Thai legends and how giants became symbols of strength and courage.

The Tale of the Yaksha Who Guards the Temple Gates

The legend of Yaksha began long ago, during a time when supernatural beings were believed to walk among humans. According to Thai mythology, Yakshas were giant spirits known for their strength and loyalty. Some of these giants were warriors who defended the gods, while others were fierce guardians who protected sacred places from evil forces.

Yaksha, the guardian of Wat Arun, is one of the most well-known and respected giants in Thailand. Standing tall at the temple gates, he is depicted with a towering frame, fierce eyes, and a menacing expression that warns all intruders to keep away. With his enormous size and brightly colored armor, Yaksha commands respect and awe. He wears a traditional helmet with pointed spires and carries a large club, which symbolizes his readiness to defend the temple from harm.

Legend has it that Yaksha was chosen by the gods to protect Wat Arun. The temple was a sacred place where monks prayed and performed rituals, and the gods wanted it to remain safe from anyone who might disturb its peace. Yaksha accepted his duty with pride and vowed to stand guard for all eternity. Rain or shine, day or night, he would remain at the temple gates, making sure that no harm came to this holy place.

Over time, Yaksha became a symbol of protection, strength, and loyalty. People began to feel safe under his watchful gaze, knowing that his powerful presence would keep away evil spirits and intruders.

Children who visited Wat Arun would look up at Yaksha in awe, imagining what it would be like to be as brave and strong as this giant guardian.

How Giants Became Guardians in Thai Folklore

In Thai folklore, giants, also called Yakshas (this is, of course, why Wat Arun's guardian is named Yashka), are often seen as guardians. The belief in Yakshas originated in ancient Hindu and Buddhist traditions, where giants were considered supernatural beings with immense power. In Buddhist stories, Yakshas were sometimes fierce and frightening, but they also had a deep sense of duty and loyalty to protect what was sacred. This made them ideal guardians for temples, treasures, and holy sites.

Throughout Thailand, statues of Yakshas can be found guarding temple entrances, often in pairs. These guardians are usually painted in bright colors and wear traditional armor and helmets, making them look both fierce and majestic. They stand with weapons in hand, ready to defend the temple and its visitors.

One of the most famous stories involving Yakshas is the tale of *Ramakien*, which you should remember is the Thai version of the ancient Indian epic, the

Ramayana. In this story, giants play a major role as both friends and foes. The most famous giant in the Ramakien is *Tosakanth*, a powerful king of the giants who fought against the hero, *Rama (yes, the very same who worked with Hanuman to save Rama's wife, Sita).* While Tosakanth was a fierce opponent to Rama, he was also respected for his loyalty and strength. Stories like these are what caused Yakshas to become symbols of both danger and protection, teaching people to respect their power and appreciate their role as protectors.

In Thai beliefs, Yakshas are also believed to guard the natural world along with their temples, watching over forests, rivers, and mountains. These giants serve as reminders of the importance of respecting sacred places and preserving the beauty of nature. Yakshas help maintain the balance between the human and spiritual worlds by keeping these places safe.

Lessons About Responsibility and Protection

The tale of Wat Arun's beloved Yaksha, along with the broader role of Yakshas in Thai folklore, teach us important lessons about responsibility and protection. Here are some of the values we can learn from these legendary giants:

The Importance of Taking Responsibility

Yaksha accepted his role as guardian of Wat Arun with pride and commitment. His sense of duty reminds us that responsibility is not just a task, but a promise to care for and protect something important. When we take responsibility for something, whether it's a chore, a project, or a promise, we show that we care and can be trusted to fulfill our duty.

Protecting What Is Sacred

Just as Yaksha stands guard over the temple, we can protect things that are precious to us, like our families, friendships, and the environment. By standing up for what we believe in and looking after things that matter, we show respect and dedication, just like the giant guardians of Thai folklore.

Standing Strong in the Face of Challenges

Yakshas do not back down in the face of danger, and they are always prepared to protect those who need it. Their bravery teaches us the value of standing strong, even when things get tough. Just like Yaksha, we can face our challenges with courage and determination.

Respecting Boundaries and Rules

Yakshas guard the temple gates to keep intruders out, reminding us of the importance of respecting boundaries and rules. By following the rules and respecting the spaces of others, we create a safe and peaceful environment for everyone.

Visiting Yaksha at Wat Arun

If you visit Wat Arun in Bangkok, you'll have the chance to see Yaksha standing tall, clad in his intricate armor and decorated with bright colors, at the entrance. The experience of standing in front of this mighty guardian is both exciting and humbling.

When you look up at Yaksha, you might feel as though he's looking right back at you, silently reminding you to be respectful and mindful of the sacred space you're entering. Yaksha's presence encourages visitors to step carefully and speak softly as they enter Wat Arun, showing respect for the temple and all it represents.

Some visitors even say a silent thank you to Yaksha before entering, acknowledging his role as a protector and expressing gratitude for the peace he provides. This small gesture helps people feel connected to the ancient traditions of Thailand and shows that Yaksha's role as a guardian is still valued today.

The Lasting Influence of Yakshas in Thai Culture

Yakshas like the giant at Wat Arun continue to inspire the Thai people to value responsibility and respect. They remind everyone of the importance of caring for sacred spaces and protecting what is important. In modern Thailand, Yakshas appear not only at temples but also in art, festivals, and even toys and storybooks for children. Through these representations, the spirit of the Yaksha lives on, teaching new generations about the power of protection and the duty of guardianship.

In Thai festivals, Yaksha masks and costumes are often worn to honor these powerful spirits. People dress up as Yakshas to celebrate their strength and pay respect to them. Children who learn about Yakshas in stories and games are inspired to be brave and kind, just like the giants they admire.

Embracing the Spirit of Yaksha in Our Lives

The story of Yaksha, the protector of Wat Arun, encourages us all to embrace responsibility and protect what is valuable in our lives. We may not stand permanently at the temple gates like Yaksha does, but we can still be guardians in our own way. By taking care of our friends, family, and community, we can bring the spirit of Yaksha into our everyday lives.

Just as Yaksha guards the temple from harm, we can stand up for what is right and protect those who need help. We can be responsible, caring, and strong, facing our challenges with courage and a sense of duty.

The tale of Yaksha at Wat Arun reminds us that every one of us has the power to be a protector, to watch over something important, and to bring peace to the world around us.

CHAPTER 11: THE MAGIC OF KRATHONGS - FLOATING LIGHTS ON THE WATER

Remember the tale of the sacred water serpent, the Naga? Well, if you do, you should also remember the annual *Loy Krathong* festival, which lights up rivers, ponds, and lakes with countless tiny, glowing lights throughout Thailand. On the night of Loy Krathong, people from all over the country gather near water to release beautiful, handmade *krathongs*, or floating lanterns. These krathongs are crafted from banana leaves and decorated with flowers, candles, and incense. Watching the flickering lights drift away on the water is a mesmerizing sight that captures the imagination and fills everyone's hearts with wonder.

But, remember that as much as Loy Krathong is a pretty festival filled with light, it is also a celebration filled with stories, beliefs, and traditions that go back hundreds of years. Loy Krathong honors the Naga and pays respect to the rivers and water spirits that bring life to the land. This festival is also a time for reflection, forgiveness, and new beginnings. By letting go of the krathong, people symbolically let go of their worries, mistakes, and regrets, opening the way for fresh starts.

Join us as we explore the magic and meaning of Loy Krathong, the story behind krathongs, and the lessons of hope, renewal, and letting go that this beautiful festival teaches.

The Meaning Behind Krathongs

The krathongs released during this festival serve as much more than just beautiful decorations; they are symbols of hope, forgiveness, and renewal. Each krathong carries a candle, representing the light that guides us through life, as well as incense, which stands for respect and prayer. The flowers on the krathong add a touch of beauty and fragrance, while the banana leaves symbolize the natural world that surrounds and sustains us.

The symbolism of the banana leaves also means that the Loy Krathong festival serves a way for the Thai people to show gratitude for the water itself. Water is essential to life. It nourishes the land, helps plants grow, and provides homes for animals. This festival is even held at the end of the rainy season, when rivers are full and farmers have planted their crops. By releasing krathongs onto the water, farmers and Thai people alike give thanks to nature for its bounty and ask for a prosperous year ahead.

Furthermore, because there is such a deep connection between the Naga and its protection of water sources, people also give thanks to the Naga by setting their krathongs afloat. They believe that the Naga will bless them with good fortune, protect their homes, and keep the rivers clean and plentiful.

The act of releasing the krathong onto the water during Loy Krathong holds other meanings as well. As each person places their krathong on the river and watches it drift away, they are encouraged to think about the things they want to let go of. These people might want to let go of a mistake they made, a worry they've been holding onto, or something they regret. By letting the krathong float away, they let go of these burdens, making space in their hearts for positivity and new beginnings.

Children often take part in this ritual by writing their wishes on small pieces of paper and placing them in the krathong before setting it afloat. These wishes might be for happiness, good health, or success in school. Watching the krathong disappear into the distance, they hope their wishes will come true, carried by the currents to the water spirits who watch over the rivers.

For families, floating krathongs together can be a bonding experience. Parents and children gather around the water, often helping each other craft their krathongs or sharing stories and traditions related to the festival. This tradition brings families closer, reminding them of the importance of supporting and caring for one another.

Lessons About Letting Go and New Beginnings

Loy Krathong carries deep lessons about how letting go and starting fresh are both necessary to life. By releasing their krathongs, people take a moment to think about the past year, the things they did well, and the things they wish they could change. This reflection helps them understand the importance of forgiveness, both for themselves and for others.

Here are some of the valuable lessons we can learn from Loy Krathong:

Letting Go of Worries and Regrets

Just as the krathong floats away on the water, we can let go of the things that weigh us down. Everyone makes mistakes, and it's natural to feel sad or frustrated when things don't go as planned. But by releasing those feelings, we can free ourselves from the burden of regret and focus on the positive things in life. Loy Krathong reminds us that it's okay to let go and forgive ourselves.

Embracing New Beginnings

Every krathong represents a fresh start. By letting go of the past, we create space for new opportunities, friendships, and adventures. Each year offers us the chance to learn, grow, and try new things. Loy Krathong encourages us to embrace these changes with hope and positivity.

Respecting and Thanking Nature

Loy Krathong teaches us the importance of respecting the environment and giving thanks for the resources that nature provides. Rivers, lakes, and forests are gifts that sustain life, and it is our duty to protect and care for them. By honoring the Naga and showing gratitude for water, we are reminded to take care of the Earth and appreciate its beauty.

Sharing with Family and Community

Loy Krathong is a time for families and communities to come together. Celebrating this festival with loved ones reminds us of the joy of sharing experiences and creating memories. It's a time to bond with family members, friends, and neighbors, strengthening the ties that connect us to each other.

Making Wishes and Setting Goals

Many people place wishes in their krathongs, hoping for good health, happiness, or success. This act encourages us to think about our dreams and set goals for the future. By making a wish and sending it out into the world, we remind ourselves to work towards those dreams with hope and determination.

How to Make Your Own Krathong

One of the most enjoyable parts of Loy Krathong is making your own krathong. In Thailand, krathongs are traditionally made from banana leaves, banana stems, and flowers. Making a krathong is a creative process that allows each person to add their personal touch, making it unique and special.

Here's a simple way to make a krathong:

Find a Base

The base of the krathong is often made from a slice of banana stem, but you can use any piece of natural or organic material that floats, such as a slice of bread or a piece of some other biodegradable material. The base should be sturdy enough to support the decorations.

Add Leaves and Flowers

Now, arrange the banana leaves (or other types of leaves) around the base to form petals. Secure the leaves with small toothpicks. Then, decorate the krathong with fresh flowers, such as marigolds or orchids, to add color and fragrance.

Place a Candle and Incense

In the center of the krathong, place a small candle (make sure there is no metal or plastic base on your candle!) and one or two sticks of incense. The candle will symbolize light and guidance, while the incense will carry prayers and gratitude to the heavens.

Write a Wish

If you'd like, write a wish or something you want to let go of on a small piece of paper. Fold it and tuck it into the krathong as a symbol of your hopes and dreams.

Release Your Krathong

Find a safe body of water, such as a river, lake, or pond, and gently release your krathong. As you watch it float away, think about the things you're letting go of and the new beginnings you're embracing.

Celebrating Loy Krathong with Others

On the night of Loy Krathong, towns and villages all over Thailand come alive with celebration. Streets are filled with music, dance, and food stalls. People wear traditional clothing, and colorful decorations brighten up every corner. Fireworks light up the sky, adding to the excitement and joy of the festival.

One of the most enchanting sights of the festival is the thousands of krathongs floating together on the water. Each glowing light represents a person's hopes, dreams, and the promise of a new beginning. For children, it's a night filled with wonder and excitement, as they join their families in celebrating the beauty of the floating lights and the magic of Loy Krathong.

Families often come together to share a meal, play games, and exchange stories. This festival is a time for laughter, connection, and building memories. Many towns also host krathong-making contests, where participants can show off their creativity by designing the most beautiful or unique krathong.

A Magical Festival of Reflection and Renewal

Loy Krathong is a festival that brings light to the night, hope to the heart, and peace to the soul. As the krathongs drift away on the water, they carry with them wishes for a brighter future, as well as freedom from worries and new possibilities.

This festival teaches us to reflect on the past, appreciate the present, and look forward to the future with optimism. It reminds us that, just like the krathong floating into the distance, we too can let go of our troubles and make room for joy, growth, and new adventures.

In the spirit of Loy Krathong, may we all learn to let go, embrace new beginnings, and cherish the beauty of the world around us.

CHAPTER 12:
THE LEGEND OF THE TIGER SPIRIT - PROTECTOR OF THE FORESTS

Now, if we follow our krathongs on their journey through the rivers they have been set upon, into the deep in the lush, green jungles of Thailand, where ancient trees stretch towards the sky and rivers flow with sparkling water, there is a powerful presence that roams silently, protecting the natural world. This is the Tiger Spirit, another revered and feared guardian (though this spirit solely protects the forests). For centuries, the Tiger Spirit has been celebrated in Thai folklore as a symbol of courage, strength, and respect for the wild. The Thai people believe that the spirit of the tiger watches over the jungle, ensuring the balance between humans and nature, guiding those who respect the land, and warning those who do not.

The Tiger Spirit is a reminder to everyone that conservation and respect for the environment are integral to our existence. Join us as we learn about how the Tiger Spirit became the protector of the forest, meet some of the people who have encountered this powerful spirit, and explore the lessons it teaches about caring for nature.

How the Tiger Became a Guardian of the Jungle

Long ago, the jungles of Thailand were untamed, mysterious, and filled with all sorts of animals, from tiny birds with colorful feathers to massive elephants that traveled in herds. The tiger, with its fiery orange coat and bold black stripes, was one of the most majestic creatures in the jungle. It moved silently through the trees, blending into the shadows, as if it were a part of the forest itself.

According to Thai legends, the tiger was not always a spirit. In the beginning, it was simply a strong and fierce animal. But one day, the spirit of the jungle saw the struggle between the jungle animals and the people who damaged their home. These people had begun to cut down trees and hunt animals without understanding the importance of balance in the jungle. The spirit of the jungle thus decided that the tiger was the perfect animal to become its protector. With its powerful presence and wisdom, the tiger would be able to guard the forest and guide people toward respect for nature.

One night, the jungle spirit appeared to a wise old tiger that had lived in the forest for many years. The spirit whispered to the tiger, "I have chosen you to be the guardian of the forest. You will be known as the Tiger Spirit, and it will be your duty to protect this land and all the creatures who live here. You must guide the people to care for the forest and respect its beauty."

The tiger accepted this great honor, transforming into the Tiger Spirit as he had been told by the spirit of the jungle. The tiger spirit gained the ability to appear in dreams, disappear into thin air, and watch over the jungle from anywhere. Since that night, the Tiger Spirit has been a guardian of the jungle, a watchful protector who makes sure that the forest remains healthy and alive.

So naturally, over the years, many people have traveled through Thailand's forests, and some have claimed to have seen or felt the presence of the Tiger Spirit. Some of these stories tell of people who respected the jungle and were rewarded by the Tiger Spirit, while others tell of those who ignored the rules of nature and faced the consequences. Let's recount some of these famous legends.

The Story of the Kind Woodcutter

There was once a woodcutter named *Chai* who lived near the edge of the forest. Every day, he would walk into the jungle to gather wood, but he always took care to never cut down more than he needed. He tried to only take dead branches or fallen trees, and he made sure to leave the forest as he found it.

One evening, as Chai was gathering wood, he felt something watching him. He turned and saw a tiger with shining golden eyes standing a few yards away. At first, he was afraid, but then he realized that the tiger was not looking at him with anger or hunger. It was the Tiger Spirit, watching over him. Chai put his hands together and bowed respectfully to the tiger.

The Tiger Spirit nodded, as if approving of Chai's respect for the forest, and then slowly disappeared into the trees. From that day on, Chai always felt safe in the jungle, knowing that the Tiger Spirit was watching over him. The villagers noticed that Chai always found the best wood, and they believed that the Tiger Spirit had blessed him for his kindness and respect for nature.

The Tale of the Greedy Hunter

But, in the same village where Chai lived, there was a hunter named *Ruang* who wanted to be known as the best hunter in the land. Ruang had no respect for the forest; he hunted animals not because he needed food, but because he wanted to show off his skill and make a lot of money selling animal pelts (or the entire skin and fur of animals taken in one piece).

One day, Ruang ventured deep into the jungle, farther than anyone had ever gone. He hunted animals without limit, leaving a trail of destruction in his path. That night, as Ruang set up camp, he heard a low growl nearby. He looked up and saw a tiger with eyes as bright as the moon, standing silently, staring at him with disappointment and anger. It was the Tiger Spirit.

Ruang was terrified. He tried to run, but no matter where he went, he felt the Tiger Spirit's presence around him. The jungle seemed to close in on him, and he got lost, unable to find his way back. After hours of wandering, he realized he had made a terrible mistake in disrespecting the forest.

The next morning, when Ruang finally returned to the village, he was a changed man. He no longer hunted for sport or greed. Ruang had instead learned his lesson, and he spent the rest of his life teaching others about the importance of respecting the forest and the Tiger Spirit who guarded it.

Lessons About Conservation and Respect for Nature

The legend of the Tiger Spirit teaches us many important lessons about the environment and how we should treat the world around us. These stories serve as reminders that the forest is not just a place to take from; it's a home for many living creatures and a source of beauty and wonder.

Here are some of the lessons we can learn from the legend of the Tiger Spirit:

Respect for All Living Things

The Tiger Spirit protects the jungle because it understands the value of every tree, plant, animal, and stream. Just as the Tiger Spirit watches over the forest, we should take care of the natural world around us. Every part of the ecosystem has a role, and when we respect each creature and plant, we help maintain balance.

Conservation and Taking Only What We Need

The story of Chai, the kind woodcutter, shows us the importance of conservation. By only taking what he needed and leaving the forest unharmed, Chai earned the respect of the Tiger Spirit. We can learn from his example by using natural resources wisely, not wasting, and thinking about leaving enough for future generations.

Understanding the Consequences of Greed

Ruang's story is a lesson about the dangers of greed (taking too much) when it comes to the environment. When we take more than we need or harm nature for selfish reasons, it can lead to problems not only for ourselves but for everyone. Respect for nature must come from within.

Protecting the Wilderness

Just as the Tiger Spirit guards the forest, we too have a role to play in protecting nature. Whether it's by planting trees, cleaning up litter, or supporting organizations that protect wildlife, every action counts. By becoming guardians of nature, we can help preserve the beauty of our planet.

Being Mindful of Our Actions

According to the legend, the Tiger Spirit is always watching, making sure that people treat the forest well. This teaches us to be mindful of our actions, even when we think that no one is watching. By taking care of our environment, we can create a world that is healthier and more beautiful for everyone.

Protecting the Forests and Wildlife of Today

While the Tiger Spirit lives in the legends of Thailand, real tigers and other animals still roam the forests and jungles of the world. Sadly, many of these animals are at risk of extinction due to deforestation, pollution, and hunting. We can honor the spirit of the Tiger by taking action to protect these animals and their habitats.

There are many ways that we can help. For example, you can:

Plant Trees

Planting trees is one of the simplest ways to protect forests. Trees provide shelter and food for animals and help keep the air clean.

Reduce Waste

By recycling, reusing, and reducing our waste, we can keep forests and other natural areas clean. Less waste means less pollution, making it easier for animals to survive.

Support Wildlife Conservation Efforts

Many organizations work to protect wildlife and their habitats. By supporting these efforts, whether through donations, volunteering, or spreading awareness, we can make a difference.

Learn and Share Stories

Just like the stories of the Tiger Spirit, sharing tales and knowledge about nature and conservation can inspire others to take care of the environment. We can help others understand why it's important to protect the forests and the animals who live there.

Celebrating the Spirit of the Tiger

By honoring the Tiger Spirit and following its example, we become part of a long tradition of caring for the environment. Whether through small actions like picking up litter or bigger commitments like supporting conservation efforts, each step we take helps protect the natural world.

So the next time you walk through a forest, listen carefully. Feel the strength of the trees, the rustle of leaves, and the sounds of animals all around. Imagine that the Tiger Spirit is watching over, ensuring that the forest remains a place of beauty and balance. Remember that we too have a responsibility to protect and care for these special and beautiful places for ourselves, for generations to come, for the animals, and for the Tiger Spirit who watches from the shadows.

CHAPTER 13: THE TALE OF SANG THONG - THE GOLDEN PRINCE

From Thailand's jungles to its enchanting kingdoms, there are many fascinating characters still to be discovered. In this story, we will explore a kingdom far away in Thailand, where a tale has been told for centuries about a very special prince named *Sang Thong*. Sang Thong was no ordinary prince as he was born with a face and body made of pure gold. And, though Sang Thong is also known as "the Golden Prince," he was not raised in the palace surrounded by riches. Instead, his life was filled with mystery, adventure, and valuable lessons that showed everyone around him the true meaning of worth, kindness, and inner beauty.

How a Prince in Disguise Proved His True Worth

Sang Thong's story begins in a small, humble village. Though he was born to a royal family, his life took an unexpected turn right from the start. Sang Thong was born with mystical golden skin, causing his family to fear the reaction of the kingdom toward him. His appearance was so unusual and dazzling that his family believed the people might misunderstand or even fear him. This worry caused them to hide Sang Thong away, hoping to keep his true identity a secret.

As Sang Thong grew older, he became curious about the world beyond the palace walls. He wanted to experience life as everyone else did, and did not want his golden skin to define him. So, with the help of a magical mask, Sang Thong disguised his golden face. To the world, he appeared to be a simple, ordinary young man with no special powers or riches. This mask allowed him to walk through villages, meet new people, and learn about life. This appearance meant he was free of any expectations.

Though he was the true prince of the kingdom, Sang Thong worked hard, did chores, and helped others. He spent his days among villagers, working as they did and living humbly. The villagers knew him as a kind and gentle boy who was always willing to help them, never realizing that he was actually the royal prince.

The Magic Mask That Hid His Golden Face

Sang Thong's mask was a powerful artifact given to him by a wise elder in the palace. This elder understood Sang Thong's desire to live a life where he could learn and grow. As such, the mask hid not only his golden face, but also his noble heritage, allowing him to experience life as any other person might.

The elder warned Sang Thong, "Remember, true beauty lies not in what people see, but in who you are inside. Use this mask wisely, for one day, your golden heart will shine through no matter what you wear."

With this advice in mind, Sang Thong set out on his journey through villages and towns. In his travels, he encountered all kinds of people. Some were kind and generous, others not so much. But no matter how people treated him, Sang Thong always showed kindness and respect. He helped those in need, shared what little he had, and never used his golden birthright to make himself seem more important.

A Contest of Strength and Skill

One day, word spread throughout the kingdom of a grand contest held by a neighboring king. The king was searching for a brave, strong, and wise man to marry his daughter, the princess. Many young men gathered from near and far, each hoping to win the contest and the princess's hand.

Sang Thong was curious about the contest, but he didn't think he would have a chance. After all,. However, his friends in the village encouraged him to join, saying, "You may not have riches, but you have a heart of gold. Surely that counts for something!"

Encouraged by his friends' faith in him, Sang Thong decided to join the contest. As he arrived, he saw many fine young men dressed in splendid clothes, all eager to prove their strength and skill. They laughed and sneered at Sang Thong's simple appearance, seeing him as no competition.

The king announced the first challenge: an archery contest. Each contestant had to hit a tiny target placed far across a field. Many missed, but Sang

Thong, remembering the training he had received as a child, took a deep breath, steadied his hand, and let the arrow fly. It hit the target perfectly, surprising everyone.

The second challenge was a test of wisdom. The king presented a difficult riddle and asked each young man to solve it. Sang Thong, having spent time learning from the wise villagers and listening to stories of old, easily answered the riddle, impressing the king.

The third and final challenge was one of kindness. The king wanted to see if the contestants possessed true compassion. When it was Sang Thong's turn, he recounted his travels and how he had helped many people along the way. His humble tales of generosity touched the hearts of those who listened, including the princess, who was watching from afar.

The Golden Revelation

After passing all the challenges, Sang Thong was declared the winner. The king and the princess were overjoyed, but there was still one thing left to reveal—who Sang Thong truly was. With a deep breath, Sang Thong removed his magical mask, revealing his golden skin.

The crowd gasped in amazement. His face, radiant and golden, shone brightly in the sunlight. The villagers and the other young men were astounded to see that the humble young man that they had underestimated was not only the contest's winner but also a prince. They realized that Sang Thong's worth did not lie in his golden skin but in his kindness, bravery, and humility.

The king and the princess welcomed Sang Thong as family, and they celebrated the day as one of new beginnings. The princess, having seen Sang Thong's inner beauty and courage, knew she had found a noble-hearted man to stand by her side.

Lessons About Humility and Inner Beauty

The tale of Sang Thong, the Golden Prince, teaches us valuable lessons about humility and inner beauty. Here are some of the important morals we can take from this legend:

True Worth Lies Within

Sang Thong's story reminds us that true worth comes from within. His golden skin was hidden behind a mask, meaning what was truly valuable about him was the kindness and humility that shined through in his actions. This teaches us that it's not our appearance or what we have on the outside that matters, but who we are inside and how we treat others.

Humility Is a Strength

Despite being born a prince, Sang Thong chose to live humbly, respecting others and learning from his experiences. He didn't boast about his abilities or his royal lineage, but instead earned respect through his actions. Humility, he showed, is a strength that can win people's hearts.

The Power of Kindness

Sang Thong's kindness, generosity, and willingness to help others were what truly set him apart. Even when others looked down on him, he responded with compassion. His kindness ultimately won him the contest and the love of the people.

Inner Beauty Is More Valuable Than Outer Appearances

Sang Thong's golden skin may have made him unique, but it was his inner beauty that made him truly exceptional. This story encourages us to look beyond appearances and value others for their character.

We Should Embrace Challenges with an Open Heart

Throughout his journey, Sang Thong faced many challenges, yet he remained open-hearted and optimistic. His willingness to try new things, even when others doubted him, shows the importance of facing challenges with courage and a positive attitude.

The Legacy of Sang Thong's Tale

The tale of Sang Thong, the Golden Prince, has been passed down through generations in Thailand. It's a story that celebrates the importance of humility, kindness, and inner strength. Sang Thong became a hero not because of his unique appearance, but rather his noble actions and heart.

Today, this story continues to inspire people to look beyond the surface and to find beauty in their own actions and those of others. Just like Sang Thong, we all have the potential to shine, not because of how we look, but because of who we are inside.

So the next time you feel nervous about facing a challenge or think that others might judge you by your appearance, remember the story of the Golden Prince. Each of us carries our own inner light, a glow that comes from kindness, courage, and a willingness to help others. Like Sang Thong, we all have the power to make a difference and to be recognized for our true worth.

CHAPTER 14: THE FESTIVAL OF THE FULL MOON - YI PENG

Golden light is an integral part of Thai culture. As Sang Thong's inner beauty became a light that glimmered as much as his golden skin, there is a festival that focuses on the power of physical light to overcome the darkness. Each year in Thailand, the night sky becomes a sea of glowing lanterns floating gently upward, like stars being born during the celebration called *Yi Peng*. This festival is also known as the Festival of the Full Moon. Yi Peng is a time of hope, wishes, and joy. It's when families and friends gather to honor the full moon, release their worries, and fill their hearts with dreams for the future.

How Lanterns Are Released to Honor the Full Moon

On the night of Yi Peng, people across Thailand, especially in the northern city of *Chiang Mai*, come together to prepare their *khom loi*—or, floating lanterns. These lanterns are made of thin paper with a small opening at the bottom where a candle or fuel source is placed. When the candle is lit, the heat fills the lantern, and it begins to rise, floating gracefully into the night sky.

Imagine standing in a crowd of people holding these delicate lanterns. As you watch the lantern glow and feel it begin to lift, there's a moment of excitement and shared connection with everyone around you. The full moon shines brightly above, lighting up the night, and the gentle breeze carries each lantern higher, as if guiding it toward the stars.

The lanterns are released as an offering to honor the moon and, in some beliefs, to send a message to spirits or ancestors. It is said that each lantern carries away any negative feelings or worries, freeing people's hearts and leaving them open to new joys. As you let go of your lantern, you feel a sense of peace as you release all your troubles and make space for hope.

The Tradition of Making Wishes for Good Luck

Yi Peng is about making wishes for the future as much as it is about letting go of worries from the past. Before releasing their lanterns, many people take a quiet moment to close their eyes, hold their hands together in a prayer-like gesture, and make a wish. It could be for good health, success in school, happiness for family members, or even a small personal goal.

In Thai culture, the belief is that if your lantern rises high and disappears into the night without faltering or falling back down, your wish will come true. As kids watch their lanterns drift upwards, they giggle and cheer, hopeful that their wishes will soar as high as the stars.

Some people even write their wishes or prayers on the lantern itself before it is released. Families gather around, helping each other hold the lantern steady, whispering their dreams and goals into the quiet night air. The act of wishing during Yi Peng brings people closer together, making them feel united in their dreams and hopes.

The Symbolism of Light in Yi Peng

The light from the lanterns during Yi Peng symbolizes hope, knowledge, and the triumph of good over evil. As people light their lanterns and watch them float away, it's as if each glowing light is carrying a positive wish, lighting up the darkness of the night.

This symbolism is rooted in the idea that, just like the lanterns, our hopes and dreams can help us overcome challenges and bring brightness to our lives. Yi Peng reminds people to stay hopeful and to believe that even in the darkest of times, there is always a way forward, just like the light of the full moon and the floating lanterns.

The Meaning of Yi Peng and the Full Moon

The full moon itself holds a special place in Thai culture, as it is thought to be a symbol of completion, fullness, and balance. The bright, round moon represents unity and harmony, making Yi Peng a perfect time for families and communities to come together, strengthen their bonds, and share a joyful experience.

In Thailand, the moon is also respected as a part of the natural world that affects life on Earth. During Yi Peng, people honor the moon for the role it plays in marking time and guiding agricultural cycles. It's a time when everyone can pause, appreciate nature's wonders, and feel grateful for the simple joys of life.

Celebrations and Festivities

The festival of Yi Peng is not only about lanterns; it's also a time for vibrant parades, traditional dances, and music. The streets come alive with colorful decorations, and people dress in traditional Thai clothing. Flowers, especially marigolds, are used to decorate temples, streets, and homes, symbolizing good fortune and positivity.

Children giggle as they watch dancers in beautiful costumes perform traditional Thai dances. Music fills the air, adding to the festive spirit, while street vendors sell tasty treats and toys. Friends and families enjoy the night, sharing food, laughter, and stories. Yi Peng is a time for joy and celebration, for young and old alike to come together and honor their shared traditions.

Lessons About Hope and Celebration

Yi Peng, with its enchanting lanterns and the glow of the full moon, teaches us many valuable lessons:

Letting Go of Worries

Releasing lanterns symbolizes letting go of negativity and worries. Just like the lantern floats away, we can learn to let go of things that weigh us down. This act of releasing our worries encourages us to move forward with an open heart and mind.

Celebrating New Beginnings

Yi Peng is a time of hope and renewal. Just as the moon completes its cycle and begins again, we too can start fresh, setting new goals and making new wishes. This festival reminds us that every ending is also a new beginning, and we should celebrate each chance we get to grow and improve.

Believing in the Power of Wishes

During Yi Peng, everyone—children and adults alike—makes wishes. This shows us the importance of hope and imagination. Wishing on a lantern is a reminder that dreams are important and that having goals gives us something to look forward to and work towards.

Unity and Togetherness

Yi Peng is a festival that brings people together. Families, friends, and communities join hands to celebrate, share stories, and help each other. This festival is a beautiful example of how unity can make experiences richer and more meaningful.

Respect for Nature

The festival also teaches respect for the natural world. The full moon is honored for its beauty and its role in the rhythms of life. Yi Peng reminds us to cherish and respect the world around us, to see the beauty in nature, and to protect it for future generations.

A Magical Experience for All Ages

Yi Peng is especially magical for kids, who watch the sky fill up with floating lights as if stars have come down to Earth. For children, the festival feels like stepping into a dream, where wishes can come true, and the night is filled with wonder. They run around, excitedly helping to light lanterns, holding onto their parents' hands as they make their wishes, and watching in awe as the lanterns float higher and higher.

Parents and grandparents share stories with the younger generation, passing down the meaning of the festival, so they may understand its importance. This shared experience across ages means the Yi Peng festival holds a special place in the hearts of everyone, young and old.

The Legacy of Yi Peng

For anyone who experiences Yi Peng, whether Thai or from another culture, the festival leaves a lasting impression. The sight of countless floating lanterns that carry hopes and dreams is a reminder of the beauty of community, the power of hope, and the importance of traditions. Yi Peng is not just a celebration but a way for people to express their gratitude, their dreams, and their unity.

So, as those who celebrate Yi Peng do, let's remember to hold onto our dreams, believe in the power of new beginnings, and celebrate life's special moments with the people we care about. Whether we're releasing a lantern or simply making a wish on a star, we can carry the spirit of Yi Peng with us, spreading light, hope, and joy wherever we go.

CHAPTER 15:
THE STORY OF KHUN PHAEN
- THE WARRIOR AND HIS CHARMS

Let's follow one of the glowing lanterns of Yi Peng up into the sky, and travel back in time with it to the Thai ancestors who are listening to the prayers and wishes their family members are sending them. If we follow this special lantern, we will end up in the lush, green kingdom of ancient Thailand, where there once lived a warrior named *Khun Phaen*. The ancestors knew Khun Phaen for his bravery, cleverness, and magical skills. The legend of his life was filled with thrilling adventures, fierce battles, and magical powers that helped Khun Phaen protect his people and kingdom. Khun Phaen is remembered not only for his strength but also for his powerful charms and amulets, which, as you can probably now imagine, were used to outsmart his enemies and accomplish incredible feats.

How Khun Phaen Used Magic to Defend His Kingdom

Khun Phaen possessed not only great skills in battle, but also the knowledge of ancient Thai magic, which gave him powers beyond what most could imagine. From a young age, he was trained in the art of combat, strategy, and spells. His heart was full of courage and loyalty to his people, and he vowed to use his talents to protect his kingdom.

One day, a neighboring kingdom prepared to invade Khun Phaen's land. The invading army was large and well-equipped, and many people in Khun Phaen's kingdom feared they would not be able to defend themselves. But Khun Phaen stood tall and confident, reassuring everyone that he would do whatever it took to protect them.

On the battlefield, Khun Phaen's presence was unforgettable. Clad in armor and carrying a powerful sword, which he had enchanted with powerful spells, Khun Phaen marched to meet his enemies in battle. To further strengthen him in battle, Khun Phaen had also created magical charms that would help him. These charms made him invisible to his enemies at times, allowing him to move like a shadow across the battlefield, surprising his foes (another word for enemies).

One of his most famous magical feats during this battle was summoning a giant, invisible force that acted like a shield, protecting his soldiers from arrows and other attacks. People said it was as if an invisible wall guarded Khun Phaen and his men. This enchanted shield gave them courage, and they charged forward with great bravery, led by their fearless warrior.

The Power of Charms in Thai Folklore

In Thai culture, charms and amulets (like the Nung Phaya which had been blessed by the ancient queen who shared its name) have long been believed to hold magical powers. These items are often created by monks or wise elders who perform rituals and bless the charms with protective spells. Charms can take many forms—small stones, carved symbols, or even pieces of clothing. When carried or worn, they are said to bring good luck, safety, or strength.

Khun Phaen's charms were legendary. He carried several amulets, each with a unique power that helped him in different situations. One of his charms was a small statue of a mythical animal that he kept in a pouch around his neck. This charm was said to give him the speed and agility of a tiger, allowing him to move and dodge attacks effortlessly.

Khung Phaen also had a charm made from the wood of a sacred tree, which he kept hidden in his clothing. This charm was said to have protected him from harm so that when he wore it, no weapon could pierce his skin. His enemies were astounded by his invincibility, for no matter how hard they tried, they couldn't harm him. This charm, blessed by monks, was a symbol of the power of faith and belief in something greater than oneself.

Khun Phaen's magical abilities have made him into a powerful symbol of Thai folklore. Many people admired him and wished to be as brave and skilled as he was. Today, people still wear charms and amulets inspired by Khun Phaen's story, hoping for good fortune and protection.

The Story of Khun Phaen's Golden Boy Charm

Khun Phaen also carried a "Golden Boy" charm, also known as *Kuman Thong*. This charm held within it a spirit that could help Khun Phaen whenever he needed. The Golden Boy was believed to have powers of sight and protection, meaning it could warn Khun Phaen of danger before it arrived. Some say that the Golden Boy could even offer Khun Phaen advice and help him make decisions.

Thanks to the Golden Boy charm, Khun Phaen often escaped from difficult situations unharmed. In one tale, he was captured by enemies and locked away in a high tower with no chance of escape. But the Golden Boy appeared to him, showing him a hidden way out of the tower. Following the charm's guidance, Khun Phaen escaped and returned home, much to the amazement of his friends and family.

Khun Phaen's Golden Boy charm became his most-trusted companion. He would talk to it, ask it for guidance, and draw on its presence to strengthen him, especially when facing tough challenges. Unsurprisingly, the Kuman Thong is a charm that is still cherished today in Thai culture, as it is thought to bring good luck and protection to its owner.

Lessons About Bravery and Cleverness

The story of Khun Phaen teaches us that bravery is as much about facing enemies or fighting in battles as it is about having the courage to do what's right, even when it's difficult. Khun Phaen was brave because he was willing to stand up for his kingdom and protect the people he loved.

Khun Phaen's cleverness was equally important as his bravery. He didn't just rely on his physical strength; he used his mind and his knowledge of magic to solve problems. In one tale, when Khun Phaen found himself surrounded by enemies in a dense forest, he used a charm to confuse his foes, making it seem as if there were hundreds of warriors in the forest. The enemy army became so frightened that they retreated, believing they were outnumbered.

This is one of the many examples of his clever use of charms and other strategies. Khun Phaen is proof that sometimes, the best way to solve a problem is by thinking creatively and using the tools we have in unexpected ways. Khun Phaen's story reminds us that, if used together, bravery and cleverness can make us unstoppable.

Khun Phaen's Wisdom and Kindness

Despite his magical powers and his strength, Khun Phaen was known to be humble and kind. He never used his charms or powers to hurt others for his own gain. Instead, Khun Phaen used these tools to protect the innocent and defend his kingdom. He treated his friends, family, and soldiers with respect, always encouraging them to be brave and look out for each other.

When he wasn't fighting battles, Khun Phaen spent time learning more about his culture's wisdom and sharing his knowledge with others. He taught younger soldiers about courage, discipline, and kindness, showing them that a true warrior is not only strong, but also gentle and wise.

Khun Phaen's kindness extended to his enemies as well. In one tale, after winning a battle, he showed mercy to those he had defeated, helping them heal and find a better path in life. He believed that everyone had the potential to be good and that showing compassion to his foes could sometimes make more of a difference than fighting.

The Legacy of Khun Phaen's Charms

The tales of Khun Phaen have inspired people for centuries. His bravery, wisdom, and magical charms have become symbols of Thai culture. Today, people still make and wear charms modeled after the ones he carried, hoping to gain a bit of his strength, courage, and good fortune.

People believe that carrying a Khun Phaen amulet brings blessings and protection. These charms are often blessed by monks and given as gifts to friends and family. Just like Khun Phaen's charms, modern amulets are seen as a way to protect oneself, overcome challenges, and remind people of the values that Khun Phaen represented.

Lessons from Khun Phaen's Story

The story of Khun Phaen is more than just an exciting adventure—it's filled with valuable lessons that we can all learn from:

Courage in the Face of Challenges

Khun Phaen shows us that true bravery means facing our fears and standing up for what we believe in. No matter how difficult a situation may be, we should remember that courage can help us overcome anything.

The Power of Clever Thinking

Physical strength isn't everything. Khun Phaen's cleverness and creativity often helped him win battles and escape danger. His story reminds us thinking outside the box and using our minds can help us solve problems in unique ways.

Kindness and Compassion

Even though Khun Phaen was a powerful warrior, he was also compassionate and kind. He treated others with respect and mercy, showing us that kindness is just as important as strength.

Faith in Something Greater

The charms and amulets in Khun Phaen's story represent faith. Believing in something beyond ourselves—whether it's family, friends, or even a little bit of magic—can give us the strength to face life's challenges.

A Hero for All Ages

Khun Phaen's legacy lives on in the hearts of Thai people. His story is told in temples, at schools, and by families, inspiring children to be brave and kind, like him. Khun Phaen may have lived in ancient times, but his spirit remains alive in Thailand today. His charms, courage, and wisdom remind us that with a bit of bravery, clever thinking, and a kind heart, we too can face anything life throws our way.

In learning about Khun Phaen, we learn more about the strength and magic that lies within us all.

We may not have magical amulets or charms, but we have something just as powerful—our own hearts and minds, filled with courage and kindness. And that, in the end, is what makes a true hero.

CHAPTER 16:
THE LEGEND OF THE PHI TA KHON
- THE GHOST FESTIVAL

Though many Thai legends recount the importance of amulets and charms in Thai culture, those are not the only thing that is significant to their belief system. Every year, in the quiet town of *Dan Sai* in northeastern Thailand, an extraordinary event brings laughter, color, and excitement to the streets. People dress in dazzling costumes, paint their faces, and wear tall, vibrant masks to celebrate the *Phi Ta Khon* Festival, also known as the "Ghost Festival." This event is one of Thailand's most unique and fun celebrations, mixing elements of spirituality, tradition, and joy in a colorful display.

Let's dive into the fascinating story behind the Ghost Festival, Phi Ta Khon, where tradition meets playfulness and the Thai people connect with the spirit world in a celebration filled with laughter and life.

How Spirits Are Celebrated in the Phi Ta Khon Festival

The Phi Ta Khon Festival has roots in ancient Thai beliefs. It's said that long ago, Prince *Vessantara*, who is a figure from the past life of the Buddha, went on a journey far from his home. The people loved their prince dearly, and they missed him when he was gone. When he finally returned, everyone was so happy that their loud cheers and laughter reached even the spirits. The spirits, hearing the joyful sounds, joined in the celebration to welcome the prince back, dancing and singing with the people.

Since then, the festival has been celebrated to honor the spirits and to invite them to join the living in a celebration of life and happiness. The Thai celebrate this festival to show respect for the unseen world and to thank the spirits for protecting the town.

During the festival, people dress up as ghosts and spirits to represent these beings. And, the costumes aren't scary! Instead, colorful, fun, and often funny! By dressing as spirits, people invite these ghostly beings to join in the celebration and remind everyone that life and death are connected in a cycle that should be honored and celebrated.

The Meaning Behind the Colorful Masks and Costumes

One of the most exciting parts of the Phi Ta Khon Festival is the amazing masks that people wear. These masks are tall, pointed, and covered in bright colors. Each mask is carefully crafted by hand, often taking days to finish, and no two masks look exactly alike. The masks are usually made from bamboo or coconut leaves and are painted with wild, vibrant patterns that make them look lively and mischievous.

Each mask has a face that is meant to look like a playful ghost or spirit. Some have long, painted noses, big grins, and bold eyebrows that give them a friendly but mischievous appearance. The bright colors of the masks are a big part of what makes the festival feel so joyful and exciting. The masks also represent the connection between the people and the spirit world.

The costumes that go with the masks are just as lively. People wear long, colorful robes that are often decorated with ribbons, beads, and bells. When the festival begins, you can hear the jingle of the bells and the rustling of the robes as people move through the streets, dancing and having fun. Some even attach small toys or funny objects to their costumes to make everyone laugh, reminding everyone that the festival is about joy and togetherness.

Children also take part, often making their own small masks and costumes to join in the festivities. It's a time when the whole family can participate, sharing laughter and excitement with each other and with the spirits.

The Parade of the Spirits

The main event of the Phi Ta Khon Festival is the parade. During the parade, hundreds of people in their colorful ghost costumes dance and march through the streets. Musicians play traditional Thai instruments, and the lively sounds of drums and gongs fill the air. The streets come alive with a vibrant energy as people sing, dance, and playfully interact with the crowd.

The parade is meant to entertain both the people and the spirits. Many people believe that the spirits join in during the parade, dancing alongside the people, even if they can't be seen. The parade serves as a reminder that the spirits are always around, watching over their loved ones and sharing in their happiness.

One of the highlights of the parade is the giant wooden phalluses, which are symbols of fertility and life. These symbols are waved around playfully, encouraging a good harvest and prosperity for the town. Although it may seem strange to outsiders, this symbol has been a traditional part of the festival for generations, and it's all in good fun and humor.

The people of Dan Sai believe that by making the spirits happy, they will bring good luck, health, and prosperity to the community. The parade and celebrations also help strengthen the bonds between the people, as everyone comes together to prepare costumes, masks, and decorations.

The Legend of the Spirits and the Role of the Shaman

In Thai culture, there is often a *shaman*, or spiritual leader, who plays an important role in festivals like Phi Ta Khon. During the festival, the shaman acts as a bridge between the world of the living and the world of the spirits. He leads rituals and prayers, asking for blessings and protection from the spirits.

The shaman also takes part in the parade, wearing a unique costume and mask that distinguishes him from the other participants. His presence is essential to the festival, as he is believed to have the ability to communicate with the spirits and ensure that the festival goes smoothly.

Throughout the celebration, the shaman reminds everyone to show respect to the spirits and to celebrate responsibly. By honoring the spirits, people hope to receive blessings and ensure a peaceful and prosperous year.

The Meaning of Joy, Laughter, and Tradition

Laughter plays an important role in the Phi Ta Khon Festival. The funny costumes, silly masks, and playful behavior of the participants create an atmosphere of lightheartedness and happiness.

Laughter is seen as a way to keep negative spirits away and to fill the festival with positive energy. This joyful attitude helps the people of Dan Sai feel closer to one another and strengthens their sense of community.

Tradition is another key part of Phi Ta Khon. The festival has been celebrated for generations, and each year, people gather to continue the tradition, passing down the stories and rituals to younger generations. For children, it's an exciting time when they get to create their own masks, join the parade, and learn about the history of their culture.

Lessons About Joy, Laughter, and Tradition

The Phi Ta Khon Festival teaches several important lessons that everyone can appreciate:

Joy in Everyday Life

The festival shows us that it's important to find joy in life and to celebrate the moments that bring happiness. By honoring the spirits with laughter and celebration, the people of Dan Sai show that life is meant to be enjoyed, even in the face of challenges.

Laughter as a Powerful Force

Laughter and humor play a big role in Phi Ta Khon, bringing people together and creating a positive atmosphere. This teaches us that laughter can be a powerful tool to lift spirits, strengthen bonds, and keep negativity at bay.

Respecting Traditions and Ancestors

By celebrating the spirits and keeping the festival alive, the people of Dan Sai show respect for their ancestors and for the traditions passed down through generations. It's a reminder to honor our roots and to cherish the traditions that shape who we are.

Embracing Community

Phi Ta Khon brings people together, creating a strong sense of community. Everyone, from children to elders, joins in the preparations and celebrations. This teaches us the value of working together and supporting one another in both joyful and challenging times.

A Celebration of Life and the Spirit World

The Phi Ta Khon Festival is a wonderful example of how Thai culture celebrates life and the spirit world in harmony. It's a festival that blends spirituality with fun, allowing people to remember the spirits with joy instead of fear. By dressing up, dancing, and laughing together, the people of Dan Sai honor the spirits and invite them to be part of the world of the living once again.

Each year, when the festival comes to an end, people say goodbye to the spirits with gratitude, thanking them for joining the celebration and blessing the town. The spirits are sent back to their world, but the memories of the festival remain in the hearts of the people, carrying them through until the next year's celebration.

Carrying On the Spirit of Phi Ta Khon

Even though the Phi Ta Khon Festival takes place only once a year, its lessons of joy, laughter, and respect are carried on by the people of Thailand throughout their lives. The festival serves as a reminder that life is precious and that we should take time to celebrate it with those we care about.

As you think about the festival of Phi Ta Khon, remember that joy and laughter are powerful forces that can brighten the darkest days. Whether we are celebrating with friends or honoring loved ones who have passed, we can all take part in the spirit of Phi Ta Khon by embracing life with a smile and spreading joy to those around us.

CHAPTER 17:
THE PRINCESS AND THE KRAHASA
- A TALE OF SACRIFICE

Let's join the spirits as they return to their world and memories, from the town of Dan Sai to the heart of ancient Thailand, where there once lived a beautiful and kind princess named *Benjamas*. Princess Benjamas was beloved and admired by her people for her beauty, gentle heart, and deep wisdom. She cared for her kingdom as if every person, tree, and river were part of her own family. The people of the kingdom adored her, and her father, the king, was proud to have such a brave and compassionate daughter.

But, deep in the forests of this peaceful land, a mysterious creature known as the *Krahasa* stirred. The Krahasa was part bird and part beast, with shimmering, dark feathers and fierce, glowing eyes. It was a powerful creature that ruled over the wilderness and the waters. The Krahasa was both feared and respected, for it had the ability to control the weather and bring either fortune or disaster to the kingdom.

One year, an unusual drought struck the kingdom. The rains that usually nourished the fields and rivers didn't come, and the rivers shrank to mere trickles of water. The crops withered, the animals grew thin, and the people began to worry. Everyone looked to the skies, hoping for even a single cloud, but day after day, the sun blazed fiercely without any sign of relief.

How a Princess Made a Great Sacrifice for Her People

Princess Benjamas couldn't bear to see her people suffering. She prayed for rain and consulted the kingdom's wise elders, hoping to find a solution to the terrible drought. The elders gathered together and spoke of the ancient legends of the Krahasa. According to legend, the Krahasa could bring rain to the kingdom, but it would only appear if someone pure of heart made a great sacrifice to summon it.

When Princess Benjamas heard this, she knew what she had to do. She went to her father and explained her plan. "Father," she said, "our people are suffering. If the Krahasa demands a sacrifice, then I will go and plead with it myself."

The king was shocked and heartbroken. He loved his daughter dearly and could not bear the thought of her risking her life. "No, my daughter," he pleaded, "you are the treasure of our kingdom. I cannot let you face such a dangerous creature alone."

But Princess Benjamas was determined. She looked into her father's eyes and said, "Father, I am a part of this kingdom, just like everyone else. If the Krahasa will listen to me, then I must try. Perhaps it will show mercy and bring us the rain we need."

The king knew he could not change her mind. Though his heart was heavy, he gave her his blessing, hoping that the Krahasa would recognize her bravery and spare her life.

The Journey to Find the Krahasa

Princess Benjamas set out on a long journey to find the Krahasa, accompanied only by her loyal horse. She traveled for days, crossing rivers, climbing hills, and venturing deep into the dense forests where few dared to go. The further she went, the darker and more mysterious the forest became. Strange sounds echoed in the shadows, and the air was thick with magic.

Finally, after many days of searching, she came to a misty lake hidden in the heart of the forest. The water shimmered under the moonlight, and the air was filled with an eerie silence. Princess Benjamas felt a chill, but she gathered her courage and stepped forward.

"Krahasa!" she called out, her voice echoing across the lake. "I am Princess Benjamas, and I have come to ask for your help. My people are suffering from a terrible drought. I beg you, mighty Krahasa, please bring us rain and save my kingdom."

For a long moment, there was no response. Then, from the depths of the lake, a figure began to rise. The Krahasa appeared, its massive wings casting shadows over the lake, its fierce eyes glowing like embers. Its feathers glistened like midnight, and it towered over the princess, filling her with awe and fear.

The Krahasa's Test of Selflessness

The Krahasa's voice was as deep and rumbling as thunder. "Why have you disturbed me, human?" it asked, its voice echoing through the trees.

Princess Benjamas took a deep breath and repeated her plea. "My people are suffering, great Krahasa. There is no rain, and our rivers have dried up. I beg you to help us. I am willing to make any sacrifice if it means saving my kingdom."

The Krahasa observed her with its glowing eyes, its expression unreadable. "Sacrifice?" it asked. "And what would you give up, little princess, for the lives of your people?"

The princess did not hesitate. "My life," she answered firmly. "If it means that my people will be saved, I am willing to give everything."

The Krahasa was silent for a moment, as if considering her words. Then it spoke again, its voice softer but still powerful. "Very well. I shall test your selflessness, Princess Benjamas. If you truly wish to help your people, then you must give up not only your life but also the promise of ever returning to your kingdom. Are you willing to sacrifice your freedom and live by this lake, where your spirit will forever watch over these lands and ensure that the rain returns when needed?"

The princess felt her heart ache, for she loved her kingdom and her people dearly. She knew that if she accepted the Krahasa's terms, she would never see her family or friends again. Yet, her love for her people was stronger than her desire to return home.

"Yes," she said, her voice unwavering. "If that is what it takes, I accept."

The Rain Returns

The Krahasa spread its mighty wings and let out a cry that echoed through the skies. Dark clouds began to gather overhead, swirling and thickening until they covered the entire sky. Thunder rumbled, and lightning flashed, casting the forest in eerie, flickering light.

Then, the rain began to fall. It started as a gentle drizzle, but soon turned into a downpour. The parched earth drank up the water eagerly, and the rivers began to flow once more. The crops were revived, and the people of the kingdom rejoiced, not knowing the sacrifice their beloved princess had made for them.

As the rain poured down, the Krahasa looked at Princess Benjamas with respect. "You have proven your selflessness, princess. From this day forward, your spirit will watch over this land, and you will forever be remembered as a guardian of the rain."

With those words, Princess Benjamas disappeared, her spirit becoming one with the land and the rain. She was no longer the princess of her kingdom, but a guardian spirit who would watch over her people for generations to come.

The Legend Lives On

The rain continued for many days, bringing life back to the kingdom. The people noticed that every time they prayed for rain, it came gently and lovingly, as if someone was watching over them. They began to tell stories of Princess Benjamas and her sacrifice, and her memory lived on as a symbol of love and honor.

It was said that on quiet nights, when the rain fell softly, her spirit could still be felt, moving through the mist of the lake, blessing the land she loved so dearly. To this day, people in Thailand remember the tale of Princess Benjamas and the Krahasa, and they honor her spirit with offerings of flowers and prayers whenever they need rain.

Lessons About Selflessness and Honor

The story of Princess Benjamas and the Krahasa teaches us many valuable lessons:

Selflessness

Princess Benjamas showed that true leadership means putting others before oneself. She was willing to sacrifice everything she loved to save her people, showing that selflessness is one of the greatest acts of love.

Honor

Honor is not just about bravery as much as it is about doing what is right, even when the choice is a difficult one. Princess Benjamas chose to keep her promise to the Krahasa, even though it meant she would never see her home again.

The Power of Sacrifice

Sometimes, making a sacrifice can bring blessings not only to ourselves but to everyone around us. The princess's sacrifice ensured that her kingdom would thrive, and for that reason the Thai people have not forgotten her love and kindness.

Connection with Nature

The Krahasa symbolizes the balance of nature, reminding us that humans and the natural world are deeply connected. Only the princess's bond with the Krahasa ensured that her kingdom could live in harmony with nature.

Legacy of Kindness

Princess Benjamas's sacrifice left a legacy of kindness and care that lived on through the generations. Her story reminds us that the good we do can continue to inspire and protect those who come after us.

Remembering Princess Benjamas

To this day, Thai people honor the spirit of Princess Benjamas in various ways. They tell her story to their children as a reminder of the values she represented. Some even leave flowers as a tribute to her memory when they visit lakes and rivers. The legend of the princess and the Krahasa is a beautiful example of Thai culture's respect for nature, bravery, and the idea of sacrifice for the greater good.

As you think about Princess Benjamas and her story, remember that sometimes, the greatest acts of love come from selflessness and sacrifice. By honoring her spirit, we can all learn to be kinder, braver, and more willing to help others, just as she did.

CHAPTER 18:
THE STORY OF THE KHMER RUINS
- A GLIMPSE INTO THE PAST

Deep in the heart of Thailand's lush green jungles and sprawling landscapes, perhaps quite close to where Princess Benajamas sacrificed herself to the Krahasa, lie the ancient and mysterious *Khmer* ruins. These magnificent temples and structures, built long ago by the Khmer Empire, offer a glimpse into a time filled with powerful kings, dedicated builders, and spiritual legends. For the people of Thailand, these ruins are a treasured link to the past, a reminder of their heritage, and a symbol of the wisdom and strength that has endured through the ages of their country.

The Legend Behind the Ancient Temples of Thailand

In the days of the Khmer Empire, which ruled parts of what is now Thailand, Cambodia, and other regions, the kings and their people had a vision: to build temples so grand that they would reach the gods, who would, in turn, protect their lands out of appreciation. These temples served as both places of worship and homes for the gods themselves (or so it was believed).

One of the most famous of Thailand's Khmer temples is called *Phanom Rung*, which is a sandstone temple that sits high on an extinct volcano in the northeastern part of the country. According to legend, Phanom Rung was constructed to honor *Shiva*, the Hindu god known as the "Destroyer and Transformer." In the ancient Khmer stories, Shiva was a powerful god who could bring not only destruction but also renewal, transforming what had been broken into something new and beautiful.

The story goes that a great king dreamt of a place where people could connect with the divine and seek wisdom from the gods. Inspired by this dream, he ordered the construction of Phanom Rung. It is said that the gods themselves guided the builders, providing them with visions of how to carve the stones and align the temple with the movements of the sun. To this day, the temple's doorways align perfectly with the sunrise and sunset on certain days of the year, a symbol of harmony between earth and sky.

As Phanom Rung rose on the hill, other temples began to appear across the land. The Khmer kings, inspired by their devotion to their gods and desire to protect their people, constructed temples such as the *Prasat Hin Phimai* and *Prasat Muang Tam*. These temples became places of worship, learning, and gathering, where people could feel close to the divine and experience the power of their ancestors.

How the Temples Connect to Thai History and Myths

Each of these temples holds stories, not only of the Hindu gods like Shiva and Vishnu (the God of Preservation), but also of the Buddha and other Thai myths. As the Khmer Empire eventually transitioned from Hinduism to Buddhism, so did many of the temples. New statues were added, and some temples were even rededicated to Buddha. The temples became symbols of the blending of beliefs, where gods and spirits from different traditions were worshiped together, reflecting the diversity and openness of Thai culture.

The carvings and artwork on these temples tell stories from both Hindu and Buddhist beliefs. At *Phimai*, for instance, there are carvings of Naga, the sacred serpent, and *Garuda*, a mythical bird-like creature that serves as a vehicle for the god Vishnu. Both Naga and Garuda are beloved figures in Thai folklore and symbolise protection, courage, and wisdom.

The ruins also tell the story of heroes and mythical creatures who protected the people and guided the kings. Many of these legends are still told in Thai stories today, linking the past with the present. For example, the story of the *Phra Lak Phra Lam* is depicted in some of the temple carvings, with scenes of battles and courageous acts like that of Hanuman, symbolizing the victory of good over evil.

These temples also served as places where wise teachers shared their knowledge with the common people. They would come from far and wide to learn about the gods and to understand the mysteries of life. These ruins stand as reminders of a time when knowledge, respect for nature, and spiritual beliefs were passed down to young minds, building a strong foundation for Thai culture.

Lessons About Heritage and Learning from the Past

The Khmer ruins are not only a source of beauty and mystery but also teach us the following timeless lessons:

The Importance of Heritage

These temples remind us that our heritage shapes who we are. Just as the ancient Khmer built temples to honor their gods and protect their people, we can also honor our history by remembering and preserving our stories. Heritage connects people across generations.

Respect for Spiritual Beliefs

The Khmer temples reflect the harmony between different beliefs. They remind us that people from different religions can share the same spaces, respect one another, and even worship together. Just like the ancient Thai people who adapted the temples to suit their Buddhist beliefs, we, too, can respect and learn from others.

Perseverance and Dedication

Building temples like Phanom Rung and Prasat Phimai took immense skill, patience, and dedication. The workers and artists poured their hearts into their work, knowing that these temples would outlast them and serve as a legacy for future generations. This teaches us the value of hard work and the importance of creating something meaningful.

Connection to Nature

Many of these temples were carefully positioned to align with natural elements, such as the sun and moon. This shows how closely people were connected to the natural world and respected its rhythms. Even today, we can learn to live in harmony with nature, understanding that we are part of a larger cycle that includes the sun, moon, stars, rivers, and forests.

Learning from History

Each stone, each carving, and each relic at the Khmer ruins tells a story. By studying them, we learn about the values, beliefs, and lives of those who came before us. Learning from history helps us avoid mistakes, appreciate our achievements, and be inspired to do better for the future.

A Visit to the Khmer Temples Today

Today, people from all over the world visit the Khmer ruins in Thailand. They walk among the ancient stones, marveling at the craftsmanship and feeling the deep sense of history that surrounds them. For visitors, it's like stepping back in time into a world where kings, gods, and mythical creatures once roamed.

The temples are not only a source of pride for the Thai people but also a reminder of their ancestors' strength, resilience, and creativity. Schools often bring children to these sites to teach them about their history, and families share stories about the myths and legends carved into the stones. Many visitors leave offerings of flowers, incense, or even small coins as a sign of respect and gratitude for the wisdom and protection these temples have provided over the centuries.

Some days, when the sun rises or sets, its rays align perfectly with the temple doorways, creating a magical moment when the whole temple seems to glow. It's as if the gods themselves are blessing the temple once again, a reminder that these ancient sites still hold a special place in the heart of the Thai people.

Embracing the Legacy of the Khmer Ruins

The Khmer ruins continue to be a source of inspiration for artists, musicians, and storytellers. They have inspired countless stories, paintings, and songs that celebrate the beauty of Thailand's past. To truly appreciate the Khmer ruins is to recognize that they are more than just historical sites; they are a gift from our ancestors. As we walk among these ancient stones, let us remember the people who built them, the stories they tell, and the lessons they offer. The legacy of these ruins is a reminder to cherish our past, respect our heritage, and continue to learn from the wisdom of those who came before us.

By keeping the stories of these ruins alive, we honor the Khmer kings, the builders, the artists, and the spiritual leaders who believed in a world of balance, beauty, and connection to the divine. Their legacy remains, urging us to look deeper, think broader, and carry forward the values that make our culture rich and timeless.

CHAPTER 19:
THE LEGEND OF THE LOTUS BLOSSOM - A SYMBOL OF PURITY

If you walk a short way from the ruins of the beautiful Khmer temples into the surrounding natural areas, you will likely find some of Thailand's peaceful ponds and rivers nearby. And, if you're lucky, you might come across a beautiful flower with soft petals and a gentle fragrance floating peacefully on the water's surface. This is the lotus blossom, one of the most beloved flowers in Thai culture. Despite growing in muddy waters, the lotus rises above, its petals untouched by dirt, as it reaches for the light of the sun. As such, the lotus symbolises purity, inner strength, and spiritual growth in the Thai belief system. For centuries, the lotus has been a powerful symbol in Thailand and Buddhist teachings alike, reminding people about the importance of keeping a pure heart despite life's many challenges.

How the Lotus Blossoms in Muddy Waters

Imagine a small, muddy pond surrounded by tall grass. On the water's surface there are bits of leaves and soil floating. It doesn't look like much, but from this murky water, a tiny green bud begins to emerge. Slowly, it grows taller, reaching up through the mud and pushing past the water's surface. Finally, after days of reaching toward the sunlight, the bud opens, and a stunning lotus blossom appears.

The lotus is known for this amazing ability to bloom in muddy waters, rising above the mud and muck to reveal its pure, spotless petals. This journey of the lotus, from murky depths to sunlight, teaches us an important lesson; namely, that even in difficult situations, beauty and strength can grow. Just as the lotus flower remains pure despite its surroundings, people, too, can strive to be the best versions of themselves, no matter what challenges they face.

In Thailand, people see the lotus as a symbol of resilience. This flower reminds everyone that even when life seems challenging, like the muddy water, we can still grow and find our way to the light.

The Role of the Lotus in Thai Buddhism

As mentioned, the lotus blossom holds a special place in Thai Buddhism. In many temples, you'll find statues of Buddha sitting or standing on a lotus flower. This is because the lotus represents purity of mind, body, and spirit, which are important qualities in Buddhism. Just like the flower, Buddhists believe that people can reach a state of purity and wisdom by overcoming the challenges and distractions of life.

According to Thai Buddhist beliefs, the journey of the lotus blossom from the muddy pond to the bright sun represents the journey of the soul. Just as the lotus rises from the mud, people should strive to rise above negative thoughts, temptations, and struggles. Buddhists believe that by practicing kindness and patience, they can achieve inner peace and a pure heart, just like the lotus.

During temple visits, you might see people bringing lotus flowers as offerings. They carefully place them in front of Buddha statues as a sign of respect and devotion. The offering of the lotus is a reminder to Buddhists of their own spiritual journey, where they must look beyond their worries to seek inner wisdom and peace.

In some temples, monks teach stories about the lotus blossom to inspire people to be patient and discover internal peace. The lotus, after all, doesn't rush to bloom. It grows slowly, patiently stretching through the water, taking its time to reach the surface. This cycle is a reminder that growth and learning take time.

The Story of the Buddha and the Lotus

Buddha's connection to the lotus is present through Thai Buddhist mythology. For example, one popular Thai legend tells of the Buddha and his stroll through a beautiful lotus garden. As he walked through the garden, he saw lotus blossoms of all colors – pink, white, and blue. The Buddha noticed that not all of the lotuses were at the same stage of growth as he walked. Some buds were still closed, hidden in the mud, while others were blooming brightly in the sunlight.

The Buddha saw these lotuses as symbols of people on their journeys. He noticed that some of the lotus buds were still in the mud, beginning to grow just like people starting on their spiritual journeys. Other lotus blooms were halfway through their journeys, and some had blossomed fully, which he believed were like people achieving wisdom and peace. Through this lesson from the lotus garden, the Buddha taught that everyone, no matter their stage of growth, could reach enlightenment if they remained pure, compassionate, and wise. His story from the lotus garden encouraged people to be patient and believe in their own journeys, knowing that one day, they too would bloom.

Lessons About Growth and Inner Peace

The lotus blossom's journey offers several important lessons that are still meaningful today. Let's explore a few of these:

Embrace Growth, Even in Difficult Times

The lotus teaches us that even when life feels messy or challenging, we can still find a way to grow and improve ourselves. Just like the lotus, we can rise above difficulties and reach for something better.

Keep Your Heart Pure

Despite growing in muddy waters, the lotus remains pure and clean. This reminds us to keep our hearts and minds pure, no matter what's happening around us. We can choose to be kind, honest, and positive even when the world around us is not, just like the lotus.

Be Patient with Yourself

The lotus doesn't rush; it grows at its own pace. Sometimes, when we're learning something new or trying to improve, it can feel frustrating if we don't see results right away. But, like a lotus flower, we must be patient and trust in our own growth.

Find Inner Peace Amid Challenges

The lotus grows through mud and water but always finds a way to the light. In the same way, we can find peace within ourselves, even if things around us are difficult. The lotus encourages us to stay calm and steady, no matter the situation.

Remember That We All Have Our Journey

Just as the Buddha saw the different stages of lotus growth, people also grow and learn at their own pace. The lotus reminds us to respect everyone's journey, knowing that each person is blooming in their own time, including you.

The Lotus in Everyday Life

In Thailand, the lotus is more than just a symbol in temples; it's also part of daily life. You'll often see lotus flowers in markets, used in cooking, or even as decorations in homes.

Some people use parts of the lotus plant for food. Lotus seeds, for example, are a popular snack, and the stems are sometimes used in Thai dishes. Eating parts of the lotus reminds people of its symbolic journey and its connection to their culture. By using the lotus in daily life, Thai people keep its lessons close to their hearts.

During festivals, you might see people making beautiful displays with lotus flowers, arranging them in ways that showcase their colors and shapes. Each display celebrates the beauty of the lotus and honors the values it represents.

The Lotus in Art and Culture

The lotus is also a popular subject in Thai art. Artists use its image in paintings, sculptures, and even jewelry. Its delicate petals and graceful shape make it a favorite symbol for creativity and beauty. Many Thai dances, for instance, are inspired by the movement of the lotus, with dancers moving their hands and arms in ways that mimic the petals of the flower as they open to the sun. By including the lotus in their art, Thai people express their respect for the flower's symbolism and are reminded of its lessons.

Keeping the Spirit of the Lotus Alive

The lotus blossom might be a simple flower, but its story carries an important message for everyone, young and old alike. By looking at the lotus, we're reminded to be kind to ourselves, to be patient, and to stay true to our path, no matter where it may lead. The lotus blossom shows us that, like the flower, we all have the strength within us to rise above any challenge. Like the lotus, we must find the calm within, reach for the light, and believe that each one of us has the potential to blossom beautifully, no matter where we begin.

CHAPTER 20: THE TALE OF THE MYSTERIOUS KINNAREE - HALF-BIRD, HALF-WOMAN

As we stand up from beside our little pond filled with beautiful lotus flowers, we will continue to explore the enchanting forests of Thailand. And, as we wander through the forest, nestled within the depths of ancient legends, we could stumble upon a magical being who is as beautiful as she is mysterious – the *Kinnaree*. Imagine a creature with the graceful body of a woman and the wings and tail of a bird. She glides and dances through the trees, her every movement as light as a feather, and her every gesture filled with elegance and grace. The Kinnaree is the beloved symbol of beauty, love, and freedom in Thai culture. Her story is woven into the fabric of Thai art, dance, and song, and her tale teaches us about the importance of freedom, the power of love, and the beauty of finding balance in life.

How the Kinnaree Danced in the Forests of Heaven

In the heavens, far beyond what the eye can see, there is a magical forest called *Himmapan*, where mythical creatures live in harmony. It's a land filled with sparkling rivers, tall trees, and vibrant flowers. Such beauty is like nothing like what we can find on Earth. Among the trees, you might catch a glimpse of the Kinnaree dancing gracefully, her wings glistening like silver in the sunlight, her laughter like soft music. Her dance is said to bring joy to all who see it, and her songs float like a gentle breeze through the forest.

Legends say that when the Kinnaree dances, the world around her seems to come alive – the trees sway to her rhythm, the rivers sparkle brighter, and even the clouds pause to watch her. Her movements are so smooth and graceful she appears to be floating. In many Thai myths, her dance is so beautiful that it is described as a gift to the heavens.

Stories of Love, Longing, and Magic

One of the most beloved tales about these mythical creatures recounts the story of a specific group of Kinnaree. The protagonist of this tale is named *Manohra*, a beautiful Kinnaree princess who fell in love with a human prince. Manohra was the daughter of the king of the Kinnarees, and she was known for her beauty and kindness. One day, while she was playing and dancing near a lake in the Himmapan forest, she was captured by a prince who had fallen in love with her at first sight. Although she was taken to live in the human world, she remained kind and patient, slowly winning the hearts of everyone in the prince's kingdom.

Manohra eventually fell in love with the prince, and for a time, they were happy together. However, life in the human world was difficult for a Kinnaree, who yearned for the freedom of the skies and the forests. The Kinnarees were not meant to live away from Himmapan, and over time, Manohra longed to return to her magical homeland. Though she loved the prince deeply, she missed her family and her home.

In the legend, Manohra is faced with a difficult choice – to stay with the prince she loved or to return to her world of freedom and magic. The story tells of her struggle between love and freedom, a theme that touches the hearts of everyone who hears it. In the end, she returns to her world, but her love for the prince remains, showing that true love can endure across any distance.

The Kinnaree in Thai Culture

The story of the Kinnaree, especially Manohra's tale, has become an important part of Thai culture. In traditional Thai dance, dancers perform the Kinnaree-Manohra dance, wearing costumes that represent the Kinnaree with feathered wings and graceful movements. As the dancers capture the beauty and grace of the Kinnaree through their performance, they tell the beautiful yet heartbreaking story of Manohra and the prince.

The Kinnaree is also a popular symbol in Thai art. In temples and sculptures, you can often see carvings and paintings of the Kinnaree, her wings spread wide, her face filled with kindness and beauty. She is a symbol that encourages people to always act gracefully and stay true to themselves.

Lessons About Grace and Freedom

The legend of the Kinnaree holds many valuable lessons for you young readers, such as:

Be True to Yourself

The Kinnaree's story teaches us the importance of being true to who we are. Just as Manohra couldn't stay away from her homeland, we should remember to stay connected to our roots and values. It's okay to explore and experience new things, but we should never forget where we come from.

Cherish Freedom

The Kinnaree's ability to soar above the trees and dance in the forests shows us that freedom is a precious gift. She reminds us to appreciate and enjoy our freedom.

Love and Longing Can Coexist

The story of Manohra and the prince shows that love can endure, even when people are separated. It teaches us that it's okay to miss someone or something that we love. True love doesn't fade; it remains in our hearts, bringing us strength and comfort, even across great distances.

Embrace Grace and Kindness

The Kinnaree reminds us to treat others with kindness, to move through life with grace, and to share joy with those around us. But, grace is not about our physical movements; the way we make others feel is just as important to embodying the core value of grace.

Balance Love and Freedom

Manohra's story shows us that love and freedom are both important. Though at times in life we might need to make difficult choices, listening to our hearts ensures that we will choose correctly. The Kinnaree's choice teaches us that we can love others deeply and still honor our own need for freedom and growth.

Keeping the Spirit of the Kinnaree Alive

By keeping the spirit of the Kinnaree alive, Thai people honor their traditions and pass down values that inspire future generations. They believe that just like the Kinnaree who danced in the magical forests of Himmapan, we, too, can bring beauty and joy into our lives by embracing our unique qualities. The Kinnaree shows us that true beauty comes from being true to oneself.

Through her story, the Kinnaree invites us all to live with elegance, to fly freely, and to cherish the love and freedom that fill our lives. Her tale is a reminder that even in a world filled with challenges, we can rise above, like a graceful bird in the sky, dancing to the song of our own hearts.

CHAPTER 21: THE KING AND THE MONK - A LESSON IN WISDOM

Though it would be lovely to follow the Kinnaree to her beloved home in Himmapan to watch her sing and dance, our journey must continue on Earth. We will continue by travelling to the heart of a kingdom filled with towering palaces and gleaming golden temples. Within these grand buildings lived a king who was both powerful and wealthy beyond measure. He also proudly ruled his kingdom with an iron fist. His people knew of his great achievements, power, and vast riches, meaning they bowed before him wherever he walked, always dressed in robes of fine silks that shimmered with jewels. But, despite all his riches, the king felt something was missing. Deep inside, he was not truly happy.

One day, the king heard about a wise monk who lived humbly in a small, simple hut outside the city. This monk, despite having no riches, was said to possess a great wisdom that could answer any question and solve any problem. People from all over the land came to visit the monk, seeking advice and comfort. Curious and intrigued, the king decided he would meet this monk and learn the secrets of happiness and wisdom.

How a Simple Monk Taught a King About Humility

The king set out from his palace, bringing with him a grand entourage (like a parade, but used specifically to escort someone very important) of servants, soldiers, and advisors. He wore his finest robes, adorned with gold and precious stones, and rode in a gilded (covered with a thin layer of gold) chariot that sparkled under the sun. The people in the village marveled at the sight of their king, wondering what brought him to such a humble place.

When the king arrived at the monk's small hut, he was surprised to find just how simple it truly was. The walls were made of bamboo, and the roof was thatched with dried leaves. There were no servants, no grand decorations, and no sign of wealth anywhere. The king dismounted his chariot, straightened his robes, and prepared to meet the wise monk.

The monk greeted the king with a warm smile and bowed respectfully. "Welcome, Your Majesty," he said in a gentle voice. "To what do I owe the honor of your visit?"

The king looked around, puzzled by the simplicity of the monk's home. "Are you truly the monk who is said to possess great wisdom?" he asked. "Your hut is humble, and you have no wealth. How can a man with so little teach me anything about happiness and life?"

The monk simply smiled and invited the king to sit on a straw mat on the ground. "Please, make yourself comfortable, Your Majesty," he said. The king hesitated, unused to sitting on the bare ground, but he agreed, curious to hear what the monk had to say.

"Tell me, Great King," the monk began, "what is it that troubles you?"

The king sighed, admitting, "I have wealth, power, and respect. Yet, I feel an emptiness inside, as if I am searching for something that cannot be bought with riches or achieved with power. I heard that you are wise and can teach me the path to true happiness."

The monk nodded thoughtfully. "Happiness and wisdom, Your Majesty, are indeed treasures, but they cannot be found in gold or jewels. True wisdom comes from understanding oneself and the world around us. And true happiness comes from kindness, humility, and simplicity."

The Power of Wisdom Over Wealth

The monk then asked the king, "Imagine, if you will, a man who has everything he desires—gold, jewels, fine clothes, and a palace. Yet, if he is alone and does not know the joy of kindness or the peace of humility, do you think he is truly happy?"

The king thought for a moment and replied, "Perhaps not. Wealth cannot buy kindness, nor can it fill a person's heart with peace."

The monk smiled. "Exactly, Your Majesty. Wealth may bring comfort, but it cannot bring lasting happiness. Happiness is a gift we give ourselves through our actions and our thoughts. Kindness, humility, and understanding are the true treasures that make a person rich."

Intrigued, the king listened as the monk continued. "Your Majesty, do you see this simple hut, the bare walls, and the single mat upon which we sit? I do not need more, for I am content with what I have. When we learn to appreciate simplicity and practice kindness, we find peace within ourselves."

The king pondered this. "But how can one find joy without wealth?" he asked. "How can a person be satisfied with so little?"

The monk took a deep breath. "Once, there was a poor farmer who worked in his fields from dawn until dusk. He had no riches, no fine clothes, and no palace. Yet every evening, he would sit under a tree, enjoy his simple meal, and watch the sunset with a heart full of gratitude. He was happy, Your Majesty, because he was content with what he had and found beauty in life's small moments."

The king was moved by the monk's story and finally realized that the happiness he sought was not hidden in riches, but in his own heart.

Lessons About Simplicity and Kindness

The monk invited the king to stay and experience the simple life of the village for a few days. He showed the king how the villagers helped one another, how they shared their food and resources, and how they found joy in everyday tasks. The king saw that the people were happy, not because they were wealthy, but because they cared for one another and lived with gratitude.

During his stay, the king learned many lessons from the monk that changed his heart forever. Here are some of the lessons that the king carried back with him to the palace:

Humility Is the Path to Wisdom

The king realized that wisdom is not measured by one's wealth or status. The monk, despite his humble surroundings, was wiser than anyone the king had ever known. Humility, the king learned, opens the door to understanding and growth.

There is Peace in Simplicity

The king felt a peace in the village that he had never known before despite being surrounded by simple things. He understood that true peace doesn't come from having more but from needing less. By appreciating the beauty in simple things, we open our hearts to joy.

Kindness Is a Gift We Give Ourselves

The king saw that when the villagers helped one another, they were not just making others happy—they were also making themselves happy. Kindness, the monk taught him, is a treasure that grows each time we share it with others.

Happiness Comes from Within

The king discovered that happiness was not something he could buy or achieve. It was something he had to nurture within himself. The monk taught him that by practicing gratitude, he could find joy in even the smallest moments.

Contentment Is the Key to True Wealth

By watching the villagers, the king learned that contentment (or, being satisfied with what you have) is a form of wealth. People who are content with what they have are truly richer than any king in fine robes, for they never wish for more..

Returning to the Kingdom with a New Heart

After spending time with the monk, the king felt a great peace within himself. He thanked the monk for his kindness and wisdom, and as he prepared to return to his palace, he vowed to live his life differently. He understood now that true happiness could not be bought with wealth or won with power. It was something that came from kindness, humility, and gratitude.

When he returned to his palace, the king began to rule with a gentle heart and a wise mind. He shared his wealth with those in need, showed kindness to his people, and made fair decisions. The kingdom flourished under his rule, not because of his riches, but because of the love and respect he showed toward his people.

The king no longer sought happiness in material things. Instead, he found joy in the simple moments, in the laughter of his people, and in the beauty of the world around him. And, though he was still a king, he ruled with a humble heart, grateful for the wisdom he had gained from the monk.

Keeping the Wisdom of the Monk Alive

The king taught his children and his advisors the same lessons in the importance of humility, kindness, and gratitude that he had learned from the monk. He reminded them that true happiness is found within, and that the greatest treasures in life are the ones we carry in our hearts.

As time passed, the king's story spread throughout the land, and his people came to cherish the wisdom he shared. Thus, the lessons of the wise monk lived on in the kingdom long after the king had passed, shaping the lives of generations to come.

A Story That Teaches Us All

The same gentle wisdom that the monk shared with the king can remind us that the greatest gifts in life are those we carry within us—love, compassion, and the joy of helping others.So, as you read these words, remember that the lessons of the monk are not just for kings. They are for everyone, young and old, rich and poor. No matter where you go or what you achieve, carry kindness in your heart, practice gratitude, and let humility guide your path. In doing so, you will find both happiness and wisdom that will last a lifetime.

CHAPTER 22: THE LEGEND OF PHI AM - THE SPIRIT OF DREAMS

As we move on from the village of the humble monk and his lessons in true wisdom, we will journey to another small Thai village, with a story much stranger than that of the king and his pursuit of happiness. In this town, people have whispered for centuries about a mysterious spirit who visits at night, bringing dreams and, sometimes, even nightmares. As was told in ancient legends, this spirit, known as *Phi Am*, was the bringer of dreams—sometimes ones that were both gentle and magical, filling people's nights with wonder. Other times, Phi Am filled people's nights with eerie dreams that stirred their deepest fears. Phi Am was a spirit who was known for dancing between light and shadow, filling the nighttime world with colors and mysteries only visible to sleeping eyes.

How the Phi Am Brought Dreams and Nightmares

According to Thai legend, Phi Am was a spirit of the night, a figure who wandered unseen, visiting people as they slept. Phi Am could bring peaceful dreams that would wrap sleepers in stories of joy and adventure, but could also stir up unsettling dreams or nightmares that helped people face their fears. People believed that each of Phi Am's dreams carried a message or a lesson, waiting to be uncovered by the person who the spirit touched.

Phi Am was said to be a spirit that was neither good nor bad. This spirit served as a simple guide through the hidden realms of the mind. Some nights, Phi Am would weave soft dreams of fields filled with lotus blossoms or forests where magical creatures roamed. Other times, Phi Am might bring visions of spooky places or mysterious sounds that would help the dreamer confront their hidden worries or fears.

As the legend goes, to create dreams, Phi Am would approach the bed of a sleeping person. The spirit would place a gentle hand over the person's eyes, whispering dreams into their minds. If someone had been feeling joyful, Phi Am would grant them a dream of peace and happiness. If someone had worries that they were hiding, Phi Am might give them a dream that revealed those feelings, bringing them to the surface so they could be understood and, one day, overcome.

The Role of Dreams in Thai Folklore

In Thai folklore, dreams were believed to be messages from the spirit world. They served as a channel of communication for spirits like Phi Am. Many Thai people believed that dreams could reveal insights about a person's future or guide them through difficult times. Elders in the village often encouraged children to remember their dreams, for they believed each dream held a valuable lesson or a hidden meaning.

Thai legends also speak of special dreams that could predict the future. It was said that Phi Am sometimes brought such dreams to warn or prepare a person for something important. These dreams, called "dream omens," were viewed as precious gifts, and their messages shouldn't have ever been ignored. If someone dreamt of a white elephant, for example, it was believed that great fortune or wisdom was on its way. Dreams of water, on the other hand, could mean that a time of change or renewal was coming.

Some dreams had personal meanings, reflecting a person's inner thoughts and emotions. A child who felt afraid might dream of thunderstorms or dark forests, while someone feeling hopeful might dream of a sunrise or a beautiful temple. As such, Phi Am's dreams were a window into the heart and mind of the dreamer, helping them understand themselves better.

Dreams were also seen as a way to connect with ancestors or loved ones who had passed away. Many families believed that Phi Am could guide the spirits of ancestors to visit their family in dreams, bringing love and comfort from the other side. It was said that if you dreamed of a loved one who had passed on, it was because Phi Am had brought their spirit to see you, allowing you to feel their presence once more.

Lessons About Understanding Emotions

Each of Phi Am's dreams, whether happy or frightening, gave the dreamer a chance to explore how they felt deep inside and learn one of the following lessons:

It's Okay to Feel Scared Sometimes

Scary dreams were not meant to harm the dreamer, but rather help them understand their fears. Children learned that being afraid is a natural feeling that everyone experiences. A dream about a dark forest or a storm might help a child recognize their worries, allowing them to talk about it with someone they trust.

Happy Dreams Teach Us to Treasure Joy

Joyful dreams reminded people to appreciate the good things in life. Dreams of laughter, sunny days, and friendly animals reminded everyone, young and old, to cherish the simple joys around them.

Every Emotion Has a Purpose

Phi Am's dreams taught that every feeling, whether happy, sad, scared, or excited, was part of being human. Just as a rainbow has many colors, life is full of many emotions. Dreams helped people accept and understand these feelings without judgment, embracing them as part of their journey.

Facing Fears Makes Us Stronger

By dreaming of something scary only to wake up safe and sound, people learned that they could overcome their worries in real life. The villagers taught their children that dreams were a way to practice courage.

Dreams Connect Us to Loved Ones and Memories

People treasured dreams of loved ones who had passed on, seeing them as visits from the spirit world. Phi Am's dreams reminded them that their ancestors and loved ones were always close in heart and memory, even if they couldn't be seen.

Phi Am's Nightly Visit

Every night, as the stars sparkled above, villagers knew that Phi Am was wandering through the streets, bringing dreams to each sleeper. Children often shared stories of their dreams in the morning, laughing about the funny dreams and talking through the scary ones. Some would draw pictures of their dreams, adding colors and shapes to show how they felt. The village elders encouraged this, saying it was a way to honor Phi Am's gift.

One little boy named Kiet loved hearing stories of Phi Am from his grandmother. Each night, before falling asleep, he would whisper a "thank you" to Phi Am, hoping for a dream filled with wonder. Sometimes, Kiet would dream of flying across the jungle on the back of a great bird, soaring high above the trees. Other times, he dreamt of a mysterious cave with glowing lights inside, a place both enchanting and a little bit scary. No matter what kind of dream he had, Kiet knew that Phi Am's visit was a special gift.

One night, Kiet had a dream that he was walking through a dark forest. He felt afraid, hearing strange noises and seeing shadows among the trees. Just as he was about to turn and run, he remembered what his grandmother had told him: "Even in your dreams, you can be brave." Taking a deep breath, Kiet faced the shadows, and as he did, they faded away, turning into friendly animals who guided him safely out of the forest. When Kiet woke up, he felt proud and brave, knowing that Phi Am's dream had helped him discover his inner courage.

A Gift for All Dreamers

The legend of Phi Am reminds us that dreams are just as important as the moments we spend awake. Thai people believed that Phi Am's dreams held wisdom and guidance, helping people young and old to understand themselves better. Dreams allowed them to explore feelings they might not understand during the day, providing a safe place to learn and grow.

Even today, people cherish the lessons of Phi Am's dreams, honoring this spirit of dreams as a part of Thai culture. They believe that dreams can show them new paths, offer comfort, and even bring them closer to loved ones who are no longer with them. Just like Kiet, children in Thailand are encouraged to remember and share their dreams, finding courage, joy, and wisdom within them.

So, next time you have a dream—whether it's about flying, exploring a magical land, or facing a scary forest—remember the legend of Phi Am. Every dream is a gift, a story whispered to you as you sleep, helping you grow, understand, and embrace all the colors of your heart. And who knows? Maybe Phi Am is visiting you too, and guiding you through the world of dreams with a gentle, invisible hand.

CHAPTER 23:
THE STORY OF THE PHAYA NAGA - GUARDIAN OF THE MEKONG RIVER

Where Phi Am could be seen as a type of guardian of the dream world, the Naga is well-known for its guardianship of Thai waters. And, deep in the flowing waters of the Mekong River, which winds its way through Thailand and other parts of Southeast Asia, it is said that the *Phaya Naga* lives deep below the surface. This sacred serpent, which you should remember for its immense size and powerful spirit, is a legendary guardian of the Mekong river. The Phaya Naga watches over the river's waters and the people who live near them. The Phaya Naga represents nature's power and serves as a reminder of the importance of respecting the rivers that give life to the land.

How the Naga Protects the Waters of the Mekong

The legend of the Phaya Naga tells of a massive, serpent-like creature with a body as long as the river itself. According to Thai folklore, the Phaya Naga has beautiful, glittering scales that shimmer in shades of green, gold, and blue, much like the Mekong River under the sun. The Naga has eyes as deep as the river and the wisdom of a creature that has lived for hundreds, maybe even thousands, of years.

Like in other parts of Thailand, people that live in the villages near the Mekong believe that the Naga guards the river from harm. It is said that the Phaya Naga watches over the fishermen, the boats that glide along the water, and even the animals that come to drink. The Naga is both feared and respected, as it has the power to create waves or calm the waters with a flick of its mighty tail.

Stories of People Encountering the Mighty Serpent

Many stories have been told about people encountering the Phaya Naga. Some of these tales are passed down from generation to generation, and often teach lessons about respect, bravery, and humility.

One famous tale speaks of a fisherman named Jai who would set out on the Mekong River every morning. Jai was known for his skill with the fishing net and for his respect for the water. Every time he caught a fish, he would say a prayer of thanks and throw a small portion of his catch back into the river to honor the Phaya Naga.

One morning, as Jai was casting his net, he saw a ripple in the water larger than any he had ever seen. The surface of the river shimmered, and suddenly, he saw the enormous head of the Phaya Naga rise from the depths. Its eyes were calm, and its scales sparkled in the sunlight. Although Jai was startled, he remembered his respect for the Naga and bowed his head.

To his surprise, the Naga spoke to him in a voice that rumbled like distant thunder. "You have shown respect to the river, and in return, I shall bless your fishing so that you will always have enough for yourself and your family," the Naga said. From that day on, Jai never returned home empty-handed, and he continued to honor the Naga with a portion of his catch.

Another tale tells of a young girl named Mali, who once dropped her favorite silver bracelet into the river by accident. Heartbroken, she sat by the water, staring at the spot where it had fallen. As the sun began to set, a soft ripple appeared, and the Phaya Naga emerged. Seeing Mali's sorrow, the Naga gently lifted its head, and on one of its scales, the silver bracelet sparkled, returned to her from the depths of the river.

The Naga's act of kindness taught Mali the importance of treasuring her belongings and caring for the river. She grew up to become a guardian of the river herself, working to keep it clean and healthy for future generations. Villagers say that her dedication was inspired by her encounter with the Phaya Naga.

The Phaya Naga and the Festival of Fireballs

One of the most magical events connected to the Phaya Naga is the mysterious fireballs that appear over the Mekong River during certain times of the year. Known as the Naga Fireballs, these glowing orbs rise from the water and float into the sky, shimmering in shades of pink, orange, and red. Thousands of people gather by the riverbanks to witness this phenomenon, which is believed to be a sign of the Naga's power and presence.

The Naga Fireballs appear during the end of the Buddhist Lent, a time when people give thanks for the harvest and pray for peace and harmony. Many believe that the fireballs are a gift from the Phaya Naga to celebrate and bless the people who honor the river. Scientists have tried to explain the fireballs, suggesting they might be caused by gases rising from the riverbed, but the villagers prefer to believe in the magic of the Phaya Naga.

Families come from all around to watch the fireballs, bringing food and offerings to share by the river. Children listen wide-eyed as their parents tell them the story of the Naga, reminding them of the importance of respecting the river and its guardian.

Lessons About Protection and Respect for the Rivers

The legend of the Phaya Naga teaches several important lessons, especially about respect for nature and the environment. Other lessons to remember include:

Respect the River and All It Gives

The Mekong River is a source of life, providing water for drinking, farming, and fishing to the surrounding communities. The villagers believe that by respecting the river and showing gratitude, they honor the Phaya Naga. This respect is shown in how they use the river responsibly, taking only what they need and ensuring that it remains clean and healthy.

Protect What Is Sacred

The Phaya Naga's role as a protector of the Mekong River reminds people of the importance of protecting the environment. By taking care of the river, forests, and animals, people honor the spirit of the Phaya Naga and preserve the land for future generations.

Gratitude for Nature's Gifts

The villagers express gratitude to the Naga by offering prayers and showing respect for the river.

This practice of gratitude helps them remember that nature's gifts are precious and should not be taken for granted. By giving thanks for what they have, they cultivate a sense of responsibility toward the earth.

Unity and Celebration

The Naga Fireballs festival brings people together to celebrate the river and its guardian. This event teaches the value of community, unity, and celebrating the wonders of nature. By coming together, people strengthen their bond with each other and with the natural world.

The Guardian Spirit of the Mekong Lives On

To this day, villagers tell stories of their ancestors' encounters with the Phaya Naga, and some even say that they've felt the presence of the great serpent while out on the water. The Phaya Naga may be a mythical creature, but its spirit lives on in the hearts of those who depend on the Mekong River.

When children grow up hearing stories of the Phaya Naga, they learn to view the river as more than just water. It becomes a source of life, a friend, and a teacher. The Phaya Naga is there to remind them that they must protect and cherish the river, just as it has protected them for generations. Through this legend, the river becomes not only a part of their physical world but also a part of their heritage and identity.

So, next time you visit a river's shores, imagine the Phaya Naga watching over it, just as it has done for centuries in the Mekong river. Perhaps, in the gentle ripple of the water or the shimmer of sunlight on the surface, you'll feel the presence of the mighty serpent, reminding you of the power of nature and the importance of respecting the world we all share.

CONCLUSION - THE ENDURING MAGIC OF THAI LEGENDS

That concludes our journey through Thai mythology and the world of powerful gods, brave heroes, mythical creatures, and inspiring tales that have shaped Thailand's culture for generations. But, these legends are far from over. In fact, the legends of Thailand are timeless, passed from grandparents to children, from storytellers to listeners, and from readers like you to your friends and family.

Why Stories Are Important in Thai Culture

Stories are like treasures that each generation passes down to the next that preserve history, teach values, and build a sense of community. Thai legends were created long before people could write things down, so storytelling became the way of remembering important events and heroic deeds. In villages across Thailand, people would gather in the evenings to listen to these stories, often told by the village elders or skilled storytellers.

As you well know by now, the role of these stories was, and still is, to connect people to each other and to the world around them. They celebrate the beauty of nature, respect for the gods, and the value of kindness, courage, and respect. The stories give the Thai people a sense of identity and pride, helping them understand where they come from and what they stand for. Even today, Thai children hear these legends in school, during festivals, and at home, keeping the spirit of the stories alive.

What Kids Can Learn from Thai Legends Today

As someone who has now joined in the Thai tradition of storytelling, don't forget the five most important lessons we have learned from these tales:

1. Respect for Nature

Remember the many Thai legends involve creatures like the Naga, the Tiger Spirit, and the White Elephant, who guard the rivers, forests, and mountains. Nature is a sacred gift, and these legends show us that every river, tree, and animal deserves our kindness and protection.

2. The Importance of Community

From the tale of Songkran (the water festival) to the story of the guardian Yaksha at Wat Arun, Thai legends celebrate the spirit of community. They teach us that working together, helping one another, and caring for our families and friends make us stronger and happier.

3. Wisdom and Humility

Thai legends often highlight the wisdom of monks, elders, and even humble villagers. Stories like that of the wealthy king and the humble monk remind us that true wisdom isn't about riches or power; it's about kindness, understanding, and simplicity. Humility is a quality highly respected in Thai culture, and these legends should encourage those who hear them to seek knowledge, listen, and treat others with respect.

4. Courage and Bravery

The adventures of Hanuman, Khun Phaen, and the Golden Prince (Sang Thong) inspire us to be brave in the face of challenges. These heroes show us that courage is not just about physical strength but also about standing up for what is right, protecting others, and believing in ourselves.

5. The Value of Inner Beauty

Many of the Thai legends we have learned about discuss the importance of inner beauty. For example, Sang Thong may have worn a magical mask, but his true beauty lay in his heart and his actions. This lesson encourages us to focus on being good, honest, and kind people rather than focusing too much on appearances.

An Invitation to Keep Exploring Thai Myths and Traditions

Our journey through Thai legends may be ending, but the adventure doesn't have to stop here! There are many more stories waiting to be discovered, and here are the top four ways you can dive further into the world of Thai mythology:

1. Visit Temples and Sacred Sites

Many of the legends we've explored are connected to real places in Thailand. Temples like Wat Arun or rivers like the Mekong are special sites that you can visit if you ever travel to Thailand. By visiting these places, you'll get to experience the magic of the legends firsthand, and you may even hear a new story or two from the locals.

2. Celebrate Thai Festivals

Thai culture is rich in festivals, each with its own special meaning and traditions. Loy Krathong, Songkran, and Yi Peng are just a few of the celebrations that bring Thai legends to life. Even if you can't go to Thailand, you can learn about these festivals, make crafts like krathongs or lanterns, and celebrate with your friends and family. This is a fun way to connect with the spirit of Thai legends and understand the joy of Thai culture.

3. Read More Thai Stories and Fairy Tales

Thailand has a long history of storytelling, and there are still many more legends, fairy tales, and folk stories to explore. You can ask your parents or teachers to help you look for more books and online resources on Thai folklore so you can discover new heroes, magical creatures, and adventures that will continue to inspire you.

4. Create Your Own Thai-Inspired Story

Imagine what it would be like if you were a character in one of the Thai legends. Would you be a brave hero, a strong guardian, or a wise monk? Creating your own story is a wonderful way to connect with the tales you've learned. You can draw pictures of your characters, write your own legend, or even make a short play based on a Thai tale. By adding your own creativity, you become a part of the storytelling tradition.

Celebrating the Wisdom and Magic of Thai Legends

The stories we've explored are filled with ancient wisdom and timeless magic that are a part of

Thailand's identity. Each tale carries a piece of Thailand's history, beliefs, and way of life. Thai legends have the power to make us laugh, think, and wonder about the mysteries of the world. They bring us closer to the past and inspire us to carry forward the values that these tales teach.

Thai legends don't just belong to Thailand; they belong to everyone who hears and cherishes them. By learning about these stories, you are helping to keep them alive. You have become part of a long line of listeners and storytellers who honor these tales and ensure they are never forgotten. Just like the people of Thailand have done for centuries, you are now a guardian of these stories.

An Invitation to Tell Your Own Tales and Keep Exploring

The legends of Thailand are a doorway to a world filled with mystery, wisdom, and beauty. As you close this book, remember that the adventure doesn't have to end. You should keep exploring, asking questions, and opening your heart to the magic of stories. One day, you might create your own tale—a story that inspires others, just as these Thai legends have inspired you. And who knows? Perhaps the Phaya Naga, the Golden Swan, or even the wise monk will be there, in spirit, cheering you on as you continue your journey through the wonderful world of myths and legends.

Thank you for traveling through Thai legends with us. May you carry the spirit of these stories with you, lighting your way and filling your life with joy, wonder, and inspiration.

ACTIVITIES

Still can't get enough of Thai legends? Use these guided activities to help you bring the magic of Thai legends to life through fun crafts, creative games, and thoughtful projects. These activities are inspired by the stories you've read, and they'll help you dive deeper into Thai culture, traditions, and mythology. Gather your art supplies, invite your friends or family, and get ready to explore Thai legends in a whole new way!

1. Make Your Own Krathong for the Loy Krathong Festival

Supplies:

A round piece of banana stem or a small, shallow bowl (that will float)

Banana leaves (or green construction paper)

Scissors and glue

Small flowers and candles

Colorful paper or stickers for decoration

Instructions:

Start with your round base. If you have a piece of banana stem, that's perfect! Otherwise, you can use a small bowl.

Cut banana leaves (or green paper) into decorative shapes and glue them around the edges of the base.

Decorate your krathong with flowers, candles, and small decorations.

Once it's done, you can float it in a pool, bathtub, or sink and make a wish, just like in the Loy Krathong festival!

Helpful hint: You may not be able to travel to Thailand for the Loy Krathong festival, but if you gather your friends and family, you can celebrate this festival together at home! Just make sure to respect the environment by safely disposing of your lanterns afterwards (remember, this is a sign of respect for the Naga!)

2. Design a Kinnaree Mask

Supplies:

Paper or cardstock

Paints, markers, or crayons

Feathers, glitter, or stickers for decoration

Hole punch and string

Instructions:

Draw and cut out a mask shape on a piece of paper or cardstock.

Color and decorate your mask to look like a Kinnaree. Think of bright, shimmering colors, feathers, and mystical patterns!

Punch holes on the sides and tie your string to both sides so you can wear your mask.

Once it's ready, put on your mask and pretend you're a Kinnaree, dancing gracefully through the skies!

3. Create a Lotus Blossom Out of Paper

Supplies:

Colored paper (pink, green, and yellow)

Scissors

Glue

Instructions:

Cut out petal shapes from pink paper and glue them in layers to form a flower.

Add a circle of yellow in the center for the stamen.

Cut and add green leaves around the base.

Your lotus blossom is ready! You can even make several and use them as decorations.

4. Draw a Scene from Your Favorite Thai Legend

Supplies:

Paper and pencils

Colored pencils or markers

Any other art supplies you like

Instructions:

Choose your favorite Thai legend and think about what scene you want to draw from it.

Sketch out the scene, adding details like the characters, setting, and any special objects (like a krathong or an amulet).

Once you're happy with the sketch, color it in and add any final details.

5. Write Your Own Thai-Inspired Legend

Supplies:

Notebook or paper

Pen or pencil

Optional: Colored pencils for illustrations

Instructions:

First, think about what message you want your legend to teach. Will it be about kindness, bravery, or wisdom?

Create a character, setting, and a challenge or adventure for your character.

Write your legend, adding details that make it magical and exciting.

If you like, illustrate your story or share it with friends and family.

6. Build a Temple Model Inspired by Thai Architecture

Supplies:

Cardboard or paper

Glue and tape

Paint or markers

Small decorations like glitter, beads, or stickers

Instructions:

Using cardboard or paper, create the base and main structure of your temple.

Add details like columns, a roof, and any unique features you want to include.

Paint and decorate your temple.

Once you're finished, admire your model and imagine it's a place where stories and legends are told.

7. Make a Phra Rahu Eclipse Art Project

Supplies:

Black construction paper

Yellow and white crayons or colored pencils

Scissors

Instructions:

Cut out a circle from yellow paper to represent the sun and a smaller one for the moon.

Place them on black construction paper as if they're being "swallowed" in an eclipse.

Draw stars around the scene, and if you like, draw a picture of Phra Rahu.

These activities are a fun way to keep the spirit of Thai legends alive and learn more about Thai culture. Whether you're making a krathong, writing your own legend, or creating a model temple, each project brings you closer to the magic of Thailand's stories. Enjoy your journey through creativity, and remember, every legend starts with imagination—just like yours!

FUN FACTS

Let's explore some extra fun and curious details beyond the legends we have discussed that make Thai culture so captivating. Get ready to be amazed by everything from mystical animals to extraordinary festivals!

1. Thailand is Known as the "Land of Smiles"

Thailand is often called the "Land of Smiles" because Thai people are known for their warmth and friendliness. Smiling is a big part of Thai culture, and each smile can mean something different—from happiness and kindness to a polite greeting or even a bit of shyness.

2. The Naga is Found All Over Southeast Asia

The Naga, or sacred serpent, is not only famous in Thailand but also in other Southeast Asian countries like Laos, Cambodia, and Myanmar. The Naga is believed to live in many rivers, but especially the mighty Mekong River as mentioned in the book.

3. Thai Dance Brings Legends to Life

Traditional Thai dance is a beautiful and graceful art form that often tells stories from legends. Dancers wear elaborate costumes, and their movements are slow and precise, so much so that each gesture has a meaning. You'll probably remember that stories like that of Hanuman, Kinnaree, and other legendary figures are often retold in dance, making these ancient tales come to life.

4. Temples are Called "Wats" in Thailand

In Thailand, a Buddhist temple is called a *wat*. Each wat is unique, with beautiful designs, tall stupas (a Buddhist shrine that often features a dome), and colorful decorations. Many wats feature images of legendary creatures and heroes, showing how important legends are to Thai spirituality. *Wat Phra Kaew* in Bangkok, for example, is one of the most sacred temples and is home to the famous Emerald Buddha.

5. Thai People Believe in the Boon System (Karma)

In Thai culture, people believe in *boon*, which is a concept that is similar to karma. When someone does good deeds, they earn positive boon, which brings them good luck and happiness. People believe that helping others, praying, and showing kindness can help build a good life for themselves and others.

6. The Mekong River is Known as the "Mother of Waters"

The Mekong River, which flows through Thailand and several other countries, is known as the "Mother of Waters." It's home to many myths and is considered sacred. The Phaya Naga is believed to live in its depths, and the river is essential to the lives of many people, providing water, food, and transportation.

These fun facts offer a peek into the rich and fascinating world of Thai legends, culture, and traditions. Each one tells a story about the values, beliefs, and wonders of Thailand, where ancient myths continue to inspire and enchant people of all ages. We hope these fun facts spark your curiosity and inspire you to learn more about the magical land of Thailand!

REFERENCES

Phongpaiboon, Somchai. Thai Legends and FolkTales.

Pornpanich, Sunantha. The Culture of Thailand: Traditions and Beliefs.

Saradee, Ratchanee. Sacred Animals in Thai Mythology.

Songsom, Chanya. Loy Krathong and Yi Peng: Celebrations of Light.

Suchart, Phra Ajaan. Thai Buddhism and Its Rituals.

Boonsri, Nattakarn. The Art of Thai Dance and Theatre.

Phumitham, Achara. Hanuman and the Ramakien: Thailand's Epic Tale.

Sangmuang, Jirachai. The Spirit World of Thai Culture.

Phoonchai, Kritsana. Temples of Thailand: Architecture and Symbolism.

Jitlada, Pakorn. Exploring Thai Festivals.

FREE BONUS FROM HBA: EBOOK BUNDLE

Greetings!

First, thank you for reading our books.

Now, we invite you to join our VIP list. As a welcome gift we offer the History & Mythology eBook Bundle below for free. Plus, you can be the first to receive new books and exclusives! Remember it's 100% free to join.

Simply click the link below to join.

https://www.subscribepage.com/hba
Keep up to date with us on:
YouTube: History Brought Alive
Facebook: History Brought Alive
www.historybroughtalive.com

Check out the other books in this series

- African Legends For Kids: Kings, Queens, Heroes, Spirits, Myths, Tales & More From Africa
- Aztec Legends For Kids: Gods, Warriors, Myths, Wonders & More From Ancient Mexico
- Celtic Legends For Kids: Heroes, Fairies, Warriors, Myths, Magic & More From The Ancient Celts
- Chinese Legends For Kids: Emperors, Dragons, Gods, Heroes, Myths & More From Ancient China
- English Legends For Kids: Knights, Castles, Kings, Queens, Myths & More From Old England
- Incan Legends For Kids: Emperors, Warriors, Myths, Treasures & More From Ancient Peru
- Indian Legends For Kids: Gods, Goddesses, Warriors, Sages, Myths, Epics & More From Ancient India
- Irish Legends For Kids: Heroes, Druids, Myths, Magic & More From Ancient Ireland
- Japanese Legends For Kids: Samurai, Spirits, Emperors, Myths, Magic & More From Japan

- Mesopotamian Legends For Kids: Kings, Queens, Gods, Myths, Wonders & More From The Cradle Of Civilization
- Native American Legends For Kids: Spirits, Chiefs, Warriors, Myths, Sacred Tales & More
- Persian Legends For Kids: Heroes, Kings, Myths, Epics & More From Ancient Persia
- Russian Legends For Kids: Czars, Fairies, Warriors, Folktales, Myths & More From Russia
- Scottish Legends For Kids: Warriors, Fairies, Kings, Queens, Myths, Legends & More From Scotland
- Thai Legends For Kids: Kings, Queens, Demons, Heroes, Myths, Sacred Tales & More From Thailand
- Viking & Norse Legends For Kids: Gods, Warriors, Myths, Heroes & More From The From The Ancient Norse World
- Welsh Legends For Kids: Dragons, Heroes, Prophecies, Myths, Magic & More From Ancient Wales

and follow us on www.historybroughtalive.com and https://www.youtube.com/@historybroughtalive

www.ingramcontent.com/pod-product-compliance
Lightning Source LLC
Chambersburg PA
CBHW072012030526
44119CB00064B/572